The Inside Story of Interactive TV and Microsoft® WebTV™ for Windows®

David Feinleib
Microsoft Corporation

Morgan Kaufmann

AN IMPRINT OF ACADEMIC PRESS

A Harcourt Science and Technology Company

San Diego   San Francisco   New York   Boston

London   Sydney   Tokyo

Academic Press
A Harcourt Science and Technology Company
525 B Street, Suite 1900, San Diego, CA 92101-4495 USA
http://www.academicpress.com

Academic Press
24–28 Oval Road, London NW1 7DX United Kingdom
http://www.hbuk.co.uk/ap/

Morgan Kaufmann Publishers
340 Pine Street, Sixth Floor, San Francisco, CA 94104-3205 USA
http://www.mkp.com

Library of Congress Catalog Number: 99-61532
International Standard Book Number: 0-12-251570-6

Printed in the United States of America
99 00 01 02 03 IP 9 8 7 6 5 4 3 2 1

Contents

The Emmy Awards 50th Anniversary Essay

Bill Gates

As I was thinking about the amazing progress made by television over the past 50 years, I started wondering what Judy Splinters would have made of it all. Judy was the puppet who, along with her 20-year-old ventriloquist partner Shirley Dinsdale, won the very first Emmy back in 1949, for Most Outstanding Television Personality. Those first Emmys weren't even televised nationally, and only shows produced in Los Angeles County were eligible for awards. Nationally, fewer than one million homes had a TV.

Yet the box with the flickering black-and-white screen and scratchy sound was already generating national controversy. Critics, who once saw TV as a fad that wouldn't last, now feared it would spell the death of radio, live sport, movie theatres, and Broadway. Indeed, when the World Series was telecast for the first time, Broadway reported a 50% drop in ticket sales. The *New York Times* issued a dire warning that "the American household is on the threshold of a revolution. The wife scarcely knows where the kitchen is, let alone her place in it. Junior scorns the late-afternoon sunlight for the glamour of the darkened living room. Father's briefcase lies unopened in the foyer."

But revolutions, once sparked, are hard to extinguish. By mid-1949 Americans were buying TVs at the rate of 100,000 a week — and more than 60 American companies were scrambling to meet the demand. Radio and Broadway continued to thrive, as did movie theatres. Instead of killing live sport, TV opened it up to a whole new generation of fans.

Yet for all this, nobody in 1949 would have dared forecast that one day more Americans would have color TVs than telephones — and that they would be watching in color and listening in stereo. Nor could anyone have imagined that most Americans would soon be able to view dozens of channels, the majority of them broadcasting 24 hours a day, seven days a week. Or that, thanks to cable and satellite, Americans would be able to travel the world yet still watch the news in English on CNN. Or that more than a billion people worldwide would one day tune in each week to see *Baywatch*, an American soap.

But what is most amazing is that all the progress of the past 50 years has been achieved with pretty much the same technology that brought you those first Emmys back in 1949. Sure, today's TVs have color screens and vastly improved sound. True, the VCR has changed the way most people watch TV. But TV still relies on the same old analog transmission technology. Most still have a cumbersome cathode-ray tube screen. And, mostly, TV remains a one-way experience. You sit in your chair watching, the TV sits in a corner broadcasting. Beyond the remote control, there isn't much interaction going on. The TV doesn't even know you are there. Nor can program makers and advertisers make a direct connection with their audience.

Now, though, the TV is about to undergo incredible technological change. During the next decade, analog technology will give way to digital technology — everything your TV does will start life as the same ones and zeros (or bits) that propel your PC. And this will not only make high-definition television (HDTV) — ultra-sharp widescreen TV without ghosting or interference — a reality. It will also merge the capabilities of the TV with the amazing versatility of the PC and the wonders of the World Wide Web, turning TV-viewing into a true multimedia experience.

At the same time, we're going to see an explosion in the bandwidth — or transmission capacity — that will be needed to make all this possible in real time. And given how rapidly digital computing technology evolved — from punched cards to graphical user interfaces in well under 20 years — it's clear that all this innovation will result in a massive acceleration in the number of new features and benefits for consumers in the TV industry. Indeed, the next decade may well eclipse the remarkable progress of the past half-century. It will certainly be the dawn of a new era of television.

What will this new era mean for the typical viewer? In a word: interactivity. Now, to some older TV viewers, interactivity will be old hat. Many Americans who grew up in the 1950s will remember "Winky Dink and You," perhaps the first ever interactive TV program. You bought a transparent cellophane overlay for your TV screen in the local store, then watched through it as the cartoon character Winky Dink faced all kinds of dangers, such as being chased to the edge of a river by a wild animal. You could help Winky Dink escape by drawing a bridge over the river on the overlay.

And in the 1970s there was Warner Communications' QUBE experiment in Columbus, Ohio. This offered participants a set-top box that allowed them to take part in game shows, participate in newspaper surveys, visit virtual town meetings, and even simulate voting in the Academy Awards. Unfortunately, QUBE proved too expensive to bring to the mass market. But it was certainly the forerunner of the various interactive-TV trials that have taken place in recent years.

The drawback to all these systems, though, was that you needed either clunky or very expensive and complex technology to make TV interact with viewers. The beauty of the coming era of interactive TV, by contrast, is that it will be based on universal Internet standards. So it will be cheap to implement and easy to use — and viewable on everything from the TV in the corner of your living room to the PC in your office to devices not yet dreamed of. This proliferation of media will help propel interactive programming towards the magic 20m viewers — the level at which advertisers really sit up and pay attention.

So what will you see when you are sitting in front of your interactive TV? Well, for now you'll first need to find some programming that's been enhanced for interactive TV. And already there are pilot schemes involving programs such as *Baywatch* and *Saturday Night Live*, plus local news programs, cable channels, and much more.

Now, you can simply sit back and watch these interactive programs on your TV just like you've always watched shows, without any interaction at all. Or you can shrink the picture a little, and bring up an L-shaped panel — a bit like the "menu bars" you see on the Web — that wraps around two sides of your screen, and which gives you a lot of different interactive viewing options. And the kind of interactivity you'll discover goes a long way beyond "Winky Dink."

Say, for instance, that you want to find out more about one of the characters in a weekly serial. Well, with interactive TV you'll just click on the appropriate icon on the menu bar to read biographies of cast members alongside the TV picture. Or perhaps you'd like to discuss this week's plot with other viewers. If so, you'll be able to click on another icon and be taken to a chatroom on the Internet. And if you missed last week's episode, you'll be able to read a plot summary while still watching this week's show.

Or perhaps you'll be watching a ball game and want to get some background statistics, check on the scores in other games, or watch a replay. And again, you'll simply click on the appropriate icon and instantly get all the information you need.

And your children, while watching educational programs, will be able to download facts and figures, research projects, ask questions in real time, perhaps even get homework assignments. All, again, at the click of an on-screen icon.

Or maybe you'll want to buy a surfboard just like the one in the movie you're watching. There may already be an advertisement for the board displayed on the menu bar by the manufacturer who is sponsoring the movie's interactive programming — and you'll be able to click on the ad to be taken seamlessly to the firm's Web site. (Again, such TV merchandising is as old as the Emmys — children watching Hopalong Cassidy bought $40 million of "Hoppy" clothing in 1950.) This kind of interactivity will be available in commercials, too, so buying advertised products will be easier than ever. And TV will rapidly become one of the major gateways for e-commerce.

Or perhaps whatever you're watching, you'll simply want to find out what's going on in the real world — the weather, the stock market, the latest ballgame score, the headlines. Or you may remember an email you need to send, or a bill that must be paid. And all that will soon be possible just by clicking on the appropriate icon.

The possibilities really are endless — and they will always include simply watching TV as you did before, without any interactivity. But how soon those possibilities become reality for the majority of viewers depends on how swiftly the TV industry starts making interactive programs. I'm very optimistic about this. In a world of deficit-financed shows — one that relies on broad syndication to make a profit — interactive TV offers many new and innovative ways to make money. And advertising will play a large part here, with program makers and broadcasters generating revenue from commissions on on-line sales.

But there's also another, perhaps more important benefit for program makers from the increased "density" offered by interactive programming — the ability to add value, and viewers, to shows being re-run in syndication.

Take the late lamented "Seinfeld." Although hard-core addicts may be content to view old episodes over and over, programmers will be able to increase the potential audience for re-runs by adding interactivity. They could, for instance, create a cartoon Jerry who could sit in the menu bar, commenting on what's going on, telling viewers about behind-the-scenes activities, filling them in on scenes that didn't make it into the show. And for very little additional investment this adds significant extra value for viewers — and for advertisers.

Interactive technology, then, will enable program makers to create entirely original programming out of re-runs. But there are also two other reasons why I'm optimistic that interactive television will take off faster than the industry ever imagined — digital TV and soaring bandwidth.

Digital TV will be a revelation for viewers. You'll see clearer pictures. Hear better sound quality. And because everything starts out as bits, you'll get seamless integration with the Internet, the Web and other on-line information — and with your PC. Because everything is just bits, it will be possible to transmit the same programming to PCs, digital TVs, or any other medium, via cable, broadcast, wireless, or satellite. And because it's all just bits, your digital TV will surf the Web as easily as it receives *Baywatch* broadcasts.

This isn't some distant dream. This fall, digital transmissions are already beginning in a handful of major U.S. markets. In a year's time, the top 30 U.S. markets will be receiving digital transmissions. By 2006 analog broadcasting will be phased out. That doesn't mean everyone will have to sell their old analog TVs — but they will need a set-top box to receive digital transmissions.

At the same time, we're on the verge of an explosion in the kind of bandwidth that will allow all this programming and information to travel instantaneously to and from your home. Increasingly you'll see cable modems, linked up to both TVs and PCs, that will allow high-speed two-way connections to the Internet and Web. New technologies based on the old twisted-copper telephone line will allow much broader bandwidth connections than were envisaged only a few years ago. And a vast amount of digital interactive programming will be transmitted by satellite constellations such as that planned by Teledesic, a company in which I have a stake. It is encircling the Earth with a web of 288 low-orbit, geostationary satellites, which will deliver broadband two-way transmissions to almost every part of the globe. This "Internet in the Sky" will go on-line in 2002.

But as we look to the future, we should learn from the past. At the time of the TV industry's birth 50 years ago, many people feared the impact of this new medium. We know now that their fears were unfounded, and that although TV has profoundly changed the world we live in, it has done so almost universally for the better. That's why I am so optimistic about this new era of TV. The power of interactive technology will allow viewers to participate in the information age — many of them for the first time — no matter where they live. No longer will TV be a one-way window into your home; it will be your two-way window into an expanding world of entertainment, information, and knowledge. There could be no better way to celebrate TV's — and the Emmys' — first half century.

Preface

Transport of the mails, transport of the human voice, transport of flickering pictures — in this century as in others our highest accomplishments still have the single aim of bringing men together.

Antoine de Saint-Exupéry, noted French aviator and writer (1939)

The personal and social consequences of any medium — that is, of any extension of ourselves — result from the new scale that is introduced into our affairs by each extension of ourselves, or by any new technology.

Marshall McLuhan, Canadian communications theorist (1964)

This book is the inside story of the people and companies that took the risk to enter the next age of television, an age brought on by the convergence of television and the Internet. It is about the change from the passive television experience we've known for the past 50 years to a new era of interactive television, a change as dramatic as that from silent movies to "talkies," from black and white to color. Television once offered only a one-way transfer of information. Now, the Web brings with it the possibility of a two-way transfer — a dialog — between the media, information and service providers, and the viewer.

The 20th century witnessed the development of the automobile, the airplane, nuclear power, and plastics. But by far the most important development was the switch from analog to digital — from continuous waves of analog signals to on–off pulses of digital signals that let us represent information of any form by ones and zeros. Digital allows the movement of a page of data, a song, or a movie scene as if it were one boxcar on a train. Moving these items in digital form allows data and images to be transported to the viewer more efficiently.

Claude E. Shannon (1916–) expounded on the precision and accuracy of digital technologies in *A Mathematical Theory of Communication* (1948), leading to the creation of the digital computer, compact disc, modern telecommunications, and now, digital television. Converting data, sound, and images to ones and zeros allows all means of communication to have a common platform. The consequence of such a seemingly modest change is a revolution in image and sound quality, variety, and interaction.

About This Book

This book is written for everyone involved in the digital transition, from the viewer, to the television station manager, to the advertisers and providers of goods and services, to the software programmers who create the interface between them. If you're involved in the programming, deployment, or development of this new businesses called interactive television, this book is your guide and bible. If you've ever authored a Web page — or if you work with someone who has — read this book. If you've ever wondered how people in the television industry make a decision — be it about business or technology — read this book. And if you're wondering about the impact of interactive services on your own checkbook, read this book. From executives making multimillion-dollar decisions about which new businesses to enter to managers and engineers trying to understand those decisions, this book is for you. Here you will find out how others addressed the hurdles and issues of the new age of television.

Part of the book is devoted to the software implementation and technical details of WebTV for Windows and the underlying architecture that supports it. However, the majority of the book combines interviews, case studies, and first-person accounts from the people who made the decisions to explore new forms of content using television and the Internet. Their thoughts, ideas, and experiences are documented here and are valuable and pertinent across all platforms, technologies, and companies. As much as possible, the book preserves the style and unique perspective of each contributor. Thus, some of the chapters are really narrative case studies, telling the story of how decisions were made. Some chapters contain overlapping information — this is simply a natural result of each contributor providing a unique perspective.

Just like much of interactive television, this book is designed to be both informative and entertaining. I hope that its focus on both technical detail and human experience provides a well-balanced picture of this brave new broadcast industry. Please send me your feedback by electronic mail to *davefe@microsoft.com*.

Acknowledgments

My role at Microsoft for the past few years was as a program manager (PM) on the WebTV for Windows team, a part of the larger Windows 98 team. One of the most challenging parts of "PM'ing" is in managing people and resources without the power of having people report directly to you. When I started this book, I somewhat naively had little reason to think that it would require all my experience as a PM — and more — to complete this project.

To everyone who helped me get through my first book and who contributed their writing, their ideas, their time, and their hard work — this is your book. What you find here is truly the collaborative result of all of your efforts. For your hard work in meeting deadlines, getting approvals, and contributing the key ideas and information in this book, I want to thank all of the contributors.

Brian Moran has served as mentor and friend for more than 7 years. For his direction, advice, and sense of humor I will always be grateful. Larry Namer has become a great friend and has been a true source of inspiration and guidance in both my personal and business affairs. Bob Mariano made possible our relationships with the television stations and station groups. Bill Veghte gave me the time, freedom, and resources to start this project and see it through to completion, well after the date I promised him I would finish it. I can only hope that the result overcomes any doubts he may have had. Thanks to Ed Stubbs for his never-ending good humor and to Gabe Newell for beginning what ultimately led to WebTV for Windows.

Chuck Mount was critical in developing HTML pages, scripts, and designs that contributed to the content you see in this book. Thanks for your friendship and your technical expertise late into the night on numerous occasions. Noel Gamboa suggested the original division of the book into three sections and helped me organize my initial thoughts and ideas.

At MSNBC, special thanks to Kevin Crumley, Peter Durham, Ted McConville, Beth Roberts, and Frank Barbieri. At Tribune, special thanks to Lou Bardfield, Ira Goldstone, Jeff Scherb, Maryann Schulze, Matt Thompson, and Gary Wong. At Sinclair, thanks to Mike O'Malley, Nat Ostroff, and Dave Smith. At Paramount, thanks to J. W. Linkenauger. At Avid, thanks to Mark Basler, Ray Gilmartin, Rich Johnson, D. J. Long, Oliver Morgan, Steve Noyes, Luis Valdez, and Kincade Webb.

For their technical knowledge and countless hours in explaining and reexplaining code and architecture details to me, at Microsoft, thanks to Lee Acton, Christopher Garry, Matthijs Gates, Chris Kauffman, Brian Keller, and Isaac Sheldon. Thanks as well to Andamo Deming for his belief in "the VBI project." Thanks to all the other members of the Broadcast PC team for making WebTV for Windows a reality. Brad Serbus proved to be a truly fantastic development lead on the Broadcast Server. George Moore and Sriram Rajagopalan delivered a great version one product, and Sean Chai will move it ahead in the future. Rick Portin and Kiran Rao contributed to the exciting content available today and will continue to do so well into the future.

Paul Mitchell and Sarah Norton contributed their thoughts and input throughout the process. Rick Portin's ideas helped make possible the stories you find here. Steve Guggenheimer spent countless hours spinning words and helping me fine-tune the introduction to this book. Through their tremendous efforts, Craig Mundie, Hank Vigil, and Tom Gershaw removed the hurdles that made possible the inclusion of WebTV for Windows with Windows 98.

My thanks to Crista Prince in the Microsoft Library. The numbers and facts that are correct in the book are due to her. Any that are wrong are due to me.

Thanks to Mark Derbecker, Bei-Jing Guo, Anupam Gupta, Aki Kimihira, Alan Oka, Jackie Potter, Fumie Sato, Jed Stafford, and Kingsley Wood for their encouragement.

I will forever be indebted to Bob Prior at MIT Press for forwarding my proposal to Tom Stone at Morgan Kaufmann. Without Tom Stone's dedication and his willingness to take a risk on something unproven, this book wouldn't exist. Thomas Park served as an excellent project coordinator and Julie Champagne as a fantastic production editor.

Megan Sheppard served as a wonderful developmental editor, turning text into prose. Jeff Hickey's copyediting skills and Elisabeth Thebaud Pong's graphics expertise made it possible for me to deliver a quality manuscript to Morgan Kaufmann. Their dedication and efforts transformed a bunch of words and assorted pictures into a book. Thanks to Steven Timm and Peter Haynes, who made possible the inclusion of the Emmy Awards 50th Anniversary Essay.

Aki Kimihira has remained my light at the end of the tunnel. For that, I will be forever grateful.

Finally, I am most indebted to my father, whose wisdom and understanding of technology and society will forever influence the way I tackle problems and explore ideas. Without him, I would never have discovered Vannevar Bush or any of a number of other great technologists who deeply affected my thinking.

Introduction

Television is changing. It is evolving from continuous waves of analog pulses into ones and zeros that represent many kinds of multimedia information in digital form. Members of the broadcast community often think of this evolution in terms of high-definition television (HDTV), a technology offering significant improvements in picture and sound quality. Conversely, members of the computer and cable industries generally perceive digital television as intelligent television — an innovative, multimedia melding of video and data. The marriage of video and data into a new genre of television known as *interactive programming* is the focus of this book.

Integrating video and data can be as easy as simultaneously displaying program listings and real-time television on a portion of the screen, as in the electronic program guide (EPG) shown in Figure I.1. Providing an instant, noticeable benefit, the EPG clearly demonstrates the advantages of digital television. Simple in concept and easy to use, it lets you search, navigate, and find out what's on, all while watching TV.

Figure I.1   The electronic program guide. (Graphic provided courtesy of MSNBC.)

The objective of interactive programming is to bring that same level of simplicity, ease of use, and benefit to the programs themselves. Figure I.2 shows an interactive version of the Microsoft/NBC news network, MSNBC.

The WebTV Experience

The EPG and interactive television programs are part of what we call the *WebTV experience*. WebTV is at once a set-top box, Microsoft's brand name for its television experience across all platforms, and the underlying architecture that enables that experience. WebTV for Windows is the implementation of that experience on the Windows 98 operating system. Moreover, WebTV for Windows, and the interactive functionality it enables, is a major implementation of what will ultimately become an industry-wide specification, currently in proposal form, from the Advanced Television Enhancement Forum (ATVEF).

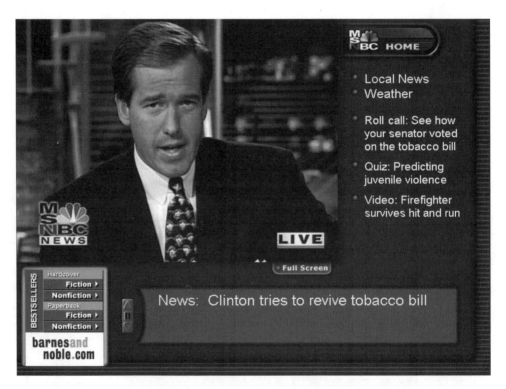

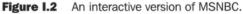

Figure I.2 An interactive version of MSNBC.

Setting the Standard

The ATVEF (*www.atvef.com*) is a cross-industry alliance of companies representing broadcast and cable networks, cable and satellite service providers, consumer electronics, personal computers, and the software industry. The standards proposed by the ATVEF ensure that consumers will have a consistent experience independent of program, transport, or receiver:

- Internet Protocol (IP) Multicast ensures that interactive programming will be able to be delivered over satellite, cable, broadcast, and other networks.

- Use of existing hypertext markup language (HTML) and ECMAScript (a scripting language supported by many Web browsers) standards ensures that interactive content can be designed once and displayed across a wide range of receivers — from the set-top box in the home to the computer in the classroom.

WebTV for Windows was designed with the ATVEF standards in mind. The update to WebTV for Windows included with the 1999 release of Windows 98 is expected to provide full ATVEF support (the actual name for the Windows 98 update was still to be determined at press time).

Taking Advantage of the VBI

Much of this book focuses on the delivery of interactive content over a portion of existing analog television signals known as the *Vertical Blanking Interval* (VBI). By using the VBI, show producers and advertisers can deliver useful and timely information with television programs today as they prepare to use the digital infrastructure of tomorrow. Such content can take a variety of forms, from simple Web site links (which today are called TV Crossover Links), embedded in a television show, to content that is delivered over the VBI and fully integrated and synchronized with a particular program (Figure I.3).

To make use of integrated interactive programming, users do not need a connection back to the Internet. However, when this technology is combined with an Internet connection, the potential addition of electronic mail, chat, polling, and electronic commerce expands its possibilities significantly. Information that is common to all can be delivered over the television signal, while purchasing and other services requiring connectivity can occur over traditional Internet links.

Figure I.3   An interactive version of *Baywatch* showing integrated video and HTML content on the left and a linked Web site on the right. (Screen shot courtesy of the *Baywatch* Production Co.)

About This Book

The book is divided into three parts:

- Part 1 contains the insights, criticisms, musings, and perspectives of industry veterans familiar with WebTV for Windows and interactive television.

- Part 2 is a technical reference that describes how WebTV for Windows and the underlying broadcast architecture work. It also explains the standards and interfaces used in WebTV for Windows as well as the standard proposed by the ATVEF.

- Part 3 consists of technical case studies of companies that have invested in delivering interactive content today — their challenges, technological innovations, and implementations are all represented here.

Interactive television opens up a new world of opportunity for the companies that participate in the analog-to-digital evolution. For consumers, interactive television combines the innovations of computing with the content of television, making possible a completely new multimedia experience — from entertainment enhancements such as on-demand sports statistics and instant replay to information capabilities that provide details about products of interest.

Today's set-top boxes and computers look noticeably different from each other. But computer manufacturers are already offering computers that look more and more like set-top boxes: sealed cases and a more consumer-like look and feel are just the beginning. Likewise, set-top boxes are starting to act more and more like computers, with greater functionality and the ability to add peripherals. The size and shape of receivers, like many other aspects of interactive television, are sure to change. But your interest in two aspects of interactive television is certain to remain constant: the *business* of interactive programming and the *technology* of interactive programming.

Terminology and Abbreviations at a Glance

Term	Meaning
Digital television	The delivery of a television signal using the common binary system of combinations of 1s and 0s. As opposed to traditional analog television, digital television provides higher quality picture and sound and supports features such as interactive programming, electronic program guides, and data delivery.
Electronic program guide (EPG)	A WebTV for Windows component that lists television shows. The EPG can be browsed and searched. Television programs can be viewed through the EPG if a TV tuner card is installed in the computer.
Internet Protocol (IP)	A standard for the delivery of data across networked computers, relying on the delivery of packets of information.
Internet Protocol (IP) multicast	A method of transmitting data used in conjunction with IP. A multicast sends information to a subset of recipients. (Broadcasts send data to all recipients, and unicasts are directed at a single recipient.)
TV Crossover Link	Links to Web sites that are delivered to an interactive television receiver through the closed caption stream.
TV tuner card	Computer hardware used to receive and display television broadcasts on a computer.
Vertical Blanking Interval (VBI)	A portion of the analog television signal. A television signal consists of many horizontal lines. During the time the electron beam that draws the picture is resetting, the image is briefly blanked out, allowing the transmission of data instead of a picture. Closed captioning is sent on line 21 of the VBI.

Business Case Studies, Interviews, and Narratives

The film *A Christmas Story* provides a primitive — yet pertinent — demonstration of the potential for interactivity. In the film, 9-year-old Ralphie eagerly awaits the delivery of a Little Orphan Annie secret decoder ring. When it finally arrives in the mail, he immediately begins to decode the message. For that moment, Ralphie truly believes he is part of the show and capable of saving the world. Although his moment of "connection" is short lived (all Ralphie gets for his efforts is the message, "Be sure to drink more Ovaltine"), the feeling of participation — that desire to interact and to be a part of the program — is what content producers are striving to create with interactive television.

More recently, Intel Corporation added a level of interactivity to its television commercials. During the 1998 Superbowl, Intel's commercials presented a story whose outcome was decided by viewer input to the company's Web site. Showtime added interactivity to its programs by providing online voting for boxing matches and online selection of movies. (Audience members vote for the film they most want to see, and the network airs the winner.)

Digital television will bring these forms of interactive television to the next level, making it possible for all audience members to feel that they are part of the show. It will blur the traditional distinction between the television show and its audience. Interactive television, with its use of online chats, simple games, the ability to provide feedback (and thus change the course of a show), and other elements of choice will change the course of television as we know it.

In this section, through narratives, interviews, and case studies, a cross section of industry members describe their own experiences in bringing together the distinct cultures of the Web and TV. Here you will find executives and managers telling you, in their own voices, about their unique perspectives and experiences to date in developing interactive television. You will also learn about new forms of content, new models for business, and new ways of delivering high-speed data that will benefit the consumer and all of the stakeholders.

Interactive Television Overview and Origins

Larry Namer, President, Comspan Communications

www.comspan.com

We hired Larry Namer, cofounder of E! Television, as a consultant on the interactive television project to help us develop the original business plans and to contact and work with television stations and station groups nationwide. He has written this chapter in his own style. It is exactly this different style that led us to hire him in the first place. In this chapter, Larry recounts the history of this consulting project, providing valuable insight into how this "enhanced TV technology stuff" will actually be used.

Introduction

It was business as usual at Comspan Communications[1] in mid-1996 with the usual assortment of TV network development projects making up the bulk of our workload. We were getting The Recovery Network (a television network geared to the needs of people in recovery from drug or alcohol abuse, eating disorders, and other afflictions) ready for a spring 1997 launch. We were also creating the business plans for HobbyCraft Network (scheduled to launch in 1999).

In Russia, our subsidiary, Bigstar, has become the leading producer of live entertainment events. Our productions include concerts (Sheryl Crow, Salt-N-Pepa, Jose Feliciano), sporting events (Champions Tennis Tour and the Harlem Globetrotters), and fashion shows (Versace, Armani, and others, utilizing supermodels such as Claudia Schiffer, Linda Evangelista, and the Wonderbra model Eva Herzigova). They were in the process of finalizing all the details for our biggest show yet, David Bowie at the Kremlin. For a company whose roots were deeply planted in the entertainment business, we were probably more Internet savvy than most.

---

1. Comspan Communications Inc. (CCI) is a business development and strategic planning consulting company that specializes in the creation of niche television networks. CCI is one of the few companies outside the key media conglomerates that has the skill set in house to do the planning of a TV network. There are thousands of companies that develop TV shows.

Several years before, I had "discovered" the Internet and became fascinated not by what it was but by what I believed it had the capability to become. It reminded me of the cable television scene in the early 1970s, when technology created the opportunity for new players to enter the TV scene and break the stranglehold that the "Big Three" networks (ABC, CBS, and NBC) had on the industry. There would soon be room for more channels, more choices, and, most important, the entry of fresh new minds in creating content.

The relatively low cost of entry into cable television allowed a whole new generation of entrepreneurs to move in and compete against the networks. I saw the same kind of situation with the Internet, where the barriers to entry were low and the level of creativity was high. Fortunes were going to be made and new "Ted Turners" would be born. I wanted to make sure that Comspan wouldn't be left behind. We immediately instituted mandatory Internet training for everyone. Our employees (all from traditional TV backgrounds) spent at least an hour on the Internet every day, just to begin to understand it.

It became increasingly obvious to us that the same disciplines that we brought to bear on the process of creating and developing television networks could (and should) be brought to the process of creating Internet ventures. At that point, we thought of the online world as just another area of business, separate and distinct from our core business (in much the same way that the Bigstar business, while extremely profitable, rarely touched on our network development business). Until we got "the Microsoft call," that is.

The phone message said that Paul Mitchell from Microsoft was calling and wanted to talk about interactive television. When I returned the call I was a bit skeptical at first, thinking that this was probably just another one of my friends playing a practical joke. Paul Mitchell sells hair care products, doesn't he? Why would Microsoft be calling us?

Billg's[2] troops certainly had the ability to pick up the phone and get Gerald Levin, chairman of Time Warner, on the line. Who better than Levin, with his highly publicized "Full Service Network" in Orlando, could answer any questions about interactive television? After a short bout of asking silly questions to make sure this wasn't a practical joke, I came to understand that Paul wasn't offering advice about adding luster and shine to my hair. Rather, he was offering me the opportunity to participate in one of the most exciting projects ever to come my way. It was a project that could change the shape of the entire television industry.

---

2. Bill Gates' e-mail address is *billg@microsoft.com*, which led to him being referred to as billg.

Ted Turner

In the late 1970s, Ted Turner, owner of a small UHF TV station in Atlanta, Georgia, WTBS, did something previously unthinkable. He uplinked his station's signal to a satellite and distributed it nationally to cable operators across the United States. For the first time a new "network" was able to compete with the Big Three for national audiences and advertisers. WTBS was known as a "superstation." Advances in satellite technology made this affordable and enabled local TV stations to reach beyond the areas they were originally licensed to serve. Turner followed up the effort with an even more unthinkable act, launching CNN as a cable-only news network that went straight to the heart, and pocketbook, of the Big Three again. With the networks clearly no longer in sole command of the technologies to broadcast nationally, new networks began to pop up at a rapid pace.

Paul was offering Comspan the opportunity to work with Microsoft on a project called Microsoft Interactive Television (MITV). Microsoft wanted to bring TV and the computer together in a manner, and with a mass of deployment, that would allow creative minds finally to address television as being more than something produced for the lowest common denominator. Paul had heard about us from Rick Portin, who was then working for Microsoft as executive producer in the MITV group. Rick and I went back quite a way together in the cable business, most recently when he was the vice president of production at E! Entertainment TV and I was the founder and president.

When Paul, Rick, and other Microsoft representatives visited us at our offices in Los Angeles, they unveiled the project in depth. *This* MITV was a new group within Microsoft that was to work with DIRECTV in creating a data service or computer-related programming service to be delivered via a channel that Microsoft had contracted for on a DIRECTV transponder. (A transponder is a portion of a satellite used to receive and transmit data.) It was not to be confused with the *old* MITV group, which had spent years and many millions of dollars creating interactive television applications for deployment on technology platforms that came to be understood as far off in the future and not economically feasible to pursue today.

Now that Microsoft had access to a transponder and the several million homes that received DIRECTV, there were many conflicting opinions about what to do with it. Paul Mitchell was given the task of heading the new MITV group and helping Microsoft redirect its efforts. The eloquent speeches Bill Gates usually gave at computer confabs could be rebroadcast, but that certainly didn't make a channel. There was even talk of downloading software updates every day so that the lucky consumer could come home from a hard day at the office and have instant access to the latest Excel upgrade or applet. Microsoft did indeed start MSTV, which broadcasts over C-band satellite and offers a limited program lineup on DIRECTV.

Summary

- The Internet is extremely similar to cable television in the 1970s, when the low cost of entry into cable television created the opportunity for new entrepreneurs to move in and for fresh minds to create content.

- The original purpose of the MITV group was to find a commercially viable use for bandwidth that Microsoft received from DIRECTV as part of a joint platform and service agreement.

Enhancing Television Programs by Adding Data

Paul, Rick, Bob Mariano (of Comspan), and I felt that none of the suggested possibilities really made for a compelling television network. We determined that we should really explore Microsoft's relatively unheralded technology developments of "enhancing" broadcast television programs by adding extra "data" to the transmission. The folks in the Windows development team were working on technology that would allow synchronizing Web pages to a TV broadcast. I was to learn much later, however, that they weren't quite sure of how or why anyone might ever use this feature. This team, under the leadership of George Moore, would later rise to prominence within the Microsoft organization when the astounding importance of the project was finally realized. The work they were doing was made part of a version of Windows planned for release in 1997. Microsoft would end up delivering the product in 1998 as Windows 98. (Ah, what it must be like to be able to change the calendar whenever you are running late.) We spent the next several months putting together a business plan that started out as an enhanced TV network on DIRECTV and eventually evolved into one that called for the use of enhanced TV technology as part of every TV show and network.

We started our thinking process by looking in to the various "interactive television" projects that were launched here in the United States. We were looking for answers to these questions: "What worked?" "What failed?" "Why?" It didn't take us long to realize that most of the greatly touted experiments in this area were experiments in technology or marketing but that none really ever got to the questions of content. Our real questions had to do with trying to figure out what the consumer would want and who would pay for the content and services provided. After all, someone has to bear the burden of any extra cost.

The First Interactive TV Trial: Qube

Warner Communications developed Qube in the late 1970s and first offered it in Columbus, Ohio in December 1977. Qube was the first broad attempt to bring interactivity to television in U.S. homes. In the late 1970s race to obtain the franchise rights to build cable systems in major cities, the Qube system was a valuable public relations asset for Warner Communications (Warner) in its battles with companies such as United Cable, Time Inc., American Cable, and Tele-Communications Inc. (TCI). As an employee of Time's cable operations during that time, I felt that Qube was really more about helping Warner get franchises than it was about creating services that were profitable or even logical.

Although Qube closed down after just a few years, many very notable people and businesses came out of the system. Although I may be right in assuming that the Warner executives were mainly interested in Qube's value as a franchising tool, it is very clear to me now that the people at Qube took their interactive TV mission extremely seriously. The graduates of Qube include Scott Kurnit (now the founder and chairman of The Mining Company), Howard Blumenthal (executive producer and creator of *Where on Earth Is Carmen San Diego?*), Larry Wangberg (now president of ZDTV, the new cable network launched by Ziff-Davis), Dr. Vivian Horner (who advised Bell Atlantic on their move into video services), Ron Castell (who became the head of marketing for Blockbuster Video), Bob Morton (who became the executive producer of the David Letterman show), and our own Bob Mariano (who served as an executive at such companies as CBS and Fox before joining Comspan).

Music Television (MTV) and *Nickelodeon* (formerly called *Pinwheel*) are among the services that came out of the Qube programming group. The Qube system was revolutionary in that it introduced a set-top box with a computer chip and some memory. Remember that in 1977, the average cable system offered fewer than 20 channels, Beta and VHS were gearing up for battle, and Apple Computer hadn't even been born yet. A central computer could poll the Qube set-top boxes, asking three questions approximately every 20 seconds: "Are you on?" "What channel are you watching?" "Are there any other buttons on your remote console that were pushed? If so, which buttons?"

Of the 30 channels that Qube offered, 10 were allocated to the off-the-air broadcast stations in the area, 10 to education and basic cable services, and 10 to pay-per-view (PPV) programs.

Movies originally released in movie theaters became the main PPV offerings. The charge for a movie was typically $3, but some less current or less spectacular movies were offered for as little as $1. PPV was important because at the time there were few videocassette recorders (VCRs) in the United States, and large rental chains such as Blockbuster Video didn't exist. The appeal of viewing uninterrupted movies months before broadcast on Home Box Office (HBO) or Showtime was considered to be an incredible revenue opportunity for the cable operator and one that would by itself justify the enormous capital expenditure in building a Qube system.

To ensure that subscribers would find the PPV offerings attractive, the Qube system did not offer pay television services such as HBO or Showtime. The polling computer would notice if you were on a PPV channel for more than 2 minutes and then bill you for the movie after 2 minutes. One of the biggest problems that the Qube system faced was that subscribers — so thrilled by the ability to get movies in their home — often "bought" well beyond their ability to pay. As a result, Qube faced serious collection problems and experienced a high rate of disconnects because people felt that, although they might love Qube, they couldn't afford to keep it.

Warner also tried to create original programs that took advantage of the methods for audience polling. Programs about public affairs and beauty contests were designed to allow subscribers to share their opinions with each other. Again, these programs were simplistic in their design. The polling computer found out which other buttons the viewer pushed on the remote console and tallied them for on-

HBO

HBO and Showtime were the first new networks to offer theatrical movies without commercials. To receive them, cable subscribers pay an additional fee above the cost of basic cable. Although HBO was not the first attempt at creating a channel of this type, it was the first to utilize C-band satellite technology to deliver its signal to cable operators. The marketing muscle and savvy of HBO's parent, Time Inc., allowed HBO to grow rapidly and become synonymous with the term "pay television." Launched in the mid-1970s, HBO was soon followed by competitors such as Showtime and The Movie Channel. However, HBO's "first-to-market" advantage has kept it the top pay television service in the United States.

screen display. More than PPV, it was these programs that provided insight into the early thinking on interactivity.

Warner eventually shut down Qube in 1984,[3] primarily because it was unable to establish long-term viability of the system. Interactive programs produced no revenue and PPV was being overshadowed by the rapid growth of the home video industry and the Blockbuster Video stores popping up everywhere. At the system's end, Warner had Qube operations in other cities, including Houston and Pittsburgh. At its peak, Qube reached around 40,000[4] homes in Columbus. This relatively small number was not capable of sustaining (economically) any reasonable level of quality production of original shows that utilized the interactive capabilities of the system. The technology itself, although ahead of its time, functioned mainly as a billing system and provided little insight into content usage and audience reaction to programming. The polling mechanism was interesting to some viewers at first, but the novelty soon wore off. Polling could not personalize the experience. You could see only how your opinion registered versus that of the mass of other subscribers. Polling primarily measured reaction to local political issues, with an occasional beauty contest thrown in. The polling itself was self-selected and had no scientific validity.

In looking back at Qube, it is quite evident that Warner approached the service mainly as a test of how to deliver and market movies on a PPV basis. Interactive TV programming was not provided a platform capable of allowing it to develop and sustain itself economically. After Warner ended Qube operations, many in the TV industry believed that interactive TV was a failure. The next big attempts at creating interactive TV platforms would not take place until many years later.

By the 1990s, homes across America were fully enabled to let the audience choose from a much wider array of programming. VCRs were common, and cable operators could choose from over 80 cable channels to offer to subscribers as part of their basic programming lineup. Computers were found throughout the workplace and in many homes. Direct broadcast satellite (DBS) services such as DIRECTV were challenging cable companies, as was the impending entry of telephone companies into video services. Cable companies had to respond. The time seemed right for another major foray into the interactive television world. Although there were several big projects in motion, such as GTE's Mainstreet in Southern California and

---

3. Warner dropped most of the system and all of the original programming in 1984. Qube boxes remained in houses until 1992. *The Columbus (Ohio) Dispatch*, March 12, 1998.

4. Qube's total subscriber count grew to somewhere just over 40,000 homes. *USA Today*, August 16, 1993.

Cox Communications' test in Omaha, Nebraska, none drew the attention of the public and the press as did Time Warner's Full Service Network in Orlando, Florida.

Summary

- Comspan originally focused its interactive television thinking on two questions: "What does the consumer want?" "Who will pay for it?"

- Qube, developed by Warner Communications in Columbus, Ohio, was the first interactive television trial, concentrating on pay-per-view (PPV) and simple polling provided by a basic set-top box. Although shut down after reaching a subscriber base of around 40,000, Qube can count notable television industry entrepreneurs among its founding members. Without giving real interactive television a chance, the public and the industry judged the trials a failure.

- By the 1990s, VCRs, DBS, and the availability of a large number of basic cable channels provided consumers with a wide array of programs. Technology had advanced sufficiently and consumers were ready for another round of interactive television.

The Full Service Network and Perceived Value

Our next investigation focused on Time Warner's Full Service Network (FSN). After just a few days of calls and interviews with people who were involved with the project in some way, we all kind of sat back and looked at each other. The basic plan for FSN seemed flawed. In hindsight, the flaws should have been rectified early on. (Notice how good I am at second-guessing. I can also predict yesterday's football games with uncanny accuracy.) For the purpose of brevity, I've simplified the story a little. In Orlando, Time Warner installed $10,000 boxes in 4000 homes. Big servers at the cable system head end controlled the billing operations and provided "on-demand" programs and services. The Tribune Company's *Orlando Sentinel*, for example, produced one of the more interesting services — local news segments. A lot less interesting were the bulk of other programs that were developed by local or in-house staff. The audience reaction to these programs was not positive, and it didn't take a genius to figure out why.

The ability to create anything that happens on a screen and holds the interest of a mass audience is an art that very few people in the world practice well.

Before you can make any judgments about whether interactive television is good or bad, you must first engage the creative brains in the process of designing and producing the programs with which you expect the viewer to interact. You need to engage the brains of Aaron Spelling, Steven Bochco, David Kelley, and others. But how do you get them interested in producing shows for 4000 homes in Orlando? You could offer them $10 million to produce a great 1-hour interactive TV special, but with only 4000 homes and no visible revenue stream, you couldn't afford to do this for very long. You would never get to do all the things you do to build audience for a TV series.

What we really needed to do was to create a scenario that made interactive television inevitable and in which the masters of the game felt obligated to participate to stay on top of their art. It had to be a scenario for which we could argue that, even if it were 2 or 5 years away, everyone still realized it would happen, because it made sense to the consumer and would generate additional profits for the participants. Money is what drives just about every industry. TV is no different. If we could show that money could be made through enhanced TV, we could then develop approaches designed to move the various parts of the TV industry. Conversely, we could also show that the people who didn't pay close attention would lose money and face extinction.

We began to look at the economic models that drive television. Subscription services such as HBO can charge a premium fee above that charged for basic cable because consumers perceive a value in having current, uncut, uninterrupted movies in the convenience of their homes. The value of a movie is built during the film's theatrical run, when heavy marketing and promotion dollars are spent. When the film makes it to HBO, the consumer recognizes the film, after exposure to ads in the paper and on television, as well as the publicity barrage that usually accompanies a major film release.

Think of how many people use the pay TV services they have. Each month they make a decision to keep the service for an additional month. They are faced with a negative option, which means that if they do nothing their service continues. To cancel they must call the cable company. At the end of each month they usually receive a guide that shows what will be on next month. The new movie offerings are usually promoted heavily. If consumers know the names of the movies and the stars, they subconsciously decide that the next month is a good month and decide not to cancel. Only when the movies offered seem unknown and obscure do consumers reflect on the actual value they are receiving for the extra fee they are paying. What they actually watch during that next month is sometimes less important that what they had the opportunity to watch.

Conversely, interactive TV has no such perceived value. In fact, most of what the consumer has read has been negative. It would not be possible to develop a business based on consumers paying an incremental fee for enhanced TV. It has no value at all to the consumer. Maybe the service provider could charge a fee after some cool content was developed and the public's perception changed, but not at the outset. We therefore had to base our business model on advertising revenues, which are the major source of dollars that flow into the television industry.

If we could show how enhanced TV services could increase the dollars flowing into the system, we could get the attention of the TV networks. If advertisers simply became interested in exploring the possibilities of enhanced services, the networks would surely respond by devoting some of their attention to the subject. If the networks became interested, the studios and production companies would take notice and become actively involved. After all, a studio or production company lives and dies by the number of shows it can successfully create, put on the air, and keep there until enough episodes have been broadcast to qualify the show as a candidate for syndication (where the real money is made). If the studios became interested, then the producers, writers, and creators of TV shows would become interested. Their job was to develop shows that the studios would feel comfortable supporting, in the hope of making a sale to a network.

N O T E

Later in this chapter, I will provide a brief outline of what I refer to as "the TV food chain," which will show how all the various parts of the TV industry interrelate.

The television industry is a competitive field, and no one wants to be left behind. The big problem we faced was that, in order to get the ball rolling, we needed to get the advertisers to take the project seriously. It couldn't be seen as just another little interactive test that they would throw a few dollars at. It needed to promise mass audience delivery and have a realistic way to deliver it. Microsoft faced the additional hurdle of having to go out to the TV industry and ask for their participation not long after it had done so with its own ill-fated interactive TV effort. In the early to mid-1990s, Microsoft had established the interactive television (ITV) group, which became caught up in the hoopla about "thousands of channels available, no bandwidth restrictions, and a video server in every garage." Consumers would be offered unlimited choices of movies and start times (and full VCR-like functionality such as pause and rewind), the ability to purchase anything over the system, and a TV channel for just about any interest. Microsoft has a large force of "evangelists" who go out and get the world excited about technologies it believes in. The Microsoft evangelists excited TV people to the point that many devoted a lot of time, effort, and cash to ITV. They and Microsoft later learned that the distribution platforms for ITV were in fact quite a number of years away.

In the advertising world, approximately 20 million homes capable of doing something is usually the number to get serious attention. The question became: "How do we get from 4000 homes in Orlando to 20 million homes nationwide — and then develop a worldwide system?" Microsoft was already providing that answer by building "TV functionality" into the Windows operating system. By TV functionality, I mean those functions that would allow the computer to become a TV receiver (after a TV tuner card is added to the computer). The system needed to provide the basics of TV operation, such as volume and color controls, instant on, and the more technical details of synchronizing a picture on the screen.

The initial project was conceived as a Microsoft/DIRECTV project that would utilize DIRECTV's satellite broadcast network. For several reasons, Microsoft stopped focusing only on DIRECTV and instead aimed the project toward the larger broadcast and cable TV universe. (One reason was the need for a customer base of approximately 20 million, which DIRECTV had not yet achieved.) Without the ability to receive data from a digital TV signal, the TV part of the operating system would also need to have the ability to decode additional data sent through the broadcast's Vertical Blanking Interval (VBI). This would be necessary to begin in the analog TV world rather than wait for broadcasters to convert their signals to digital.[5]

Summary

- Time Warner started the Full Service Network (FSN) trial in the mid-1990s, based in Orlando, Florida, with approximately 4000 subscribers that the company equipped with $10,000 boxes.

- The creation of a successful interactive TV scenario faced two critical hurdles: promising and delivering a mass-market ITV user base totaling in excess of 20 million viewers and involving the important content producers and developers who have mastered the art of holding an audience's attention through television.

- The economic models that drive television were a logical way to understand how to create such a scenario. Subscription services such as HBO

5. The Federal Communications Commission (FCC) has actually set a firm timetable for all broadcasters to make this change, although there is some question about whether broadcasters will adhere to the schedule.

can charge a fee because of the perceived value of the content they carry (movies that have been hyped over and over, conveniently delivered to consumers' homes uncut). Conversely, ITV has no such perceived value. A successful ITV model would have to be based on advertising, the main revenue source of the TV industry.

The Mathematics of Enhanced TV

Here is a lesson in the mathematics of deploying enhanced TV presented by a TV person (not by a Microsoft marketing person). I want to present facts that are real or generally accepted, so as to leave as little room for debate as possible:

- There are approximately 40 million computers in U.S. homes today.[6] I don't believe that people would get rid of their home computers (they would only replace them). If we forecast no growth at all, there would still be 40 million homes with computers in 3 years.

- The replacement cycle for a home computer has been approximately 3 years. The cycle is becoming shorter, but we will assume it stays the same.

- Most of the home computers in the United States are running a Microsoft operating system. Even should Microsoft be broken up into separate companies, the Windows-based operating system will still run the majority of computers. I used to be a big Apple Macintosh devotee, but even I have come to realize that Apple missed the opportunity to become the leading operating system.

Forget the percentage of people that may actually install a TV tuner card on an existing computer that was upgraded to Windows 98. Some will, but we will consider them a bonus. Most computer manufacturers are offering some products with tuner cards preinstalled. More manufacturers plan to do so next year. If TV people create some cool enhanced TV content, computer manufacturers will include TV tuner hardware, because it's relatively cheap to install at the time of manufacture. For computer manufacturers, this seems to me like a no-brainer. For the relatively low cost of adding tuner functionality, they can turn a computer into a TV and go after the market represented by 230 million[7] TV sets (U.S. only), as well as the growing home computer market.

6. According to the *National Survey of Hardware Ownership Methodology*, July 1997, there were 99.4 million households and 42 million had computers.

7. There are actually 98 million U.S. homes with TVs and an average of 2.36 sets per home, according to Nielsen Media Research (figures compiled during the 1997–1998 TV season).

Assume one-half of the people who replace their home computer purchase one with a TV tuner card. We then have 20 million TV-ready[8] computers sitting out there in just 3 years. I predict that TV-ready computers will become ubiquitous, as CD-ROM drives are today. Just a few years ago, when you replaced your home computer, manufacturers asked if you wanted to add a CD-ROM drive. Today, most new computers come with a CD-ROM preinstalled. TV-ready computers will become a common piece of equipment in millions of homes.

This approach gets a great many enhanced TV-ready units deployed in a relatively short period of time but does not address the issue of the demographic composition of the group likely to use a computer as a TV. My 12-year-old daughter Nicole and 11-year-old son Jon would do it without thinking. Simply by observing the way they watch television, I could see that they didn't have the built-in prejudices of an older generation. Often they would be watching TV and on the Internet at the same time. Screen size seemed less important than the density or intensity of the media experience. They are more active viewers. They do not think of television as the only screen in the house. They grew up playing video games on a small TV in their bedrooms and then surfing the Internet on a 17-inch monitor. They would often open up an America Online chat room with several friends and then comment on what they were watching on TV. I would do it only for some shows that aren't very intellectually challenging so that I could watch TV and answer my e-mail at the same time. Most people of my generation and almost all of my parents' generation aren't about to trade in a 60-inch screen to watch baseball on a 17-inch computer monitor that they have to boot up instead of just turn on. It would also be necessary to have a way to experience enhanced TV on devices larger than a computer monitor.[9] Again, TV producers want to reach the largest audiences possible.

How can people over the age of 30 view enhanced TV shows? A number of companies have developed add-on boxes, such as the WebTV Plus box, which will allow viewers to use their existing big-screen TVs to watch television and surf the Internet at the same time. These companies predict sales of several million of the boxes in the next few years. Then there are the announced deals to put Windows CE (the operating system that runs handheld and other consumer devices) into the cable television set-top box. A Microsoft deal with TCI calls for at least 5 million of these to be installed in the near future.

8. Editor's Note: TV ready is a term we have coined to denote computers with TV tuner hardware, thus making them capable of receiving television. Think of TV ready in much the same way as you think of your television as being cable ready.

9. Editor's Note: A computer with WebTV for Windows and the proper video hardware (which a number of video card manufacturers are now including as a standard feature) can display its output to a television.

Other systems that deliver additional data or enhanced TV content are out there competing heavily with each other. Intel has a system called Intercast, which also delivers data through the VBI. Windows 98 includes Intercast reception capabilities, which allow enhanced TV shows broadcast in the Intercast format to display on a Windows 98 computer. Wink and WorldGate also have systems that can do similar things and are signing deals with cable operators and networks and even TV manufacturers to incorporate their technology. Just as Intel and Microsoft started out with incompatible systems and have now come to agreement on standards, I predict that the rest of these players will do the same. As a TV producer, I make one show and it plays just as well on a Sony television as it does on an RCA television. When it comes to creating enhanced content, I want to do the same. Write once and then be available to the masses.

No matter how pessimistic you want to be with the numbers, you still conclude that there will be enough enhanced TV-ready units out there within a relatively short period of time to satisfy the advertising community and get it to support the development of enhanced content. This will attract advertisers, which also gets the networks' attention, and so on down the TV food chain. Yet you have still to create something to go on these devices that will be of value to the consumer.

Summary

- Delivering TV reception capability in computers via Windows will probably establish an interactive TV base audience numbering in the range of 20 million to 40 million in the next 2 to 3 years.

- Such deployment does not address demographic issues. Although the concept of watching television on a computer is not a difficult one for people under the age of 30 to accept, it won't fly for people over 30.

- Set-top boxes and televisions with integrated interactive capabilities are already being deployed, albeit in smaller quantities. The key is that a significant number of devices capable of receiving and displaying interactive content will be widely deployed within the next 2 to 3 years.

Interactivity That Worked

Our next step was to find examples of interactive television that worked. We did indeed find the perfect example of what interactive or enhanced TV should be. In the 1950s (yes, the years of Elvis) there was a children's TV show called *Winky Dink and You*. This was an animated show with fun little characters that you came to know and enjoy. You made it your business to watch the show because it was good.

- Important Point #1: The show has to be good in and of itself.

If you were a lucky kid, your parents bought you the Winky Dink game, which consisted of a piece of plastic shaped like a TV screen (ironically, this was called a "magic TV window") and several crayons. The writers of the show were aware that several million kids had the game and they would weave usage of it into the plot. For example, when Winky Dink came to a river, they would stop the action and say "Hey kids, Winky Dink can't cross the river, put up your screen and help him out." You put the plastic on the TV screen (static electricity held it in place) and then used a crayon to draw a boat or a bridge. Miraculously, Winky Dink hopped across the river. As a kid who chose to participate, you felt that you helped him. You felt that you actually participated in determining the outcome of the show. It was a deeper and more committed experience. During the commercials, I would find myself coloring in the things I drew, thus keeping me with the show (and the commercials). The kid who was not interested in interacting with the show could simply do nothing. Winky Dink still hopped over the river. The show was still fun. I will take this time to confess to my mother that sometimes I didn't "just forget" to put the plastic on, but that I thought it would be even more fun to draw directly on the screen. (Please don't spank me.) Parts of the Winky Dink kit are shown in Figures 1.1 and 1.2.

- Important Point #2: The viewers must decide to opt into the interactive mode (as opposed to opting out of it).

The decision to participate was something that you needed to initiate proactively (that is, put up the plastic). Viewers who simply wanted to watch the show didn't have to do anything. Interactivity was not forced on them. Most of the time, most viewers want to do nothing. Sometimes some viewers want to do something. Keep this in mind all the time: Don't turn off the masses in order to appeal to the few, but also give those who want to interact at some level the ability to do so.

Let's examine this experience more closely. We added a layer of density (the plastic) over a linear television show and were able to provide an optional interactive experience utilizing the capabilities of that layer of density. In the new computer devices, we have the ability to have two inputs: The TV source (roof antenna, cable) plugs into one input and the Internet connection (phone line or cable modem) into the other. The equivalent of Internet-delivered information or elements can also be accomplished by delivering them via the VBI. We can have both sources appear on the screen at the same time. Let's put a Web browser over a linear TV show and voilà!

WINKY DINK '98 (sorry, Windows marketing folks, for renaming your product).

Figure 1.1   Part of the *Winky Dink* kit. (The author gratefully acknowledges Harry W. Prichett and Edwin Brit Wyckoff, the creators of the *Winky Dink* character, for their permission to reprint Winky Dink–related material here.)

Whatever the capabilities of the Web, they become the capabilities that we can use to interact with the TV program. So as the Web becomes more sophisticated, the level of enhancements can increase accordingly. Right now, the amount of data we can deliver via the VBI is restricted. (The number of lines is limited and some are already used for private forms of data delivery or for transmission of test and reference signals.) Once the TV world goes digital, these restrictions disappear and we will have plenty of bandwidth available to deliver enhancements or interactive elements as part of the TV transmission itself. Only when we need to "connect" to the outside world (chat, e-mail, transactions, polling, and so on) will we need to have a return path on the Internet.

We had a coherent case for why TV people should begin to work with the technologies available. Simply said, why wait for digital when the key questions are essentially the same? We set out to find a few daring individuals and companies that wanted to get a jump on their brethren and work with us on some demonstrations.

Everyone essentially agreed that adding layers of content would work with certain genres of programs such as news, sports, and documentaries. It was also clear that

Figure 1.2   An advertisement for the *Winky Dink* kit. (Image reprinted with permission from Hollywood Ventures Corporation. © 1999 Hollywood Ventures Corporation.)

game shows could take advantage of the viewer's ability to play at home and serve as a way to lure viewers back to the television. Although some TV people wished otherwise, I believe that TV viewing in households with young adults (ages 12–24) and an Internet connection has declined at least 40% in the past 2 years. From observing my kids and their friends, I could see that this wasn't just some geek phenomenon. Before they "discovered the Net," these were the same kids who spent all their time watching *Nickelodeon* on cable. Their time on the Internet was coming from their TV time. My conversations with other parents indicate that this is a fairly common experience.

Summary

- *Winky Dink and You,* a black-and-white television show first broadcast in 1953, is the first example of interactive television. Through use of a Winky Dink kit that included plastic and markers, viewers could interact with the show.

- Television programming must be good in and of itself. Show-specific enhancements can add value but only if the underlying program is good.

- Interactive programming should always be an option, not a requirement.

Exploring the Genres

Let's examine some of the more obvious ways to enhance the various genres of television programming. Keep in mind that I am not stating "Here is the definitive treatise on what enhancements should be, or which enhancements will work." Rather, I feel the way the early TV pioneers must have felt during the late 1940s. They all came from radio, so early TV programming was simply pointing cameras at radio shows. Only after 1953 did some daring individuals examine the creative possibilities to the point where they felt that they could actually create shows specifically for television. After 1953, television provided creative opportunities for people like Rod Serling, Paddy Chayefsky, and Sidney Lumet. Shows such as *Hallmark Hall of Fame,* "Marty," and *Your Show of Shows* are still considered among the best TV shows ever made. To many TV historians, this was the dawn of the "golden age of television." In terms of interactivity and enhancements, today we are in the television equivalent of 1947, having done the obvious in bringing the TV and Web experiences together. When more brains, and particularly new brains that are not confined by years of doing it just one way, are applied to the creative issues, we will advance quickly to the "golden age of interactive TV."

Here is a quick example of how a "new brain" (my daughter Nicole) can enlighten the thinking of a long-time TV professional. Early on in examining interactive television, I decided that "branching" or creating multiple endings to stories was never going to get enough interest to be affordable to produce. Great storytellers take you on a journey. The journey on TV typically has one road. I always thought of enhanced TV as having a single road as well. The enhanced component would take only one direction with the information or messages it would deliver. The thought never occurred to me that this was more a function of the storyteller adapting to the constraints of TV technology than the storyteller's desire to travel only one path. When my daughter saw the enhanced version of *F/X: The Series* (discussed later in this chapter), she didn't like it as much as my son.

"You did this for boys, not girls," she said. "That's because boys tend to watch this series more than girls," I responded, confident I had put her query to rest. "Well, why don't you create two different sets of enhancements. One for me when I log on, and another for Jon when he logs on. Maybe then girls will get to like this show more." I was getting TV lessons from my daughter. She was right. There is no technical reason that there can't be multiple sets of enhancements meant to appeal to different groups of viewers. There could even be levels of enhancements just as there are levels to a video game. This could certainly be a way of expanding traditional demographic viewer patterns. New brains, new ideas.

News

Television news is served up in short bites that are designed to hold the interest of the generally interested viewer. For the most part, it is assumed that most viewers just want the basic facts and aren't looking for the in-depth story. With the exception of news analysis shows, the news is designed to deliver an overview of the top stories in 30 minutes or less. The news director is often faced with the problem of having too much information and must make editorial decisions about what to leave out. Utilizing enhanced TV technology doesn't allow the news director to devote more time to a story, but it does allow him or her to devote more depth.

Here are some simple examples:

- A news photographer returns from the scene of a dramatic accident with some compelling photographs. Confined by time, the director chooses one and eliminates the others. But enhanced technology allows the news director to choose one photograph for the linear TV broadcast and post the rest on the Web or deliver them via VBI. The interested viewer can choose the "more photos" button on the browser and have the chance to see this story in more depth.

- A politician is on the news telling us how she views a specific issue. We can connect the interested viewer with data on that politician's voting record on similar issues.

- As a news anchor reports an air strike in Bosnia, we can let the interested viewer pull up a map or even connect directly to a chat room in which other interested viewers are sharing opinions.

Another way to approach news is to use it to enhance TV program viewing:

Although this suggestion might upset many TV writers and producers — and hey, I consider myself a producer — I submit that not everything we create is so deep and so compelling that viewers must keep their eyes glued to the screen all the time. Just watching people watch TV is a good way of validating this notion. My father watches TV while reading the newspaper. I watch TV while I read a report or answer my e-mail. My kids watch TV, do their homework, and talk on the phone at the same time. As a TV station or network executive, I have a vested interest not only in attracting viewers but also in keeping them tuned in to my channel. Since the advent of the remote control, this has become a difficult task. Viewers change channels even during shows they like because they are also interested in other things. For example, although I might be watching a perfectly good movie of the week, I will switch to ESPN to get the scores of my favorite teams. My father might interrupt his viewing to check some stock listings on Bloomberg. A farmer in the Midwest might tune away from *Homicide* to check the tornado warnings on The Weather Channel.

Why not stream the data related to the viewer's most common information needs right in the VBI of the channel so that the viewer can choose from a series of tickers? This allows viewers to layer the screen with not just the program they want but also the *information* they want. Rather than clicking away from the channel, viewers can stay right where they are. Ultimately, keeping viewers results in higher Nielsen ratings, which produces higher revenue, which results in a higher value for the writer and producer on future projects. More money or more work typically can help heal the ego bruises.

Sports

Now here is where you can get even my father to enjoy the benefits of enhanced TV. Why must he wait for the network to put up the 10-minute ticker in order to find out what the rest of the National Football League (NFL) is doing? He can just click the "scores" button and get them whenever he wants them. He can also quickly get the statistics on the player who just scored the big touchdown.

A set of enhancements could be designed for particular demographic segments of the audience. By watching in the "enhanced for novices mode," those viewers can receive enhanced pages that explain the finer points of the game, thereby making it more accessible and enjoyable.

When technology improves, my father can choose a second camera angle from among a dozen "extra" cameras at the football stadium and be able to watch a streaming video feed coming from the camera isolated on the quarterback.

Documentaries and How-to Shows

People usually watch documentaries because they are especially interested in the subject matter. For example, during Ken Burns' *The Civil War*, a history buff might find it useful to have battlefield maps appear on the screen, whereas the more general viewer simply wants to watch the documentary. A student watching a documentary on the sinking of the *Titanic* might want to find out if any other documentaries are scheduled that chronicle the disaster in more depth. It is easy to provide this information by building that data right into the transmission.

No one will disagree that someone interested in a hobby show may want the ability to hit the "plans" button and download the diagrams that show exactly how to build that model railroad or even print out a 20%-off coupon to buy that cool new diesel engine.

Game Shows

There is no disputing the popularity of shows such as *Wheel of Fortune* or *Jeopardy*. As a TV producer, I would be interested in anything that helps me keep my most loyal viewers. There is no denying that some fans would welcome the opportunity to play along with the show. Although playing against the studio guests may not be practical at this time (most game shows are taped and replayed, making live home play impossible), it is certainly possible to have home viewers play against other home viewers. If I were the producer, I would use this technology to broaden the demographics of the viewing audience. For instance, I'm sure my 12-year-old daughter and 11-year-old son would be more interested in watching this show if they could play a scaled-down version of it designed for kids their age. There is no reason that there can't be different levels of enhancements for various levels of skill.

Summary

- News, sports, documentaries, and game shows are all excellent candidates for the addition of enhanced content.

- Viewers can receive content that is unrelated to a particular show — such as news headlines and weather information — through optional tickers that enhance a channel's regular programming.

Getting Started

Most people believe that the genres of television programs I've described so far could be enhanced. Therefore, it became important to the MITV team to prove that all shows, even the more complex genres such as comedy, action, adventure, and drama, could be enhanced. If we were to get members of the TV industry to react, then they had to see that enhancement was going to be a part of the whole TV pie, not just a slice. A lot of people asked why we didn't just start with the easier genres such as news and sports. On the surface this appears logical. However, in Hollywood there are certain strong and respected voices that must be convinced if you have any hope of moving the TV industry in a new direction. The "voices" that shape the industry belong to people like Aaron Spelling, Steven Bochco, David Kelley, and, more recently, Chris Carter. These are the creators of television's most popular shows. We had to convince them that interactive programming was not just a limited tool for news directors at local TV stations.

A prior example was color television. All the TV networks began reoutfitting their facilities for color TV broadcast when they saw that color was "an enhancement" for all TV programs. We wanted to get a few TV shows to work with us in creating enhanced versions of their shows. The method for selecting the shows was not terribly scientific: We wanted to work with shows that we felt lent themselves well to enhancement (meaning that we could readily think of some fun things to do with them). More important, we wanted to work with producers or companies that we felt really "got it" and that would be enthusiastic about creating enhanced content for their shows.

Doing a TV show on a regular basis is difficult. Series TV episodes are usually the result of many 16-hour days. The last thing we wanted to do was invent something (enhanced TV) while working with a production company that felt we were just getting in the way and causing them extra work and even longer hours. So, rather than try to go top down (get a network to support it and have them just tell the producer that they wanted this done), we decided it best to work with producers directly and win their support first.

Many TV executives and creative types were warm to the idea at first. Although some people considered my previous TV work (most notably *Movietime*, which later changed its name to *E!*) to be nothing more than video wallpaper (pictures that decorated a room without much intellectual substance), now even my supporters began doubting my sanity. "You want to do *what* to my show?" was a frequent response to our pitch. "How can people focus on more than one thing at a time?" was another common response.

The more egotistical producers would understand how this might be OK for other shows but certainly not for theirs. Their shows were so "deep and rich" that the viewer needed to pay total attention to the original show. They could not stop paYing 100% attention. Not even to sneeze. When I heard this, I often wondered how long it had been since they actually watched anyone watch TV.

To get started, we consulted with friends to see if they could give us a lead on a few TV executives or producers who might be excited by the opportunity to explore a whole new approach to TV. My former partner at *E!*, Alan Mruvka, volunteered a show that he created. *Pacific Blue* was on USA Network every Sunday evening. It was about cops on bikes at the beach. Some people refer to it as a poor man's *Baywatch*. Although Alan wasn't part of the production team, he did introduce us to Gary Nardino[10] and Bill Nuss, the show's executive producers.

Gary was quite a bit older than Bill, so we assumed that Bill would be the one who would be more comfortable with the concept of interactive programming and with the use of computers in general. We were wrong. It was Gary who was a great student of how today's audiences were watching television and had a better sense of who his audience was (for *Pacific Blue*) and what they would respond to. Without much convincing, both Gary and Bill agreed to work with us on creating an enhanced TV demo of a complete episode.

Next, Stan Kamens, a well-known talent manager, suggested we speak with some people at Big Ticket Television (a subsidiary of Spelling Entertainment). Led by the creative talents of former HBO executive Bill Sanders, Big Ticket was Aaron Spelling's[11] foray into the world of half-hour sitcoms. Its first hit was *Moesha*, which appeared on United Paramount Network (UPN).

Sanders (whose chapter appears later in this book) turned out to be one of the most computer-literate executives we encountered. He met our proposal with great enthusiasm and introduced us to the show's executive producer, Ralph Farquar. Ralph also "got it" right away, having been a producer who (like me) studied the TV viewing habits of his family. Ralph knew that his young son could handle much more stimulation than most TV was providing. Ralph wanted to be among the first to learn the use of this new technology. He agreed to let us join his team and create an enhanced version of *Moesha*.

10. Gary Nardino was a respected TV producer and studio executive who had a long and successful career before his death in 1997. One of his most popular shows was *Happy Days*.

11. Aaron Spelling is one of the most prolific creator–producers in TV history. Some of his key hits are *Love Boat*, *Melrose Place*, and *Beverly Hills 90210*.

Rysher Entertainment (a subsidiary of Cox Broadcasting), led by Rob Keneally, also "got it" right away. Rysher let us work on *F/X: The Series*, a show inspired by a successful theatrical film called *FX*, in which a special effects expert in films uses his skills for crime fighting.

Now the trick was to figure out exactly what we were going to do with these shows. Paul Mitchell and Rick Portin were fortunate to hire two producers who came from the TV world but were also familiar with the new technologies and how they might be applied to television: Kris Evans and Marie-Rose Phan-Le were the first two people to join the team and were assigned the task of producing the enhanced television versions of *F/X: The Series*, *Moesha*, and *Pacific Blue*.

Pacific Blue

Kris was given *Pacific Blue*. She had to figure out both what the enhancements would be and how to integrate herself and her team into the production process. The first task was relatively easy. The second task, integrating into the system and getting full cooperation, turned out to be another story. Whereas the production executives agreed to be part of the program, getting the attention of the writing staff and other key people turned out to be much more difficult. It was essential that Kris and her team be kept in the loop so that the enhancements they conceived and created were relevant to the direction the story took. Many scenes that are written and even shot don't make it into the final edited version of a show. Scenes are often rewritten right before they are shot. Close coordination was difficult, and it didn't help that the executive producers didn't convey their support to the show's staff.

Fortunately, an executive at the USA Network, Doug Holloway, recognized the potential in what we were doing and brought our project to the attention of then USA President Kay Koplowitz. Kay came to Microsoft and had a technology demonstration. To say she understood how this could benefit her network would be an understatement. Kay became a big supporter and later even agreed to let us work on enhancing USA's entire Sunday night lineup, which they marketed under the name "Sunday Night Heat." Kay saw the potential for enhanced television to engage viewers in a way that regular television couldn't. She felt that some of the technology could change the "produce all shows for the lowest common denominator" mentality that was prevalent in most TV production and allow TV creative people to develop shows with layers of density. The viewer could choose to click (with a remote control) "deeper" into any show, instead of clicking away from a show, as viewers so often do. There could be opportunities to create shows that would satisfy the "inquiring mind" and the "couch potato" at the same time.

With the open support of Doug Holloway and Kay Koplowitz of USA, the relationship between Kris and her team and the folks at *Pacific Blue* miraculously improved, and the first enhanced full episode of any TV show was produced. The enhancement of *Pacific Blue* was not a definitive work but rather a first attempt at integrating extra material into the primary story by use of data delivered by the VBI. Today I can look at what was done with *Pacific Blue* and realize how reminiscent it is of early television production. Early TV pioneers had to create not only shows but also technology to accomplish the goal of producing entertaining experiences. *Pacific Blue* was a start, but we had a long way to go.

One example of technology that had to be invented to meet the creative needs of early TV producers was the effect of fading out at the end of a scene. For producers to stage scenes just for TV, as opposed to just keep rolling the cameras, they needed to "fade" out of one scene as a natural transition to another. In creating enhanced TV, we came across the same kinds of issues. Things we were normally accustomed to doing as TV people had not yet been invented for the Web (such as the ability to fade out of one page and into another).

Kris was faced with having to work with people who weren't quite sure why she was there. Moreover, back at Microsoft, things weren't quite stable. First, no one really understood exactly what would be needed to make this all work as seamlessly as the TV show itself. The methods for synchronizing story-related pages with their associated content had to be invented as Kris was producing. The internal politics at Microsoft posed a second challenge. The value of this project was beginning to be recognized by the higher ups, and where the MITV group was to report was the subject of some debate. After the Broadcast PC initiative (the internal name for WebTV for Windows) became part of Windows 98, the value rose again and the debate increased.

Even with all these difficulties, Kris managed to complete the first show on time and very close to the original budget. In June 1996, the first episode was screened for the cast and crew of *Pacific Blue*. Once they saw it, they got it immediately. The writers saw how the technology could be deployed to enhance the storytelling process. It was amazing how the ideas began to flow for what to do on the upcoming episodes.[12] Unfortunately, Windows 98 was delayed, USA was bought by Universal, and there were no new enhanced episodes of *Pacific Blue*. Screen shots of the enhanced versions of *Pacific Blue* are shown in Figures 1.3 and 1.4.

12. After seeing the enhanced episode, the writers and the cast felt that they could have done much more than they did with integrating enhancements into the story. They thought the pace could be quickened and that more details about a great deal of the gear (bicycles in particular) could be included. They even wanted to integrate props from the show (a Personal Digital Assistant or PDA) into the enhanced space.

Figure 1.3 An interactive version of *Pacific Blue*. (The author gratefully acknowledges Gary Nardino and Bill Nuss, executive producers, for their permission to include *Pacific Blue* material here.)

Moesha

Marie-Rose Phan-Le had a bit easier road ahead with *Moesha*. Everyone from the production executives to the writers supported her project. Paul and Rick rewarded her by assigning her to produce an enhanced episode of *FX: The Series* at the same time. Enhancing *Moesha* presented some new and interesting creative challenges. It was a comedy, and comedy relied on setting up the joke for the punch line and on tight timing. The writers were cautious about having any additional story elements appear on the screen at any time near the payoff of a funny scene. In fact, they created a special screen (with a gently moving, subtle pattern) to say: QUIET, WE ARE TELLING A JOKE.

Marie-Rose and the *Moesha* team came up with a few interesting uses of enhanced TV technology that sparked Paul, Rick, Bob, and me to come up with even more complex uses that could particularly be applied to creating a financial reality for the whole project. For example, the *Moesha* demonstration uses the "thought bubble."

Figure 1.4   Another scene from the interactive version of *Pacific Blue*.

When Brandy, the actor who plays Moesha, said something on screen to her little brother, a picture of Brandy appeared in the enhanced TV space[13] with a thought bubble over her head showing what she really wanted to say (as shown in Figure 1.5). This use quickly gave us a new device that we knew television people would understand and relate to on the basis of the economics of the business.

Summary

- A valuable part of enhancements is that they offer layers of additional information and content to the viewer. Instead of using their remote to click away to other programs, viewers will be able to click deeper into a show.

- Spend some time watching others watch TV. Today, no one just watches TV. Kids, in particular, do their homework, talk on the phone, browse the Web,

---

13. There was no technical reason why the enhancements could not be laid over the TV picture itself. However, most TV people felt that the show and the enhancement must be distinctly separated. The format most TV people favored was an L shape that appeared in the upper right part of the screen and fit around the TV picture. There was no science or other research applied to this. It just seemed to be the logical configuration.

Figure 1.5   A screen shot from the interactive version of *Moesha*. (The author gratefully acknowledges Bill Sanders for his permission to include *Moesha* material here.)

and play games with the television on. It's silly for producers and network or station executives to believe that viewers tune in and stay tuned in.

- Executive support that isn't visible doesn't help. Before starting on an interactive television project, make sure that the senior level contacts with whom you're working have made it clear to the individuals producing and making the show that you're part of the team.

Show Me the Money

Series television is usually produced at a loss (to the production company). Only when a series reaches critical mass in the number of episodes produced can it be syndicated and then become profitable. Let me explain, using *Moesha*, UPN, and Big Ticket in an example that uses totally fictitious numbers.

The network, UPN, pays a license fee of $500,000 per episode to Big Ticket (the production company) for the right to show the episodes on their network exclusively for a period of time. The per episode cost to produce could actually be $650,000, causing Big Ticket to lose $150,000 per episode. This is known as deficit financing. If *Moesha* were to be an unpopular series and be taken off the air after just 22 episodes (usually the number of episodes produced for 1 year's airing), then Big Ticket would take a loss of $3.3 million (22 × $150,000). Why would Big Ticket make a deal knowing that they were losing money on every episode?

Because the reward for success is so huge that a production company can have a few "losers" mixed with a winner or two and still show huge profits. If *Moesha* is a success and gets to the point where it has 100 episodes produced, it becomes a candidate for syndication.[14] Big Ticket can now sell these episodes to TV stations around the country (or even to a cable network). Over 200 TV markets in the United States have stations that could buy *Moesha* reruns. If Big Ticket can sell the show to these stations for an average of $10,000 per market, per episode, then they will see a revenue stream of $1,000,000 per episode. This now changes their loss of $150,000 to a profit of $850,000. The numbers for shows such as *Seinfeld* are even more dramatic. The TV trade paper, *The Hollywood Reporter*, wrote that Jerry Seinfeld turned down a $100 million fee just to appear in the 1998–1999 season. The popular belief in Hollywood is that the value of an episode of *Seinfeld* is over $10 million.

The "golden goose" in TV is syndication.

So, let's use enhanced TV technology to make a syndicated show even more valuable.[15] If the number of actual viewers can be increased beyond the estimated audience rating that the syndication fees were originally based on, then the show becomes more valuable in subsequent syndication runs. I will use *Seinfeld* as an example.

As a *Seinfeld* fan, I look in the TV listings and see that a local station is running the famous "Soup Nazi" episode of *Seinfeld*.[16] Because I have already seen that particular episode, I also look to see what else is on. If there is something of interest, I will tune to that. If not, I will default to the episode I already saw. I think this is the way the average viewer reacts to the program choice decision.

As the TV producer, there is something I can do to make the *Seinfeld* fan choose the rerun as the primary viewing choice rather than as a default. I can put cartoon Jerry

14. Syndication — or reruns, as we used to call the second (or tenth) run of a TV series — means that shows are sold to broadcast stations or now even cable networks for airing during the times not being filled by network feeds. For example, an NBC-affiliated station in a particular city gets its programming from the NBC network to fill its prime time (and some other) program slots. This is usually from 8 to 11 P.M. daily. The station buys programming to fill the rest of the day not programmed by the network.

15. The value is based on what ratings a TV station feels it can get with the show. Ratings are the factor that determines the advertising rate a station can charge.

16. The "Soup Nazi" episode is one of the most famous in the history of the series. The story is about a local restaurant where the soup is so good the owner can impose dictatorial control over potential customers.

in the enhanced TV space (just as on *Moesha*) and have him tell some of the jokes that didn't make it into the episode. He can tell us funny things that happened when they shot that episode. He can expose the bloopers (mistakes). In short, he can refresh the content of the episode. As a fan, this is now a new experience for me. I want to hear Jerry's story about things related to making that episode. It is now my first choice. Next time around, the TV producer can have cartoon George in the enhanced space, and later Elaine, the popular female character. They can constantly be updating the show and providing me, the viewer, with a new experience every time I come back.

Although the original episode can't be refreshed, the enhanced space can be changed frequently and economically. We found that on a show such as *Moesha*, an entire episode could be enhanced for less than $30,000. This is a low price — about 5% of the shooting cost — and a mere pittance compared with the show's value in the syndication equation. Of course, these numbers don't reflect rights fees desired by the talent, but in the end everyone will share the additional revenue.

The enhanced *Moesha* episode polled the audience about certain plot points (for example, which shoes best matched Moesha's outfit, as shown in Figure 1.6) and

Figure 1.6 Choosing the shoes that match best in an interactive version of *Moesha*.

used the enhanced space to show the contents of letters that couldn't be seen clearly otherwise. (Imagine how the last aspect could be used to add clues to mysteries.)

Here are some other ideas that we came up with after looking at Marie-Rose Phan-Le's work on *Moesha*. Remember that her assignment was to explore the possibilities of using the enhanced TV technology, not to produce a definitive work:

- Downloading in the background discourages the viewer from changing channels (for fear of breaking the download). The viewer can't even change channels during a commercial, because the download might be occurring in the background.

- The availability of downloads can create a new category of viewer — one that initially cares more about the supplemental content than about the show itself. As a by-product of this interest, the viewer might become a fan and tune in more regularly.

For example, Brandy is a popular singer whose new album is due next month. MTV and radio play won't begin until that time. If Brandy and her record company agreed, we could offer the new single as a download sent via the VBI in tonight's episode. Anyone downloading it would have access a month ahead of other fans — a nice "present" for *Moesha* viewers. UPN gets a powerful promotion tool for *Moesha*, and the record company benefits from the promotional dollars spent by UPN.

Even today, many in the TV business consider the enhanced *Moesha* a high point. When Intel and the American Film Institute (AFI) recently held an enhanced TV workshop, Rick Portin was asked to demonstrate the *Moesha* episode as a prime example of how enhanced TV technology can be integrated into the storytelling process.

F/X: The Series

I'm not going to go into great detail about the next show to be enhanced — *F/X: The Series* — because I hated it.

It was my worst nightmare come true. I encouraged sensitivity to the story. I begged that they not get carried away and think that the enhancements can overshadow the TV show itself. I fought for use of subtle coloring in the enhanced space so as not to pull the viewer's eye away from the show. But what I saw was a bright green enhanced screen with a mind-boggling amount of activity in the enhanced space. After watching the whole demonstration, I couldn't even tell you what the show was about. The screen looked like a Nintendo game. It was a horror. I placed a screaming phone call to Rick and Marie-Rose.

The next day I happened to bring my 11-year-old son, Jon, into the office. He discovered the *F/X* demonstration on the conference room computer and thought it was the coolest thing yet. He didn't think it was "too much" and in fact he wanted more. He asked, "Why *can't* it look like a Nintendo game? I love Nintendo!" He made me realize something I thought I knew:

Interactive television today is TV in 1947.

We know nothing for sure. There are no experts. There are no rules. A reasonable number of people have figured out how to fill the TV space with some well-done shows. A more limited number are beginning to understand how to create some interesting things for the Internet (or the enhanced space). And very few are good at — or even understand — both. A new visual language is being developed. We are at the baby-talk stage.

Summary

- Production companies sell shows to networks at a loss. This is because one big hit that goes into syndication can result in huge profits, more than enough to cover the losses on shows that didn't do as well.

- Syndication is the "golden goose" of television. Producers can refresh the enhanced content for a given show at a very low cost relative to the cost of producing an entirely new episode. Each time a show is rerun, different interactive content can be provided to attract viewers who have already seen the episode.

- Don't make assumptions about how to use the new medium. Your kids (or someone else's kids) may be the best predictors of what will work and what won't.

Types of Interactivity

The jury is still out about how much viewers care about story-specific enhancements. Again, I think we need to move from 1947 to the golden age of television. More brains must be applied to the process and only then will we have enough creative content developed to make some strong judgments. However, I will put my butt on the line by telling you a few enhancements that I *know* should be part of every TV show. I can't say that a majority of viewers will use any of them at any given time, but I will say that some viewers will use some of them some of the time. As a TV producer, I want to use every tool available to me to attract viewers and keep them.

Chat

The buzz around the new media world is about how great the Internet is at building communities of interest. I believe that fans of a TV show are themselves a community. And they're a vocal community. Think about how *Seinfeld* fans would go to work the next day and constantly be asking their coworkers, "Did you see what Jerry did last night?" Fans of *Moesha* are equally interested in discussing her choice of boyfriend, her clothes, and Brandy's new album. Fans of *Melrose Place* have parties on show night, just to share the experience with other fans. TV provides the chatter that happens around the coffee machines of corporations across America. Although several TV professionals thought that enabling the viewer to chat during a show was disrespectful, I say let them chat away. If chat makes the show more fun and enjoyable, let them do it (as long as Nielsen[17] can continue to measure their viewing).[18]

On any given day there are more fans of *Seinfeld* than there are fans of Yahoo. (This is my own unscientific theory, which says that fans of *Seinfeld* are loyal and emotional, whereas Yahoo users are more likely to defect to another search engine without as much as a good-bye.) I don't see any brand loyalty on the Internet yet. Before I buy a book, I check out both Amazon.com and Barnes & Noble and buy from the site that offers the book at the lower price. Even the supposed devotees of Amazon don't seek out other devotees. On the other hand, fans of a TV show like to communicate with each other.

E-Mail

Fans of the show might want an easy and convenient way to send fan mail. Other fans might want to tell the writers their thoughts on the direction of the show. The writers themselves might want the fans to give them direction on a certain story point and might solicit e-mail on that subject. NBC is enhancing *Saturday Night Live*; it recently invited viewers to send in questions, which would be answered the following week.

17. Nielsen is the "bible" of audience measurement. The success or failure of a show is measured by its Nielsen rating. As a producer, I would never do anything that could jeopardize the rating.

18. Microsoft's WebTV for Windows team provided some sample code to Nielsen so that they could monitor viewers using WebTV for Windows. This was a big moment for Comspan, because it showed that our assignment to help Microsoft understand the "TV world" was having an effect on Microsoft thinking. They understood that Nielsen ratings were part of the TV food chain and decided to recognize what exists as opposed to trying to change the system. Technically, Microsoft could have started its own ratings service.

Backstory

This is a particularly good device for series television. In today's hectic world, the viewer can't always watch week to week without interruption. I have trouble catching up with the story in shows like *Melrose Place*. Here's a possible story line, which, although not real, exemplified the kind of confusing actions that may be experienced if you are not viewing regularly. Heather Locklear[19] enters a room, and a guy says hello to her. She clocks him with her purse. I sit there and wonder what the heck is going on. He just said hello. I didn't see the previous week's episode, so I am unaware that this is the same guy that she was going out with but that she found in an embrace with her best friend. To someone who saw the previous show, the scene makes perfect sense. To me it needs explanation. I should be able to hit the Backstory button and have a screen pop up on the side that tells me the dynamics of the scene. The writers of the show could very well anticipate that a viewer who missed last week's show will not understand the scene and use the enhanced space to speak to just those viewers without imposing on the rest.

Another way to use the Backstory feature is to provide extra material about a subject that isn't covered in depth during the show. For example, in the enhanced *Moesha* episode, the story dealt with an historical period known as the Harlem Renaissance. The writers felt that in 22 minutes[20] they never really explained the Harlem Renaissance in the kind of depth that they wanted to. They gave the viewers who wanted more information the option of receiving it. Again, this is another way to have television shows that can be designed to appeal to other than the lowest common denominator. There are many people who do not watch much television because they feel that it doesn't deal with issues at a very high intellectual level. In TV terms these people are known as "light viewers" or "I only watch PBS" viewers. The Backstory feature might appeal to this group and increase their total time using television. Although some might argue that more TV viewing is not such a good thing for our society, I guarantee that you will hear no such argument in the boardrooms of our TV networks.

Buy It (Transactions)

I love shopping on television. However, with enhanced TV technology, everything on the screen could theoretically be offered for sale without bothering me one bit.

19. Heather Locklear is the star of the show, whose character is often involved in dramatic, and sometimes overly dramatic, conflicts with other characters.

20. Twenty-two minutes is about the average number of minutes in a 30-minute TV show, after subtracting advertising and promotions.

Let's say that you're watching *Home Improvement*[21] and are intrigued by a TV cabinet that Tim Allen is building. You could activate the broadcast enhancements, press the "Buy It" button (OK, maybe we call it "Product Information"), and receive the plans to build the cabinet, the parts list, dimensions, and a coupon to take to the nearest hardware store (and where it is located) for a 10% discount. For you, the show has now taken on an added value because of the enhancements. For me — hey, I didn't turn on the enhancements. I just wanted to watch my favorite show.

Perhaps you want to purchase some of the attractive clothes your favorite stars are wearing — or simply identify the designer. Maybe that *Pacific Beach* cop is riding a cool and unusual bicycle and you want to know more about it or find out where to get it. Enhancements can provide this service without getting in the way of passive viewers. Technically, you could even set this up so that the information goes into a sort of shopping cart that is not available to view until after the show ends.

Story So Far (SSF)

Many times I come home slightly after 9:00 P.M. and miss the beginning of the movie of the week (MOW). I tend not to watch these movies because I frequently can't catch up on the story quickly, so I move on to a channel that doesn't have a traditional beginning, middle, and end structure. *MTV* and *E!* are good examples of channels that are more or less environments that you tune to as opposed to specific shows. You can enter and exit these channels freely without losing track of vital story points.

If the producers of the MOW took the plot and summarized it in sync with the running time of the show, I could press the Story So Far (SSF) button and learn what I missed right up to the point where I came in. The story and the show are now a bit more accessible to me. I might just watch instead of tuning away. If I stay with the show, the producers and the network have scored a victory. The same type of device can be used to "bookmark" or create placeholders within the story for viewers who have to go to the bathroom or answer the phone during the show. They click when they leave and click again when they return. Text pops up that tells them what happened while they were gone. Like many of the features of interactive TV, this feature can be sponsored.

More Like This (MLT)

Every TV show (except *Seinfeld*) is about something. Why not find two or three books that deal with the main theme of every show and let the viewer who wants to

---

21. *Home Improvement* is an ABC comedy starring Tim Allen. It is among the highest rated shows on TV. The show is about a fictional TV show hosted by Allen, who gives tips on home improvement techniques and do-it-yourself projects.

go deeper into that subject have easy access to those books? A link to Barnes and Noble's Web site or to Amazon.com could be established, allowing the viewer to purchase the books instantaneously. This could also be done for videos or music. If you are watching a Civil War documentary, you might want to read a book, watch a video, or find out if other shows on the same topic will be broadcast later in the week. Such information and access could be made available through the More Like This feature.

Although enhanced TV has the potential to provide any number of compelling features, it is those I have described here that I will bet the farm on. It doesn't take a genius to know that they are useful and will provide utility to some percentage of the viewers. Seeing how my kids have diverted a great deal of what was TV time to the Internet, I want to use anything I can to make my TV projects more valuable, fun, and accessible. I don't care if 30% or just 1% of the audience uses the enhancements at any given time. Whatever the number is, it is more than I would have had. The more useful and fun I can make the show, the more viewers I will have and will keep. This translates into higher ratings and more revenue. The more revenue there is in the pot, the more money a TV producer can ask for from the network.

Summary

- Anything a producer, network, or station can do to maintain a viewer's interest is worth doing as long as the value of the number of viewers derived outweighs the cost of providing the interactive content.

- There are a number of basic interactive services that make the medium extremely compelling. Some require a back channel. The services include

    Chat centered on a particular show.

    E-mail feedback available from directly within a show.

    Backstory providing information about what happened in a previous episode or providing more depth about a scene.

    Buy It button, allowing you to purchase any placed product when you see it.

    Story So Far, which fills you in on the story so far or while you were out of the room.

    More Like This, which shows you Web links, books, videos, and other types of media related to a portion of the show.

Working with Television Stations and Networks

Another part of our work with Microsoft was to establish relationships with TV-station groups and networks — for several reasons:

- Microsoft needed an end-to-end test of its ability to send data within the Vertical Blanking Interval (VBI) of a TV signal and then receive and display it on a Windows 98 client.

- Local TV stations offered a unique opportunity because they are typically one of the most profitable parts of the TV food chain. We could not hope to get the best brains in television thinking about and doing enhanced TV unless we got the local stations involved in the process.

- Data inserted in the VBI did not have to be limited to just data that enhanced specific TV shows. It could be anything from news, sports, or weather feeds to personalized stock market data. Much clogging of the Internet can be attributed to lots of computers trying to receive essentially the same information. Broadcasting the data through the VBI could eliminate some Internet traffic jams and free up the bandwidth.

- Only the local broadcaster can have its signal received by all TV sets within a market. Cable or satellite can't make this claim. Think of the possibilities for a local broadcaster who had the unique ability to send data to all devices in its market that can receive and decode VBI signals. (And "devices" means more than TV sets: laptop computers and wristwatch receivers can also receive VBI signals. A host of new business opportunities becomes available.)

One of the things we did learn in this part of the project was that enhancement of the story was just one part of the value. We could think of just simply enhancing the experience of watching TV. Here is a simple example. If we were the owners of a TV station, it would be in our interest to be able to hold a viewer's attention, even if the particular show he or she was watching was not enhanced. The economics of enhancement may not permit local stations to enhance all shows, so they will be dependent on receiving a majority of their enhanced shows from the network with which they are affiliated.

Through our subsidiary Steeplechase Media Inc. (SMI) we created the SMI viewer (Figure 1.7), a generic viewing environment designed to allow anyone watching the channel on an enhanced TV-ready device to enjoy the experience in a different way than someone watching on a standard TV. Regardless of the show on at the moment, the viewer can enter a chat room with other viewers watching the channel. Viewers

Figure 1.7   A screen shot of the SMI viewer.

can send e-mail. They can access a Web site for the station. The station can also transmit news headlines, sports scores, and weather information to viewers through the VBI. The information is displayed via a ticker while any show is on. Although the feeds don't necessarily relate to the show, they help the station keep viewers.

Sometimes viewers are watching a show that they really do find interesting and compelling. However, they do have other interests and needs for information. For example, when watching a "movie of the week," I sometimes switch to ESPN to get sports scores, to CNN to find out what the United Nations peacekeeping troops are doing in Bosnia today, or to CNBC to check the stock market. A farmer in the Midwest might switch to The Weather Channel to find out the latest on the tornado coming his way. SMI's viewer can allow the TV viewer to choose to have certain information, such as news tickers, displayed on the same channel. For the station, anything that stops someone from changing channels is a big benefit.

Viewing Themes

Another feature that we developed arose from the cultural differences between us TV folks in Hollywood and those computer people (notice I didn't say geeks) at

Microsoft. When we sent a copy of the SMI viewer to Microsoft, Dave Feinleib called to let us know that we sent some bad code. The SMI viewer was blurry. *It took us nearly 2 months to get this exactly to the right point of blurry.* As a TV station, the video we would be displaying was never predictable. Set patterns and colors on the viewer would look fine on one show but yet totally clash when set alongside the next. The blurred-out viewer with buttons that "lit up" when you moused over them was the best design solution in our way of thinking. Not so at Microsoft. Dave likes definition and clarity. So we compromised by creating a feature called "Themes," which allows the viewer to choose the art plate that lives over the viewer. We can have the blurry viewer, Dave could have the clean and clear one, my kids could have one that looks like Nintendo, and my father could have one that looks like an old TV set.

Choice. What a concept!

Summary

- Enhancements don't have to be tied to a specific show. A viewing environment can provide generally useful information in the form of tickers and headlines, including news, sports, and weather.

- By offering multiple viewing environments in the form of themes, content providers can target distinct demographic segments of the viewing audience and provide both a different look and feel and different sets of information.

Conclusion

What in the world is Steeplechase?

Steeplechase Park was an early Disneyland. It was an amusement park in the Coney Island section of Brooklyn, New York. It was known around the world, and people traveled from all over to enjoy it and to sunbathe on the beaches that surrounded it. Just a block away is the original Nathan's Famous hot dog stand. I grew up not far from there, and it is one of the fond memories of my childhood. In fact, just about everyone over 40 who grew up on the East Coast thinks back on Steeplechase Park with fond memories. When they see my Steeplechase Media business card, they smile. Unfortunately, the park burned to the ground in the 1960s. All that is left today is the structure for a ride called "The Parachute Jump," which was first a part of the 1934 World's Fair and later moved to the Steeplechase site.

That, however, is not the point. When it comes to planning a cable network, it is hard to fool me. I can look at a TV show and come close to estimating what the budget should be. I will be off a little but never a lot. This comes from experience. When dealing with enhanced TV, we had no such experience to fall back on. How long will it take? How much will it cost? How do we produce the enhanced version in parallel with the TV show itself? These were all questions without answers yet.

Steeplechase Media started out as Comspan's lab. It is a company designed to specialize in the creation and production of enhanced television. It allowed us to think of ideas and then see if they were practical and applicable. Today, Steeplechase Media is an independent company (we own part and the employees own the rest), which is now trying to make a business out of enhanced TV production. It has taken great pains to identify the few people out there who are fluent in both television and new media.

Rick Portin is no longer executive producer of Microsoft Interactive TV. He now heads up Steeplechase Media on a day-to-day basis. (I'm still the chairman.) We have recruited some really good producers and writers. We typically collaborate with more traditional Web development companies because we don't see the need to keep HTML people working directly for us. The same is true for fulfillment, database creation, and back-end processing. We see SMI as an enhanced TV studio that sets up deals with TV shows or networks and then brings in the best people to supplement its core staff of creative people. (Of course, we do have some highly qualified technical folks of our own just to keep us ahead of the curve and also to make sure the webmasters don't take advantage of us TV folks.) As TV people, we want to create enhancements just once that will work on any device. After all, when we create shows for television, they will play just as well on a Zenith as they will on a Sony. We don't have to change the code. This is the way it will need to be if enhanced TV is to maximize its reach and potential. The impending arrival of common content standards will be a first step in this direction.

In August 1998, the Documentary Channel — a new cable TV network scheduled to launch in mid 1999 — signed an agreement with Steeplechase Media to create an entire enhancement plan that would provide a fully enhanced channel at launch. The original business plan for the channel is interesting, in that it planned for enhancement from the inception of the idea. The agreement with Steeplechase will make that a reality, with the result being the very first made-for-enhancement network. Mark Derbecker of Steeplechase led the team that developed the enhancement plan and addressed the myriad technical issues that arose. The work on the Documentary Channel (Figure 1.8) is taking enhancement technology and creativity into a new era.

Figure 1.8   An interactive version of the Documentary Channel.

Glossary:
The TV Food Chain and Its Major Components

Because venturing out into the TV world will be a new experience for a lot of you (I am assuming most of the readers come from the computer industry), here are some brief definitions of the key positions and entities that make up the TV business.

Jobs

Executive producer: Has overall responsibility for delivering the show for air. Will often have more than one producer reporting to him in order to keep a weekly series schedule.

Producer: Responsible for coordinating a specific episode and all the department heads necessary for the production.

Creator: Designs and develops the series idea and format, frequently writes the pilot and reviews all scripts. May write some episodes.

Head writer: Responsible for the overall continuity of writing for the series. The head writer approves all other writers' episode ideas and scripts. Frequently writes episodes of the show. (Recently this position has come to be known as "showrunner.")

Director: Designs the production staging for both actors and technicians, including all camera work.

Agent: Business representative for all talent (actors, actresses, writers, directors, and others) involved in the production. The agent is the interface between contracted talent and the studio business affairs department.

Manager: Another business representative for the talent, primarily responsible for overseeing the talent's entertainment career objectives.

Publicist: Represents the show and artists to the press and media, coordinates interview requests and personal appearances.

Entities

Studio: Producing organization for the show. Underwrites the costs of the series and frequently owns or rents the production facilities: stage, sets, lights, cameras, costumes, and makeup. Frequently hires a production company to produce the show for it, using some of its own facilities.

Network: Licenses all programs for national televising to local stations and/or cable systems. Fees paid to production companies typically cover 80% of the production costs. Transmits its advertisements along with its programs and specified slots for local TV ads.

Guild and union: SAG (Screen Actors Guild) and technical trade unions stipulate minimum work conditions and work fees for all talent and production personnel.

Advertising agency: Agencies represent corporations who advertise on television by planning and producing the commercials and by purchasing the time from the stations or network.

Production company: The major studios — Warner Brothers, Fox, Paramount, Universal, and Sony — produce many prime-time shows, but their work is augmented by independent companies such as Carsey-Werner, Gracie Films, Rysher Entertainment, and Spelling Entertainment.

CHAPTER 2

Tribune Company

www.tribune.com

This chapter provides the business and management perspective on Tribune's interactive content efforts and Tribune's work with Microsoft. This chapter is based on our work with Jeff Scherb and his team in 1997–1998 and on an interview conducted at his Tribune Tower office in Chicago on June 24, 1998. Scherb introduces several key concepts, including the role of cultural change agents in the digital era and the need to pre-purpose rather than repurpose content. Chapter 18 provides a detailed look at Tribune's technical efforts.

"The Enhanced TV project enables us to learn about what's possible and about how we might need to operate in the future. It's important for us to play with it now, because we want to have the ideas, not copy the ideas," says Jeff Scherb, chief technical officer of Tribune Corporation. Scherb, along with Ira Goldstone, vice president of broadcast engineering, has led the interactive television efforts at Tribune and has managed Tribune's corporate relationship with Microsoft.

Tribune began working with Microsoft on the interactive television (ITV) project in support of what Scherb describes as "a bigger picture strategy." The main goal was to create new kinds of content that leveraged data from Tribune's vast media assets. (Tribune owns 18 TV stations, four newspapers, and a content syndication business, with content ranging from comic strip and advertising distribution to television listings.) Scherb and Goldstone visited the Microsoft Home, a building where Microsoft demonstrates its leading-edge technologies, and decided that they definitely wanted to participate in the ITV project.

Tribune transmitted the company's first interactive broadcast in March 1998, with content that enhanced the pre–Academy Awards show. Concurrent with the release of Windows 98, Tribune officially launched its production channel enhancement service, which provided news headlines, sports scores, camera shots, and other information on a regularly updated basis. Tribune has been able to leverage a significant portion of the content developed by Tribune Interactive, the company's Web arm, simply by using a variety of content templates and basic scheduling tools.

Scherb is candid about Tribune's expectations for the ITV project. Senior management made the decision to work on the interactive TV project independently of whether they thought the technology in Windows 98 would be a commercial success or not. "Obviously, we believe that Microsoft has more of an ability to make something a success than your average company, so if it becomes a success, that's great, but it actually wasn't material to our decision process."

Tribune focused solely on WebTV for Windows for their interactive television efforts. Although Tribune looked at other technologies, they didn't invest time and resources in them because "this wasn't a decision about 'let's pick a technology and build a commercial product.' This was a decision about 'let's learn some things.'"

Scherb believes that there will be a day when the device in the living room is an interactive device. "It's a high-bandwidth device and among the things you can do with it are things that today you would think of as couch potato TV viewing, as focused, user-driven, Web browsing activities, and all kinds of things in between that are hybrids of those two. We believe that's going to happen." Scherb and other members of senior management don't believe that such a device will become common next year or the year after. "But for a 150-year-old company we try to play for the long term." For a company typically thought of as traditional and conservative, Tribune has been extremely aggressive and open minded about its foray into the world of interactive television.

The Tribune Business Model

Tribune tends to operate its various businesses independently. The television group, for example, is highly profitable and has excellent profit margins in the industry, as does the newspaper group. But today, with one exception (the individuals who work on the television station Web sites are paid by the publishing group), there's little crossover of ideas, resources, or technology between the groups.

The company has published newspapers for 150 years and, as one of the early television operators in the country, has been producing television programs for 50 years. The key hurdle Scherb sees in moving forward is determining how to bridge the cultural barriers inside the company and then move it into the digital era. "We do things a certain way and we've got to start to change the culture." Scherb's real goal at Tribune is to be a cultural change agent.

Questions and Expectations

Behind its interest in developing and broadcasting interactive content for WebTV for Windows was Tribune's desire to use the technology to help find answers to a number of critical questions:

- In what ways will Tribune be fighting a horizontal marketplace battle rather than a number of vertical battles?
- How can Tribune work to prepurpose content rather than repurpose it?
- What kinds of products can Tribune produce with the different skills, interests, expertise, and content-creation capabilities that the company has?
- How will Tribune have to change culture across different units?
- How will Tribute operate in the future?

The Coming Horizontal Battle

Scherb says, "We believe that the convergence of all these technologies in the media are going to force us to fight a more horizontal battle." Rather than bringing all of the company's media assets to market independently, Tribune plans to leverage its audio, video, text, and graphics assets through a single, more uniform product. Accordingly, Tribune has invested heavily in technologies that enable content sharing across the company. "We're…bridging the gaps between TV and print people," Scherb says.

For example, the *Digitally Interoperable System of Content Sharing* (DISC) — currently in a pilot phase in Chicago — allows users to view assignments and content available in all Tribune newsrooms. It allows someone at WGN, Tribune's Chicago station, to use a browser to get a list of Tribune content providers, including WGN-TV, WGN Radio, the *Chicago Tribune* newspaper, CLTV (Tribune's 24-hour Chicago news station), *Exito* (Tribune's Spanish publication), and Tribune Interactive. Figure 2.1 shows the DISC infrastructure.

For phase two, Tribune wants to provide even more content, allowing, for example, immediate streaming of available video footage. DISC will also be integrated with the Associated Press (AP) Preserver System, which is AP's print newsroom photo archive. A producer at WGN-TV who needs a still shot, for example, could pull it directly from the AP system. Development of both DISC and the interactive TV project will help Tribune become more of a single horizontal army instead of a number of vertical armies.

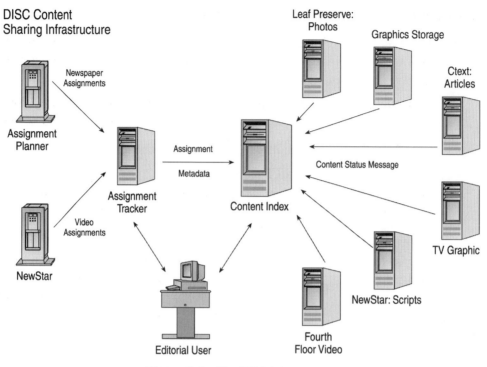

Figure 2.1   The DISC infrastructure.

From Repurposing to Prepurposing

Tribune operations today are similar to those of many large media organizations: One part of the business will cover a story. Another then wants to use the story but must first reformat it for the new medium. For example, suppose WGN-TV does a story in video that Tribune Interactive later wants to use on a Web site. The Web producer must rewrite the story and use the material in an effective way for the Web. The videos, for example, might be used as voice-overs rather than as a complete story.

Scherb visualizes a future in which Tribune's content can be used across all media without excessive manual intervention and reformatting. He calls this a change from *repurposing* to *prepurposing*.

Prepurposing requires that content staff develop an awareness of the other ways in which their shots and stories can be used: TV camera people, for example, could get shots that — while not needed for the TV news show — could be used by Web designers when creating a stand-alone story. Ultimately, Scherb wants content staff to prepurpose a majority of their content not only by collecting it the right way but also by *producing* it the right way.

Thus, prepurposing really consists of two steps:

- In the short term, building awareness among those involved in the content collection process (news and TV reporters, for example) about the variety of media across which their content is used.

- In the long term, building wider awareness about the content production process. With this awareness, content can easily be used across all of the media without significant modification.

> What do I tell the WGN camera operator so that the footage is easily useable everywhere if we want to use it? I don't know yet. When it comes to reusing TV stuff in multiple places, I think we're just starting to play with that. I don't know if we've learned anything yet.

As Scherb points out, the learning process has no set time frame. The process is continual because everything — the media, the distribution method, the technology, the viewer interest — is constantly changing. He says, "I don't think the world will ever be at a steady state where we can catch up to it and finally say, 'Whew! We've learned it all.'"

The Vertical Blanking Interval (VBI) Project

More than anything, working on ITV has created awareness of new forms of media among Tribune's people. It's shown, in a small bandwidth, some of the things that are technically possibly in the world of digital television. Scherb sees the Vertical Blanking Interval (VBI) as a "real-world laboratory for learning early on about digital television."

Tribune's entry into the WebTV for Windows arena consisted of two phases:

- A pilot phase, during which Tribune personnel learned the technology and broadcast a fully enhanced, live show, with the content closely synchronized with the video.

- An ongoing production phase, during which Tribune produced interactive content on a 24-hours-a-day, 7-days-a-week basis. The content, which is loosely (if at all) tied to the video programming, is current and provides an enhanced viewing experience to the consumer.

Tribune risked little in doing the project. Its primary investment was in the time and work provided by the engineering staff, the content producers, and the people in

Bandwidth

Granted, there are some major differences, especially with bandwidth. Tribune's stations currently use three to five lines of the VBI, or about 28.8 to 48 kilobits per second (Kbps) (the speed of a high-end modem), for broadcast of interactive TV content. Digital TV, by comparison, uses a 19.39-megabits-per-second (mbps) data stream, of which a major portion can be used for data. The space available for transmission of data with digital TV is three to four orders of magnitude greater than for VBI.

the publishing group. If the project had failed completely, Scherb and his staff would have learned something from failure:

> The people here are very smart. You put them together and you want them to talk about the right subjects together, they'll talk. There wasn't a risk that we would bring them together and they would fight like cats and dogs. This is a very civilized company with very smart people. They don't always have the opportunity to talk about common projects and problems, so they don't do it as much as we'd like, but they can do it.

> When we got into it, we never said, "This is going to be a success. We're going to make X." You couldn't write a spreadsheet that said, "Here's the business model that says it's worth doing." We don't have a clue.

Pilot Hurdles

Originally, Tribune hoped to develop and broadcast its initial WebTV for Windows interactive content offering for the Rose Bowl in January 1998. Later, Tribune wanted to do enhancements for an automotive show. Tribune ended up doing the pre–Academy Awards show in March 1998. Although there were some stumbling blocks in working with Microsoft, Scherb feels that they were by no means insurmountable. Software delivery schedules, for example, tended to slip, which posed some management challenges:

> Early on, in November [1997], we got everybody all charged up and they were gung-ho to do this joint project and "three weeks from now, we're going to have all this software working!" But a lot of people thought, "Hey, this is cool. We're doing some media stuff with Microsoft." So that kept them interested.

But Scherb makes it clear that Tribune got into the project knowing it was an experiment, and he and his staff were prepared for almost anything:

We didn't really know what was going to happen. We didn't know how well it was going to work or how it was going to be to work with Microsoft. We didn't know lots of things. The delays in the software were inconvenient, but looking back on it, they weren't material.

Production Mode

It's still a pilot project, but it's got more of a production focus to it. You have to do this every day. You've got to do it on a regular enough basis so people want to tune into it. If viewers never get any fresh info, it's useless.

Tribune is now in production mode with its interactive content and is attempting to broadcast content on a regular basis. Scherb expects that he and his team will learn a lot about the production process, particularly about the integration required with the newsrooms. For example, Tribune wants to have enhancement capabilities integrated into its existing television newsroom systems, such as Tektronix Newstar and AP News.

Tribune will provide a wide variety of updates during the day. Initially, the service will be a hypertext markup language (HTML)–based ticker service that is only loosely tied to the video programming. Tribune eventually wants to have enough automation and network support in place to key the enhanced content to its news shows automatically. For example, when a news anchor starts talking about a story, an HTML enhancement on that story would appear in real time, synchronized with the video. For news shows, where the viewer gets only a brief headline, Tribune will provide the rest of the story for reading off line. The user won't need to dial up to the Internet — the story will have already been downloaded to the local hard drive during the news program.

Continuing the content that WGN is doing on a regular basis will cost us money. There will be people assigned to it. We're making an investment now. In the overall scheme of Tribune Company operations, it's a rounding error. Perhaps even in the scope of WGN-TV, it's a rounding error, because they're a pretty big operation. But we are investing people and time in it.

For entertainment programming, such as the Tribune science fiction show *Earth: Final Conflict*, enhancements could provide a significantly deeper viewing experience. Viewers could begin to feel like participants when given the capability to explore some of the technical detail of the spaceship. With *Star Trek*, for example, the books detailing the Starship *Enterprise* technical manuals are already a way to provide a deeper experience. "Does that concept work in this [interactive TV] medium so that it gets people to tune in more, to have a more complete science fiction experience?" Scherb doesn't have all the answers but he is sure of one thing: "We have to experiment with all that stuff to find out."

A Success

The enhanced TV project was a real success, because it got great conversations started. Although the stations all have Web sites, working with interactive TV has created awareness about a future form of integrated media. Although the Web sites are good and are competitive with those of other stations, they've always remained separate from the actual newsroom operations:

> It's been something the promotion department does. Maybe the newsroom contributes to the stories and so forth, but it's not an integral part of the newsroom. Now Tribune is having good conversations and good thinking in the WGN newsroom by news executives and people asking what's possible. They ask, "What kind of updates and data and information might we want to offer through this new channel?"

Working on interactive TV has also been beneficial for senior management at the company:

> Originally, senior broadcast management wasn't focused on VBI content transmission at all. They were focused on building the WB television net-work, on acquiring more stations, on running the TV stations profitably, and doing their best-in-the-business job. There wasn't any selling process

TV Listings

The VBI isn't the only space that Tribune has explored. Program guides, as demonstrated by the recent TCI–News Corporation deal, will be a critical viewer portal in the future. Tribune Media Services (TMS) built a guide data loader that provides information for the WebTV for Windows program guide. Scherb recounts the experiment and the result:

> The people who would say they took a risk were the TMS people and the investment they made in building their own loader. Now, they're asking, "Where is the business model going to be? How am I going to get my money out of it?"

One area of particular interest was the advertising space available in the guide:

> I think TMS has a terrific asset in its listings business that's only going to get incredibly more valuable as the world gets more digital. They really understand the landscape and how things may play out in the business scenarios. They've gotten an understanding of some of the opportunities that they're going to try to develop, which they didn't have before working on the project. It's been extremely valuable from that point of view.

internally. When it started, it was, "We're going to use some of your bandwidth. Do you mind?" Senior managers now look back and think, "We did this and it's cool and we're learning from it."

Business and Content Issues

Tribune has two key objectives in developing new business models in the interactive programming space:

- To find a balance between maintaining viewership and conducting transactions
- To derive replacement revenue for existing advertising models

Making a *Real* Business

For Scherb, the question is not if or when interactive content broadcasting will become real, but how "real" is defined:

> We know how to define real. Real — that's easy. Real for us is defined as something we can make a profit at because we sell advertising on it. That's nearly all our business is — our TV and our newspaper businesses operate that way. In TV, if you can't sell time on it and make a profit, it isn't real. In newspaper, if you can't fill up an ad hole on a page, it's not real. If that's the measure, the Internet's not real yet. It is, to some extent, but profitability for most Internet businesses is hard to come by.

Although Tribune obtains a significant amount of revenue from its Internet businesses, they aren't yet profitable. One clear barrier, for example, is the limited number of receivers currently in consumers' hands. For starters, computer makers have to incorporate TV tuner functionality into a large number of the machines they ship. In addition, other content companies will need to enter the interactive TV business to make it successful. "Other people need to push the content and get people to use it. It's got to get on WebTV and WebTV for Windows." Scherb believes that interactive TV could become "real" for Tribune by late 1999, in terms of having a reasonably sized audience that an advertiser would take notice of and care about.

Balancing Enhanced Content with Core Programming

The broadcast side of Tribune does have some concerns, because the new medium is different from traditional television programming. Scherb says, "The goal of our programming people is to keep your eyes absolutely glued to the program." Crossover links — a WebTV and WebTV for Windows feature providing clickable

Selling the Sellers

Tribune sells a combination of national and local advertisements. For some products, such as Metromix, its Chicago arts and entertainment guide, Tribune has dedicated salespeople. Tribune also does a significant amount of cross selling and up selling. Some of Tribune's more traditional advertisers have been advertising in the newspaper — often in the same section — for years, and they are likely to limit themselves to that arena. But Scherb says, "I think we've done a pretty good job of selling the benefits of Internet advertising." Some advertisers are willing to try the technology but are not yet making any major commitments. Like Tribune, they view the technology as something they can learn from:

> The advertisers aren't saying, "Now, that's a market that I need to reach. Got to be there." In the traditional equation of an advertising decision, it's "Is it the demo I want? Does it give me the CPM I need?" We don't have the answers to that yet and that won't happen this year. Maybe next year.

---

links to Web sites as part of a television program — "are completely contrary to that philosophy." That's one of the problems that the company wants to address in working with interactive television. "Right now, the value of a rating point on any of our TV stations, but particularly our big ones, versus the CPM we get for Internet advertising makes it silly for us to try to divert eyeballs from *Earth: Final Conflict* or *Buffy, The Vampire Slayer.*"

Tribune wants to use the enhancements to leverage its existing programming, making it more compelling so that viewers will tune in regularly and spend more time watching the programming.

At the same time, the company doesn't want to divert focus from the core programming. "The last thing we want to do is to have somebody tune in for a minute and then go off to the Internet because there's a link in the program — and never come back." On the other hand, if the viewer makes a purchase based on that link, with the right business model Tribune could potentially be looking at additional revenue. "We have to do the math and see if that revenue (from the transaction) would be better than the advertising revenue."

As with other parts of the business, there's a balance to be found between maintaining viewership and conducting transactions. The key is in figuring out where the math breaks down. "If every advertiser were doing transactions, how much do we get per 30-second spot versus how many transactions could you do in 30 seconds? You need to have viewership because you need to have a way to draw people to the transactions." Finding that balance is Tribune's biggest business issue. The next issue is *when* the technology will generate revenue.

The television business is based on ratings. Ad rates are based on ratings. If ratings fall because Tribune's viewers are clicking off, revenue falls. Scherb says, "It's a clear cause-and-effect relationship." One of Tribune's key goals is to develop models that enable the company to derive replacement revenue for the traditional advertising business from the targets of those clicks.

Bridging Cultural Gaps

As a result of working on the interactive television project, groups at the company that never before had a reason to talk are now talking. Scherb succeeded in establishing a good dialog between newspaper people, technical people, and broadcasting people. "That isn't something that happens every day in companies like this, because each group is focused on its own operations." Once everyone understood the basic functionality and technology, the groups established a great dialog about the kind of interactive product the company could offer and why. "That goes toward satisfying my original reason for getting into the project—this kind of culture, learning, and cross-group interchange and synergy."

> We really wanted to involve a whole range of people, because who knows? Nobody knows what the product really needs to be. It's a whole new area. We want to educate our editorial and news people on what's possible and see what they think a product might be. We want to do the same with the Internet people and with the technical people. We purposely tried to round up a range of diverse people.

Although making the right technical decisions is important, Scherb's real goal is to use his technology and media experience to bridge the gap and to do everything possible to prepare the people, the management, and the culture of Tribune to be more competitive. He measures his success on how he changes the company from a cultural, operational, educational, and focus point of view. "It's not 'We saved X number of dollars by negotiating a good deal with Microsoft for Office,' though that is also part of my responsibility."

The ITV project also helped Scherb's staff think about other Tribune projects, such as DISC. "As we're doing the specs for the DISC project, we come up with examples '... remember when we did the Oscar show? We tried to do this and if we only had had that we could have . . ..'"

Cross-Industry Cultural Gaps

> In television you don't get a second chance. If you put out a show that sucks, people will tune it out and not tune back. You put out software that sucks people say, "Oh, well, next release." They'll fix the bugs. TV is about extremely slick production values. It's unthinkable to get it wrong. So this "it sucks, but it'll get better" mentality is a tough one for the TV guys to deal with.

One of the hardest challenges for Tribune is for the 150-year-old company to adapt to rapidly changing technologies. Scherb hopes to bring some of the software company culture that he has experienced in his career into what is a traditional media company:

> Some company cultures are very deliberate and thoughtful and planned and you don't just kind of say, "What the hell, we're going to go for this" and just do it. With a software company you just say, "We have got to have this product." You just decide it. You don't know what the plan is. You just go out and go for it.

Tribune is a conservative company and it manages expectations and results extremely well internally:

> We think them through. There are very few notable failures in companies like this. That happens in software companies, but it's a risk/reward thing. You take the risk and sometimes you get the big-bucks reward.

Scherb points out that a major gap exists between the level of reliability that broadcast engineers expect and the level that software provides. A broadcast engineer understands the need for a 24-hours-a-day signal and knows that it must work without fail.

> They're starting to learn about bugs, unreliable software, and are starting to be willing to take some risks, but it's just different. This is a conservative company, which is why it's very profitable, reliable, and well regarded on Wall Street. We can be counted on to turn in results.

Tribune has learned a number of things during the project and is planning to continue interactive programming in the future. In Scherb's mind, the key learning experience has been a cultural one:

> We could sit down and write a document describing some of the cultural things we've learned, and we could end the project there. I think TMS wants to continue because they think it's cool and it associates the Tribune

name with a cool technology, adding promotional value. They believe people are going to want to see data presented in this channel.

Conclusion

Looking 5 to 10 years ahead, Scherb believes that TVs and computers will have essentially the same guts but will be packaged in different boxes. "When you have a 19-megabit data stream in Digital TV, of which you can use a large portion for things other than pictures, and when everybody's got a back channel through their telco (telephone company) or some other way, then this becomes really interesting."

Scherb can see a day when Tribune offers a wide range of premium channels, including perhaps a Tribune Education Channel — a truly interactive experience with 5 megabits of the digital bandwidth used for delivery of interactive content and a back channel that's fast enough to allow real program interaction. It's still all primarily based on streaming video, rather than something like a fully interactive experience. Scherb sees the VBI pilot leading to that future. "That's why it's important for us to play with it now, because we want to have the ideas, not copy the ideas." To the degree that Tribune is learning what's possible, "that'll spark the next idea. To the degree that we feel good about the learning and the cultural synergy in our company, we'll take the next leap to try the next thing."

CHAPTER 3

MSNBC Interactive:
Telling Stories with Software

www.msnbc.com

This chapter describes the experiences of Frank Barbieri, senior interactive producer, MSNBC Interactive, and his team as related in an interview at his office in Redmond, Washington on June 2, 1998. It offers a brief history of MSNBC and its efforts to date on the Web and in cable programming, and it highlights some similarities between interactive CD-ROMs and interactive television. It then explores how MSNBC Interactive is creating an interactive television service for WebTV for Windows. A technical case study of the WebTV for Windows content efforts of MSNBC is provided in Chapter 19.

Bill Gates' December 7, 1995 announcement that Microsoft would focus on the Web was the perfect opportunity to add a new angle to the already successful partnership of Microsoft and NBC News. Microsoft's existing content relationship with NBC allowed it to offer some news properties, such as *Dateline NBC* and *NBC Nightly News*, on the Microsoft Network (MSN). The new relationship — MSNBC — would leverage the MSN News interactive space and the expertise and global reach of NBC News as a news provider, resulting in the opportunity to tell stories through software.

After a few weeks of prototyping, MSNBC Interactive, which is responsible for the Web site and the WebTV for Windows interactive service, took the WebTV for Windows service live on June 15, 1998, in time for the launch of Windows 98.

MSNBC Interactive operates from Redmond, Washington, with a staff of about 200; the cable network operation is based in Secaucus, New Jersey, and is staffed by approximately 400 people. (They are both commonly referred to simply as MSNBC — for example, the MSNBC Web site, rather than the MSNBC Interactive Web site.)

Start It Up

Barbieri describes the launch of the MSNBC cable network and MSNBC Interactive as one of the most aggressive startups of his career. The MSN interactive news team went from approximately 40 to 60 people working on a single interactive product to a staff of 600 people working on a 24-hour-a-day, 7-day-a-week cable news television station and Internet news service.

MSNBC Interactive operates from Redmond, Washington, with a staff of about 200, while the cable network operation is based in Secaucus, New Jersey, with approximately 400 people. MSNBC combed the country looking for the most talented individuals for its team. In particular, Barbieri searched for people who were able to *tell stories using software* and could work with both the news producers of NBC and the software developers of Microsoft.

The interactive television service is the perfect opportunity for the mission of the joint venture: one platform marrying television and Web-based content. The first 2 years of the venture, in a sense, have been in preparation for the coming convergence. The people of MSNBC have a significant amount of experience in Web site production and automation that they can leverage into the new platforms and spaces.

Barbieri believes that the unique medium of interactive television gives producers and editors an opportunity to present stories to users in a way that isn't possible on any other medium. Software enables MSNBC producers, through interactive television, to deliver personalized information, localized content, huge databases of supplemental facts, and deeper access to a wealth of data from one central navigational point. "In its very essence, interactive story-telling is the marrying of several great cultures," he says.

Bringing Independent Cultures Together

The marriage so far has been full of conflict and opportunity. MSNBC combed the country looking for the most talented individuals for its team. In particular, Barbieri searched for people who could tell stories using software and who could work with both the news producers of NBC and the software developers of Microsoft.

The MSNBC Web site brings together the three traditionally independent cultures of broadcast news, print journalism, and software development. Members of each culture have their own way of communicating with others and of interacting with external forces. They also have different user bases. Barbieri likes to call the crossroads of the cultures the "eureka zone." That zone includes broadcasters who understand software development, software developers who understand broadcast news technologies, and print journalists who understand broadcasting. In the eureka zone, they all get together, forming the vision that brings structure to the interactive environment.

The initial challenge for MSNBC was to establish a language that allowed coders to talk to journalists. Journalists don't necessarily understand what a "requirements specification" is, what software tools are necessary, the complications of production cycles, and, in turn, the implications of all of those pieces. Conversely, software developers don't necessarily understand the importance of timeliness or of what you see is what you get (WYSIWYG) editing and other features in tools. "Just having that constant push and pull of what's important, and arriving at what is now a well established common language and thought process, took about a year. That was a year of staring across tables from each other, asking, 'What's this all about?'"

Hiring

Barbieri calls the perfect candidate an *entrepreneurial journalist* — someone who demonstrates a unique ability to gather resources around a story and create systems or processes for getting the story to the users, someone who has a highly distilled sense of audience and a voracious appetite for the techniques that feed an audience its information. Good candidates must apply both software and news resources to story problems to solve them. An entrepreneurial attitude is also crucial for successful interactive ventures.

During interviews, Barbieri starts with a broad perspective and elicits how candidates might combine resources: "You are presented with the task of telling a story about the state of welfare in the United States. You have the complete dedication of all of the NBC News resources and all the software development resources of Microsoft. What do you do?" If the question seems overly challenging, Barbieri might offer a few helpful hints: "There's a database of state laws on welfare. What might we do on the Web? We know that the Office of Management and Budget has produced a report that shows welfare expenditure data across 30 years. What might you do with that? There's an NBC tape archive stretching back 40 years. What might you do with that?"

A good candidate will list five or six content areas in a plan of attack. Barbieri looks for an answer similar to the following: "I would team a videotape editor or a producer from the NBC side with some average people and get them to use a welfare calculator I made in JScript for the Office of Management and Budget numbers. I would get them to feed back the reaction about what their exposure in welfare payments is or what the welfare situation would be like for them."

The wrong answer is a blank stare accompanied by a quick, "Look, wow, I don't know, I would assign a reporter and I would write a story and put it on the Web."

When it comes to resumes, Barbieri tailors his expectations to the requirements of the position. For some jobs, journalism experience is a must; other jobs (such as tools development) require hardcore programming experience. According to Barbieri, the ideal candidate has some overlap: "When, for instance, we have a JScript and SQL coder who worked on a newspaper, just that little bit of interface with the news culture is helpful when working on a very unique development cycle — one that's not really replicated anywhere else in traditional software production." A journalist who has done some Web pages, CD-ROM publishing, or coding is a person who understands logic systems and informational architectures and can present data to users.

The Development Cycle

When MSN began, it exhibited a mixture of the cultures of both the software developer and the journalist. The typical software development cycle is a curve that ramps up, plateaus for a little bit, and then hits the floor. When a product is released to manufacturing (RTM'd), the software developers take a breather.

In the case of the original MSN launch, the date of which was tied to that of the launch of Windows 95, the journalists understood that they had to start the process again the next day. But the software developers experienced a startling realization: The software–journalism development process plateaus and goes down slightly but continues on forever (Figure 3.1).

The MSNBC Web site is, in fact, a huge piece of software — an application — that requires maintenance. It always needs rebuilding. After launch, it required a series of cyclical maintenance and support tasks that were really tiny software develop-

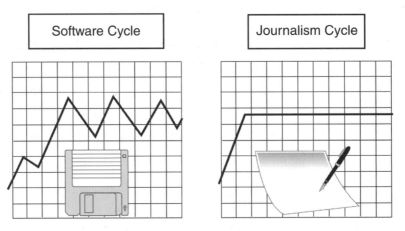

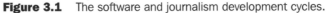

Figure 3.1 The software and journalism development cycles.

ment cycles. MSNBC does an entire software cycle — conception to test to release — in anywhere from 2 days to 4 or 5 months.

Relative to typical software development cycles, the MSNBC interactive cycles are extremely short. Each cycle starts out with a brief brainstorming and specification session. During that session, the team members decide on an initial schedule for development, testing, and delivery. Barbieri refers to this type of work as *disposable development* because it has an extremely short shelf life. If the team takes too long to ship the software, it misses its window of opportunity. "You have to get the software and content out quickly so you can service a need. That's a two-month window. That's what keeps us competitive. If we're not shrinking the development cycle and if we're not *smart* about shrinking the development cycle, our competitors are going to beat us."

Keith Rowe, former technical director of MSNBC, referred to the plateau as the *maintenance cycle*. "It's like working on the engine of a car as the car is driving down the road at 60 miles an hour." MSNBC has been on that road for over 2 years.

The Daily Schedule

The MSNBC interactive team begins the day with a brief meeting that answers the following questions:

- Where are we going to focus our resources?
- Which stories are important?
- What pieces of the stories can we tell interactively?
- What support can we expect from NBC News?
- What support can we expect from the MSNBC developers?

After discussion, the team sets delivery deadlines for its 1-day development cycle. Two factors dictate whether a story is likely to be used:

- Its flexibility. Can the story fit into existing templates and be easily enhanced with graphics, interactive quizzes, and polls?
- Its timeliness. If a breaking story can't be presented in a timely manner, it's not worth publishing.

Producing Great Content

Barbieri believes there are three keys to producing great content:

- Focus on what you're going to present. A lot of Web sites want to be everything to everybody, and they end up being nothing to anyone because they haven't keyed into their particular strengths.

- Be honest about your strengths and weaknesses. This is harder than you might think. Especially with a new medium, everyone wants to think that they're everything to everyone — that they have the ultimate design or implementation.

- Create supportable and reproducible systems for content generation — and that's where software comes in. Without robust and well thought out underlying systems, something the size of the MSNBC Web site could not be supported. If you don't go to the software for your solutions, you will be very frustrated with both the quick evaporation of institutional knowledge and the hard work of maintaining a complex, large-scale Web site or interactive interface.

Although the interactive and on-air teams are separate, both are always looking for opportunities to cross-promote each other's content. The interactive producers participate in the broadcast meetings, communicating with their broadcast counterparts on story generation, content sharing, and cross-platform opportunities. Bringing the Web and television teams together is one of the main missions of the joint venture and is something in which MSNBC is heavily invested.

To get feedback about the Web site and its interactive television content, MSNBC continuously conducts focus groups and performs usability testing. MSNBC also does market research that compares its content with its competitor's content so that it can fine-tune the Web site and interactive programming to achieve the best possible market share. Currently, MSNBC has the highest market share of all news Web sites, a tribute to the quick response of MSNBC to the input of its users. One key innovation was the implementation of a news browser navigation interface that allows users to navigate from any one point on the site to any other point on the site, with just a single click. MSNBC has already implemented the core functionality of this simple yet extremely effective interface in its enhanced television content and will implement more of it in the future.

From CD-ROM to Interactive Television

Like many individuals involved with interactive storytelling, Barbieri began his career when CD-ROMs were the most prevalent storytelling device — before use of the Web was widespread. "When I started doing CD-ROM functions based on storytelling with a journalistic background, I realized that people could access and experience stories in a way never before possible."

While getting his master's degree at the University of Missouri, Barbieri recognized that the university had a related set of media assets — a television station, a radio station, a newspaper, and a magazine — but that the assets never really worked together. CD-ROM offered the opportunity to bring a diverse set of storytelling approaches together through a single interface. As with interactive television today, the key then was that users could learn as much — or as little — as they wanted about a particular story.

Content producers on the brink of the interactive television revolution face the same daunting task that Barbieri faced in moving from CD-ROMs to the Web. "You have to be willing to re-examine what you're already doing. You have to be nimble and flexible enough to exploit new opportunities, and you have to be driven to do so. If you don't do it, somebody else will."

Moreover, just as there are those who doubt the viability of interactive television today, so too were many skeptical about the Web. "Back when everyone was doing CD-ROM production married to Macromedia Director and the Apple Media Tool, there was a small band of people who said that the Web would be big. And there was another band of people, a larger band perhaps, who were married to CD-ROM production and who were familiar with the tool-set and the content. Where are those people now? If you don't explore, if you're not always pushing, if you're not always self-examining, if you're not flexible enough to turn on a dime and reallocate resources for new opportunities, then you're going to be lost in this business."

One key to the MSNBC interactive television content is that on the back end, both it and the Web site use the same databases and automation to produce the content. Moreover, the user interface is consistent across both platforms. Rather than having associated content viewed on another device, that content will be available in context with a television video-driven viewing experience. Existing Web franchises, such as the live-vote section on MSNBC, will become interactive franchises, and more interactive franchises will be developed around voting, surveys, and other forms of user participation.

Advertising and Storytelling: A Fine Balance

Barbieri thinks of consumers as *actualizers of service*, forever hungry for more information, independent of whether it is provided as part of a news or drama show or as part of an advertisement. "If you're watching an interactive television production and you get your localized weather, as a consumer, you've received a consumable that is of value to you. Of equal value to you may be the fact that a Toyota commercial comes on and you can look up a local dealer because you've been thinking about buying a car anyway, and see what Tacoma trucks are in stock. That's almost the same level of gratification."

The media theory of "uses and gratification" suggests that everybody approaches information — be it advertising, news, information content, or public relations material — expecting to use it and to receive gratification from it. "In the ITV [interactive television] space, for instance, it's completely consistent to expect a user to have uses and gratification that live in the content space with news and information and in the advertising space with promotional and buying opportunities." To Barbieri, MSNBC's target ITV users are sitting in their living rooms, needing to use and get gratification from both news and advertising.

For Barbieri, it's a myth that the public is stupid. "The public is a lot smarter than we give them credit for. They just know what they like. If you miss exactly what they like, then you're the stupid one. I have a little bit more of an optimistic take on the consumer and I'm a little bit more sanguine in their ability to recognize the difference between content production and advertising or interactive commerce." Barbieri believes that the greatest evolution in what television presentation will do is its impending move from the passive to the active, which is what will really drive the advertising market forward. That transition will also drive content generation at MSNBC. "People, when given the chance, will engage in active participation with this space, and that's what I'm banking on."

There is great excitement among the staff at MSNBC, which believes it is one of the first groups to explore the interactive television medium. Moreover, MSNBC staff has the resources and ability to be pioneers in this area. On a practical level, Barbieri and other producers at MSNBC believe that anything the organization does now to foster relationships that bridge the diverse cultures involved will help the venture's long-term digital television efforts.

Although the tools and organization of the content will change over time, the interactions necessary between broadcast and interactive producers will stay the same. Barbieri says, "The key is to get everyone thinking. It's starting to swim when we know we've got the whole channel to cross. It's really about setting the stage for the future."

NBC and Interactive Programming

Jonathan Boltax, Manager and Producer,
NBC Enhanced Broadcast Group,
with David Feinleib, Microsoft
w w w . n b c . c o m / e t v

This chapter evolved from interviews with Jonathan Boltax in New York in June, 1998. All of the experiences, ideas, and information that made this chapter possible came from Jonathan and his group. Thus, throughout the chapter, where "we" is used, it refers to Jonathan and his staff at the NBC Enhanced Broadcast Group.

This chapter describes the framework and assembly of the NBC Enhanced Broadcast Group and offers insights into some of its design and creation processes.

Enhanced Broadcast Group: A History

The focus of the NBC Enhanced Broadcast Group (EBG) is the creation of enhanced (or interactive) television content for a wide range of NBC programs.

The EBG was created 2 months before the 1996 Summer Olympic Games in Atlanta, for which we produced more than 50 hours of live coverage. We were new to the production of interactive television, which made for an intense but invaluable learning experience. The broadcast included over 500 hypertext markup language (HTML) pages and about 40 to 50 templates focusing on basketball, swimming, gymnastics, and diving. We chose the Olympic Games (Figure 4.1) because we were confident in the technology at that point, and it was a good opportunity to utilize a major sporting event to launch the technology. The 1996 Olympics broadcast was the first television network broadcast using Intel's Intercast technology.

Figure 4.1 Screen grab from *1996 Olympic Games from Atlanta* using Intercast 1.6 technology. Credit: Sung Chang.

NBC Enhanced Broadcast Staff

The EBG initially had four people. It currently consists of 12 full-time staffers: a manager–producer, three graphic artists, three software developers, three associate producers, and two writers. The EBG also works closely with NBC's Web and broadcast operations, utilizing assets from both groups.

The entire EBG group is usually working on two to three shows at a time. For each project, the group divides into smaller teams of three (an associate producer, a graphic designer, and a software developer) plus a producer. The manager–producer oversees all work, and the writers float among all shows.

The EBG works in an area lovingly called "the Pit." New technology results in a never-ending flow of equipment and software, and the Pit has become the EBG's repository for it. The Pit is where hardware and software are configured and tested. There are dedicated workstations for broadcasting and receiving data feeds. The Pit also houses traditional video equipment, an editing station, and ever-larger piles of videotapes. The Pit was once a newsroom, and its open design has been conducive to the work flow of the EBG. During production, it allows interaction between group members. During live broadcasts, it assists in the smooth flow of assets and information between all involved.

Maximizing Existing Assets

The 12 people currently dedicated to the EBG are a deceivingly low number. The success of the group is also tied to the enormous number of available NBC resources, including Web and television production assets. For example, the EBG group utilizes the NBC Web site, NBC.com. For all broadcasts, we work closely with the TV production staff.

The U.S. Open golf tournament, broadcast from the Olympic Club in San Francisco, demonstrates how we have used television assets to take our enhancements to the next level. Part of the enhanced broadcast included *fly throughs* of the holes. (Fly throughs are aerial panoramas from tee to hole.) When a golfer approached the tee, we would trigger the "hole-by-hole" enhancement. Part of this enhancement consisted of an animated GIF fly through of the appropriate hole. The stacked-gif was based on existing film taken from a helicopter for NBC Sports. Such coordination between the television division and our group is extremely important and allows us to create high-quality, value-added interactive broadcasts.

Personnel: The EBG Ideal

The skill set and production flow of the EBG have changed over the years. Initially, the group consisted of a producer, a graphic artist, and two individuals coding HTML and creating the live Olympic updates. But as the underlying technology has evolved, so have the skill requirements. Knowledge of basic HTML was sufficient for the first broadcasts in 1996. However, with the introduction of Internet Explorer versions 3 and 4 (new versions of Microsoft's Web browser) and other new technology, the group began to need highly skilled developers.

Today, anyone developing content and tools for the group is at a minimum a Web developer with knowledge of HTML, JavaScript, and Cascading Style Sheets (CSS). These developers, known as "coders," must be able to administer back-end servers for hosting online chats and write software that parses statistics and information from databases. For example, our live statistics feed for Women's National Basketball Association (WNBA) broadcasts relies on a Kron script that retrieves and parses a WNBA live statistics feed at game time. Other important skills include the ability to understand broadcast technology, such as passing data through the Vertical Blanking Interval (VBI). The ability to maintain data insertion equipment and test the data feed's end-to-end passage is another key skill necessary for the group's success.

Recruiting individuals for the EBG is not an easy task — it is almost impossible to find someone with enhanced broadcast experience. Therefore, having a diverse group of people who understand television and multimedia becomes vital. Although those skills are hard to find, we are fortunate to employ four people with television backgrounds and three with CD-ROM backgrounds. This synergy has been vital to our success.

In addition to needing people who understand television and multimedia, we look for two key qualities when hiring staff members for the EBG:

- Creativity. Candidates must be open to new processes and new ideas. Because our group is small, a software developer cannot just write code. The developer must be creative as well.

- Patience. The software is not "bulletproof," and the tools to deliver the content are in their infancy.

Broadening Our Scope

The 1996 Olympics broadcast proved to be a success on both a technical and a content basis. However, we still had an enormous amount to learn about interactive television. We felt the best way to explore interactive television further was to produce content in a variety of genres. We divided the programming we would enhance into four categories: news, sports, drama, and late night. News and sports seemed to be a natural fit because of the data-like aspects of the content already being provided. The genres of drama and late night television, however, were more of a challenge.

Table 4.1 lists the enhanced broadcasts produced by the EBG since the 1996 Summer Olympics. Because we test with a wide variety of technologies, we enhanced some shows using Intel Intercast, others with Wink Communications, and more recent ones with WebTV for Windows and WebTV Plus. (Shows listed twice spanned more than one season.)

Figure 4.2 shows an interactive version of *Saturday Night Live*, and Figure 4.3 an interactive version of the 1998 U.S. Open golf championship.

Table 4.1 NBC Enhanced Broadcasts

Season	Show	WebTV for Windows	Intel Intercast	Wink	WebTV+
Fall 1996	The NFL on NBC		x		
	Homicide: Life on the Street		x		
Winter 1997	Dateline NBC		x		
	The NBA on NBC		x		
Spring 1997	CNBC (24 hours a day, 7 days a week)		x		
	The Tonight Show with Jay Leno		x		
Summer 1997	1997 U.S. Open golf championship		x		
	CNBC		x		
	The Tonight Show with Jay Leno		x		
Fall 1997	CNBC		x		
	The NBA on NBC		x	x	
	The Tonight Show with Jay Leno		x	x	
Winter 1998	CNBC		x		
	The NBA on NBC			x	
	The Tonight Show with Jay Leno		x	x	
Spring 1998	CNBC		x[a]		
	The Tonight Show with Jay Leno			x	
	Saturday Night Live	x			
Summer 1998	1998 U.S. Open golf championship	x			
	Saturday Night Live	x			x
	The WNBA on NBC			x	

[a] Intercast 2.0.

Continues

Table 4.1 NBC Enhanced Broadcasts (Continued)

Season	Show	WebTV for Windows	Intel Intercast	Wink	WebTV+
Summer 1998 (continued)	*The Tonight Show with Jay Leno*			x	
	Notre Dame Football	x			
Fall 1998	*Saturday Night Live*	x			x
	The Tonight Show with Jay Leno			x	
	The Fiftieth Annual Emmy Awards	x			x

Figure 4.2 Screen grab from *Saturday Night Live* using WebTV for Windows.
Credit: Jennifer McCoy.

Figure 4.3 Screen grab from the *1998 U.S. Open* golf championship using WebTV for Windows. Credit: Jennifer McCoy.

Creating Templates

From the start, we felt that the only way to ensure robust, updateable content within a broadcast medium was to create *templates* for all broadcast initiatives. A template is a shell that holds the graphical and program coding for the content we create. It is a framework for the enhancements. When we are broadcasting live, templates allow us flexibility and nimbleness. Plus, templates can be reused throughout the entire enhancement season. For example, the templates for *The Tonight Show with Jay Leno* are used on a daily basis, whereas templates for *Saturday Night Live* and sports shows are used on a weekly basis.

Here are the guidelines we follow in creating our templates:

- Create compelling content. As in any other entertainment medium, content is king. If you compromise content for the sake of the template, don't make the template.

- Design clever templates that make the enhancements, themselves, an experience. On the Web, you click on a link and wait for the content to download. For many implementations of enhanced television, once a user sees the content and associated links, the content is already located on the user's hard drive. You can truly leverage your templates by anticipating what users will be ready for and by giving them enough outlets to keep them involved while you download more data.

- Make good — not excessive — use of color. Be sensitive to the fact TV is a never-ending, ever-changing array of colors.

- Coordinate the design of the enhancement with the look and feel of the television show. Viewers of *Homicide: Life on the Street*, for example, are accustomed to the show's distinctive look and feel. We wanted viewers to feel part of the show but didn't want to distract them. We wanted them to focus on the show itself and utilize the enhancements to take the intensity of the show to the next level. To achieve these goals, we created enhancements that maintain the look and feel of the show.

- Design in flexibility. As a broadcast season progresses, you will want to make both minor and major adjustments to your templates. Scalability must be a foresight. Also, for live events, you might want to create and broadcast content on the fly. We must be prepared for anything and everything. A flexible template allows you to react to these situations accordingly.

Schedules and Cycles

There are two major phases of enhancing a show: the template cycle and the enhancement season cycle.

The Template Cycle

The template cycle is a 4- to 6-week preproduction phase in which the team takes the enhancement framework from conception through implementation to testing:

Week 1

- Establish a broad outline that details plans to enhance the show. The outline also helps the team understand the flow of the show.

- Brainstorm as a group and with people from the television production about appropriate enhancements. Create a subgroup of four people: the producer, associate producer, software developer, and designer. They further develop the enhancements and begin conceptualizing the graphical composition and layout of the templates.

Week 2

- Select the final graphical composition and make decisions based on technical realities communicated by the software developer. The graphic artist creates compositions. Ideas from the brainstorming session are fine tuned.

Weeks 3 and 4

- Choose a layout. The graphic artist begins to design the templates. The producer and the associate producer begin creating the content. The software developer begins to program the content.

Weeks 5 and 6

- Undertake revisions and testing. Run all content through the broadcast tools, making sure the content parses correctly, and perform numerous test broadcasts.

The Enhancement Season Cycle

The enhancement season cycle is a production phase during which the team produces and delivers content on a daily or weekly basis. It offers some of the best examples of the differences between software development as it's practiced on the Web and interactive programming for television.

In software development, the shipping date for a product is often flexible. In Web site development, the launch date of a particular site sometimes allows for flexibility. In television, however, shows must be aired at a specific time. An enhanced broadcast falls into that model as well. An enhanced show is tied to the on-air time of the television show. We do not have the luxury of delaying the launch of the enhanced show. Therefore, if necessary, we must cut our losses during the production week. If a part of the enhanced broadcast will not be developed in time, if need be we will drop it and move on.

Other differences:

- Content amounts. Unlike the Web, where content producers tend to err on the side of providing too much — rather than too little — information, content producers for interactive broadcast might not use a quarter of the content they created (depending on the flow of a live broadcast).

- Camera shots. In live television broadcasts, it is easy to change the camera shot. Enhanced television does not offer that flexibility, because of the unbelievably difficult task of making sure your content will not grossly conflict with any part of the broadcast. (Creative template development and careful preparation prevent such conflicts.)

Interactive Programming: From Infancy to Adulthood

Two questions are repeatedly asked in the industry: "Why give people enhanced broadcasts?" and "Why would they want that extra stuff?"

Enhanced content is already happening but taking a different form today in mainstream television. Tune to CNBC, any sports broadcast, or any news program. Additional facts, figures, numbers, and graphics are already supplementing the television picture. Enhanced broadcasts take these already implemented concepts to the next level. Interactive content is all about giving the viewers *choice*.

Viewers might want low levels of interactivity during broadcasts such as news tickers and polling, or they might want higher levels of interactivity. As a viewer, you can now customize your screen with statistics, games, and graphics. Picture this: A basketball game is about to begin. You can customize your screen to match the home team's look. You can trigger applause, boos, and catcalls through your entertainment system's speakers. As you wave your interactive pennant, you're

Four Steps to Interactive Programming

If the Internet is considered to be in its infancy, enhanced television hasn't even left the womb. To ensure a smooth delivery, follow these steps:

- Create a natural extension of the programming. Viewers should walk away from an enhanced broadcast thinking, "I just watched TV."

- Make it simple. TVs are dumb devices. To watch television, you click a button or press a switch. Enhanced broadcasts can add significant value but should maintain TV's ease of use.

- Entertain. Television does an unparalleled job at entertaining. When creating an enhanced broadcast, keep the word "entertain" stuck in your mind.

- Reach a million viewers. A million viewers tuned into an enhanced broadcast will prove the viability of the medium. One million viewers is a short-term goal that will put ITV on the map for good.

interacting with other fans who are watching the game, arguing about foul calls and play selection. You then focus a camera you control on your favorite player while you're getting real-time game statistics of this and every other game that is being broadcast that day. Your living room is instantly transformed into the arena. Also, don't forget to purchase videotapes, jerseys, etc., from the enhanced TV store.

Or, consider this scenario. As your favorite golfer steps up to the 18th hole, you're right there with her — but in a gaming environment. You must make the same decisions as the golfer as you judge wind factors, slope, etc. You participate not only with the professionals on television but against all cyberspace viewers as well.

Enhanced TV can already create these experiences or simpler, more passive experiences. And the beauty of it all is that with one simple click you can return to full-screen television.

It's your choice.

Behind the Studio Gate: Why Interactive TV?

Bill Sanders, Executive Vice President, Big Ticket Television

Understanding emerging technologies is all about asking the right questions. Bill Sanders, executive vice president of Big Ticket Television, tells you what those questions are. Although Bill has written this chapter in the context of the television studio, you'll find that the questions and answers he provides are remarkably applicable, no matter where you work: at a network, a Web production company, a television station, or a studio. And as a consumer, you'll get a clear understanding of the business and content questions that will affect you in the years to come.

The billion-dollar question is not "Will the studios jump in and create interactive programming?" The question is "When?"

Making television interactive is a quantum leap, with the potential to increase viewer involvement, loyalty, and ratings. It's also a way to enhance the bottom line with new sources of revenue from advertising and direct sales. Why, then, are many television studios not poised to jump right in?

These are uncertain times for the traditional television production studio. Its costs keep rising. Its buyers, primarily the networks, are hard pressed to pay more for series programming when their ratings are being siphoned off by new competition. The networks look to contain the rising costs and offset their expenses with future revenues by owning more of their own programming rather than by licensing several airings from the production studios. Clearly, the business models of both buyer and supplier are evolving.

A Television Studio Primer

In its traditional form (shown in Figure 5.1), the TV studio acts as the financier, packager, and production entity, bringing creative and physical elements of production together. Although it owns the shows it produces, it must rely on others in

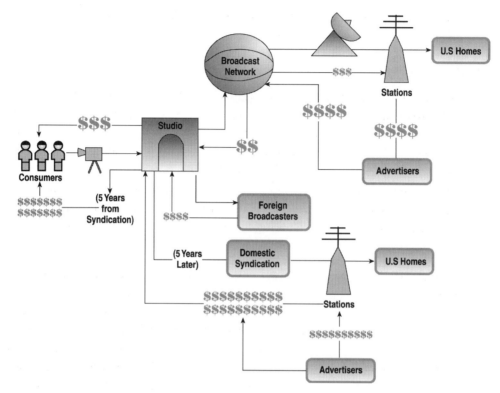

Figure 5.1   The traditional television model.

the industry, ranging from old-line or new-style networks, local stations and station groups, or cable and satellite program services, to exhibit its product physically.

The studio licenses its high-cost, high-quality programming to the network for a specified number of airings over a specified period of time, for a fee that is much less than its actual production and overhead costs. The network receives advertising revenues that it does not share with the studio. If the show is a hit and the ratings and resulting revenues go sky high, the studio doesn't make an additional dime from the network run.

However, the studio's business model is based on the show being successful enough, and running long enough, that the studio can recoup its costs through foreign and syndicated distribution, to which it retains the rights. (In fact, one hit can repay the investments in numerous other unsuccessful pilots and series and long-term contracts with writers and talent.) Generally, a studio also does the actual distribution, although it may contract distribution out for a fee or a percentage to an independent distributor or to another studio's distribution arm.

The Network–Studio Battle

Increasingly, networks (program distribution services) are willing to take on the costs and risks of fully financing and producing in house the programs they air. According to *Broadcast & Cable* (June 8, 1998): "[Networks]… will have to reinvent the business … [by holding] down program costs by producing in-house whenever possible." They are also balancing the cost of high-priced hits such as *Mad About You* by airing more low-cost, self-produced newsmagazines such as *Dateline NBC*. These low-cost shows can also be produced and repackaged year-round, generating better ratings — and revenues — in the summer months, while also stemming erosion to cable and other competitive fare.

By making deals directly with creative talent (producer–writers, actors, directors), networks hope to capture the "back-end" profits traditionally earned by the studios from U.S. domestic syndication, foreign airing or format rights, merchandising and licensing, TV and movie spin-offs, and, now, Web sites and electronic commerce. Because a studio with no physical means of exhibiting its product needs to get its shows on a network before it can reap the later rewards of syndication, the network possesses tremendous leverage when deciding whether to put a show on its schedule. With the repeal by Congress of the financial interest and syndication rules that prohibited use of such leverage, the studios have found themselves increasingly in the position of giving an ownership position to the network to get the show on the air. The new television model is shown in Figure 5.2.

The studio's new logic is that a network partner with a stake in a show's future profits is more likely to give that show a better chance to thrive (or at least survive). To put it more fatalistically, the studio believes that owning half a camel is still better than owning none. Unfortunately, while having a network share more in the up-front investment lowers a studio's risk, it also lessens its future reward. Once, a single hit could erase countless failures; now, it might take two hits to do the same. And as any student of show business calculus understands, the odds of creating two hits are not simply twice that of creating one hit.

Finding New Revenue Streams

Studios must seek new ways to increase their revenues. They can try to air their own shows directly by starting or buying their own networks, but this is an expensive

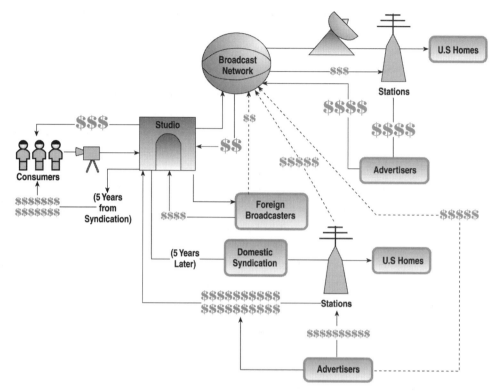

Figure 5.2   The new television model.

gamble that only the biggest companies can make. They can try to lower their costs, but, as some major league baseball team owners have learned, if you sell off all your high-priced talent, you can end up with a low-cost team that no one will come to watch. And they can search for new ways to augment income from their existing properties.

One avenue might be the advertising revenue and direct sales from electronic commerce (e-commerce) generated by adding interactivity to a studio's programs. This represents new up-front costs with an untested and unknown payoff down the line. It also runs directly into another problem with the network that licenses the program. The networks, squeezed by declining ratings on one side and increased production costs and license fees on the other, must also seek new ways to generate more revenues from their existing broadcast properties and licenses. They are not in a position to give away blithely rights to potential sources of new income. A studio could offer a network a lower license fee in exchange for retaining various interactive rights. But how does a studio place a financial value on those rights, when it is already financing a deficit of anywhere from $250,000 to $500,000 or more per episode just to produce the show for broadcast? Add to that the actual cost of interactive elements and the costs are significant.

Network television increasingly resembles the studio producing feature movies. The first network airing of a television show is similar to the first theatrical run of a feature movie. The largest investment of money, publicity, and promotion (on and off the network) is spent on the initial airing, but the bulk of the profit comes from subsequent showings and what used to be considered "ancillary" uses. (In place of pay-per-view, home video, pay cable, and TV exhibition in the movie world, substitute "off-network syndication" in the television world.) In both arenas, the rest of the profits, and an ever-increasing percentage of those profits, come from similar "downstream" sources: merchandising, licensing, theme park rides, sequels, and spin-offs, among others. While the audience is "in the theater" watching the big hit, there's the opportunity to promote the rest of the product line and to "sell them popcorn," which is a way to make money from the viewer doing something else while still watching the show. (Does this sound a bit like enhanced TV?)

The first exhibition is the engine — if it has sufficient fuel, then the rest can trail behind the bandwagon. The producer can't reap the profits of syndication, merchandising, or interactivity, for that matter, without the initial showing (and promotional push) by the network broadcaster. The networks use this leverage to garner the lowest possible license fee or secure the most subsequent rights (or obtain both). Increasingly, networks also try to secure the interactive rights.

The networks must also look to protect themselves in success. They would like to prevent situations such as the renewal of *ER*. When the initial license agreement expired, Warner Brothers commanded $13 million per episode from an "NBC held hostage." As a defense, the networks have yet another reason to try to own the shows outright or at least to negotiate for longer series deals up front. When a studio is negotiating for its very survival with issues like these on the table, the lesser issue of interactive rights is not high on the agenda.

As noted earlier, many studios, in turn, have launched or bought networks of their own (Fox, Disney/ABC, the WB, United Paramount Network, USA) or have entered into partnerships with networks to guarantee exhibition of the programs they produce. Even the definition of a "network" has changed. Now, any loose, informal organization of stations, or even cable outlets, that funds, buys, licenses, and then exhibits some form of ongoing programming (even an occasional college football game) constitutes a "network."

Clearly, then, the studios and production companies that do not have guaranteed exhibition of their own programs are not in charge when it comes to unilaterally exploiting the network broadcast of their shows. If a studio seeks to change the financial equation in any way, it will find itself in a conversation with its network "partner" about both the creative and economic aspects of such an "enhancement." This goes for "enhanced" or interactive TV as well. A studio that risked adding interactive elements on its own could find its investment squandered.

Key Questions

An important question in the world of interactive and digital television is this: Who owns the bandwidth used for interactivity? If a production company encodes links to Web sites or to lookup tables (which can then tailor the embedded link to the individual market or even the individual viewer) in its programs, can the network strip these pointers out or substitute its own?

Networks would argue that studios don't own the bandwidth, just their own bits of content (their intellectual property), which are distributed on that "channel." Will networks allow producers (studios) to embed more data within the show, whether in the coming digital bitstream or through existing analog forms such as the Vertical Blanking Interval? Or will new partnerships be struck? Given the new business environment, networks might "let" studios invest in producing interactive add-ons but could insist on sharing any new revenues.

If not allowed into the party, or if the network's price of admission is too steep, will some studios try to circumvent such possible barriers by encoding pointers within their programs that trigger interactivity in external media the networks don't control, such as a studio-produced Web site? In turn, what prevents the network from stripping the links out or adding their own (or both)? These and many other sticky issues need to be addressed and negotiated. In the meantime, this is a pioneer's business, one not for the faint-hearted (although, as always, the lawyers will come out all right).

In the near term, networks are unlikely to incur the watchful eye of Congress by trying to augment revenues by carving out additional space in their bitstream to sell for data broadcasting; stock, weather, sports, and news services; paging; cellular; telephone; or other data services. But they will not let the studios carve out bits within their programs to do the same. Given that the traditional production studio's place in the food chain is clearly evolving, only if these issues can be resolved or negotiated will the studios have the opportunity to add interactive (that is, "more") content to their programs.

That's the primer on the business side of the discussion. Economic history is filled with examples of new technologies that were wildly successful but that top business minds of the time thought consumers would have no use for or little interest in buying. Just as the spreadsheet was the "killer app" for the personal computer, making the PC extremely popular and viable, the models and technologies discussed elsewhere in this book for interactive television could well turn out to be that "killer app."

If a studio with a visionary outlook and a workable business arrangement with a network (or its own network) went forward in producing interactive elements for its shows, just what would the studio do with interactive television? And why would it do it?

Interaction: The Real Meaning of Multitasking

In early 1997, representatives of Microsoft's interactive television division approached Big Ticket Television to determine whether any of Big Ticket's shows might be candidates for interactive enhancement. As a new, fairly small production company (albeit part of an established, large organization), it made sense for Big Ticket to explore technologies that could bring it greater attention, technical and creative expertise, and leverage in the marketplace.

Big Ticket's *Moesha*, a comedy starring the talented and popular singer Brandy, was the clear candidate for enhancement. The top-rated comedy on the emerging UPN network, the critically lauded show about middle-class African-American family life from the viewpoint of a smart, inquisitive teenage girl, had all the right elements going for it. Its audience was young, progressive, and largely unserved by most network programming. The show's production had a cutting-edge style with extensive use of trend-setting music, fashion, and language. Perhaps most important, its producers, Ralph Farquhar, Sara Finney, and Vida Spears, saw the entertaining and enriching possibilities provided by interactivity and embraced the opportunity to use it on their show.

The producer's embrace is no small thing.

The "Threat" of Interactivity

Most Hollywood television writers are extremely protective of their words. Anything that might interrupt or detract from a viewer's attention to their carefully crafted story or jokes would not be looked upon as an "enhancement." Indeed, when first introduced to the notion of interactive television, some of TV's top writers exclaimed, "If my show could be any further 'enhanced,' I would have already done so!"

Fragile Hollywood egos aside, there is some merit to such reservations. Giving TV viewers the ability to get further statistics on a batter during a baseball game or ordering a transcript on line from a news interview program are obvious, valuable enhancements to the experience of watching such shows. Much less obvious is what can be added to the viewing experience of a narrative-driven show to enhance it. If the writer's intention is to involve the viewer in the predicament of the characters, to write compelling, emotionally stirring drama, trenchant dialog, clever conversations, or even side-splitting, broad physical comedy, anything that takes the viewer out of the moment could be seen as detracting and, worse, as counterproductive. Thus the obvious question for producers is, "What else could a viewer possibly do while engrossed in my show?"

Time out for a reality check.

Those who have watched teenagers watching TV in the late 20th century truly understand the meaning of "multitasking." Today's generation of young people were brought up on music videos, Sony PlayStations, pagers, voice mail, Reader Rabbit CD-ROMs, chat rooms, call waiting, and, most important, the remote control. Thus, the notion of sitting down in front of the set to absorb oneself, uninterrupted and without distraction, in a half-hour or hour program from start to finish is not realistic.

The young viewers are quite capable — and desirous — of talking on the phone, doing their homework, and downloading e-mail from America Online (AOL) while also watching *Dawson's Creek*. Or, clicker in hand, they flip between, and still follow, the story lines of three sitcoms at the same time. This behavior tells us that these viewers want more information, more density, and more interaction in their television-using experience.

Frankly, producers and network programmers are conceited to insist on the power of their shows to hold a viewer's attention when their audience's behavior so clearly belies it. Once past this psychological hurdle on the part of content providers, the bigger issue is the business model. Viewers increasingly want to get more content, be more involved, and do more things while watching a program. If the program is not being subsidized on a subscription or pay-per-view basis, can the traditional, advertising-supported "free" model still work when viewers can so easily miss, intentionally or not, the commercial message? It's one thing to have viewers distracted when watching the show — it's disastrous if they're "saving up" to play with the interactive elements when the commercial is on. (Of course, ads will be interactive too, but that won't be addressed here.)

From a network (and a 1960s) perspective, perhaps interactive enhancements are not part of the problem but actually part of the solution. Or, if you can't beat 'em, join 'em. Assume that the other choices presented to the interactive viewer (or to use a current, if clumsy, term, "viewser," from viewer and user), be they informational, transactional, games, chat, fan club, or whatever, are all related to the show, and carry advertising for the same sponsors. Assume further that these enhancements enrich viewers and their appreciation of the show, or at least satisfy their apparent appetite for diversion, but then also lead them back to the show. If tomorrow's viewers are going to be flipping around anyway, why not capitalize on that kind of TV usage?

From the studio's point of view, anything that adds to the viewing experience of its programs, that encourages involvement, enthusiasm, and, most important, ongoing habitual viewing of a series, is obviously a good thing. A show's writer–producer might look upon ads as the cost of telling the story. Whether the writer–producer will make the same allowance for a studio's desire to add interactive enhancements, let alone actively and creatively embrace them, will no doubt vary on a case-by-case basis. There's a trade-off between the increased ratings (or ratings retained that might have been lost) and the cost of producing the enhancements. This equation probably won't be easily measured or clearly defined in the early stages, so again a leap of faith may be required.

If, through negotiation or just largesse, the networks allow the studios to use extra bandwidth for interactivity, the studios will have an opportunity to enhance the entertainment, commercial, and long-term residual value of their shows.

Interactive Television:
Value for the Studio and the Consumer

For the consumer, the studio, and even the community at large, enhanced TV can enable a richer, deeper television viewing experience. This could promote greater viewer involvement and loyalty, create a sense of belonging, decrease alienation, and even inspire the formation of virtual communities linked by their shared allegiance to a TV series they enjoy together. It's the "water cooler factor" to the nth degree.

In more down-to-earth, bottom-line terms, adding interactivity to a studio's production can

- Generate additional revenue streams, all possibly shared with the broadcaster or exhibitor.

- Create tremendous merchandising opportunities. For example, with *Moesha* (which young people watch partly to keep up on the latest fashions), a viewer might click on the Moesha character and see a pop-up screen that described the clothes she was wearing or even be able to order them directly on line.

- Enable use of sponsorships, tie-ins, promotions, Web advertising and so on within the interactive content, either with the same advertisers involved with the regular program content or with additional advertisers.

- Keep reruns "ever green." The product can be refreshed in subsequent runs by updating the interactive elements. This gives viewers an added reason to watch reruns, both in the network cycle and later in syndication. Updating HTML programming is much cheaper than new full-fledged TV production. This adds tremendous value to any show and is almost reason enough by itself for a studio to embrace interactivity.

- Heighten awareness, increase profile and demand, and yield more value to programmer and consumer. While interactive TV is still young and stirring curiosity in the public consciousness, just the fact that a show is enhanced will draw interested viewers to sample it. Its "interactiveness" can be promoted on air and in conventional media, as well as on the Internet.

- Provide research opportunities. Feedback from the consumer to the producer can be used to improve and better tailor the program to its "constituents'" desires. This could be active, in the form of interactive questionnaires and prompted or unprompted e-mail to an address featured in the enhancements. Again, some useful information about viewers can also be gathered passively without any input from them at all.

The consumer, meanwhile, can

- Play games related to the show. In the *Moesha* enhanced demonstration (involving Moesha's participation in a modeling contest), viewers played a "fashion do's and don'ts" game and used the cursor to put together various ensembles of shoes, tops, and bottoms, which were then judged for their fashion sense.

- Take part in polls. Again from the *Moesha* demonstration, viewers were able to vote for their favorite during the modeling contest, with the results tallied as percentages on the screen in real time. The experiences of Internet Web site providers show that there are also strong opportunities here for networks, studios and advertisers to learn more about their viewers, because of the two-way nature of the medium, both actively from polls and the like and passively.

- Use other services, such as transcripts and other downloaded information, links to related interests and to other shows, travel, books, music, and so on. The only limits here are in the imagination of those involved.

Interactivity: When, What, Who, and Why?

Here is the multibillion-dollar question: Given what the studios could do, if the networks allow them to do it, will the studios jump in and do it?

Yes.

Or they will perish, and deservedly. As would any other provider of television programming, be it studio, network, cable, or direct broadcast satellite service.

Television will become an interactive experience because it can. Because the potential added revenues are irresistible to business. Because the younger generations brought up on interacting with their computers already "get it" and want it.

But it's the wrong question. The right question is *When?*

For a studio to answer that, it must have a sense of who the audience will be. Initially, these viewers will be able to use enhanced TV:

- WebTV Plus owners (and perhaps owners of similar competing set-top formats) and WebTV for Windows users with Windows 98 and TV tuner cards in their computers. (It is hoped that both installed bases will grow simultaneously.)

- Digital TV set owners, beginning in fall 1998 (assuming that consumer electronics manufacturers provide an interface that allows interactivity beyond program guides and timers for DVHS recorders).

These viewers will be able to afford enhanced TV:

- A fairly small, select, niche audience of prosperous, educated, nontechnology-averse, professional young male early adopters.

- Institutions such as corporations, universities, and well-endowed schools. Bars and restaurants that show sports events are likely to be early buyers of digital TVs because of their larger, clearer, enhanced wide-screen picture and terrific sound capabilities. Whether they would use, or encourage the use of, any included interactive capabilities in the sets is unknown but unlikely. Interactivity is an individual activity or a way to bring together small groups of familiar people like a family.

These types of programming fit the following demographics:

- Sports events, sports magazines, and event wrap-ups. If coupled with higher resolution, wide-screen, surround sound digital TV, especially big event sports such as those of the National Football League, National Basketball Association, baseball World Series, heavyweight boxing, and the Olympic Games.

- Live events, such as rock concerts (and it should be mentioned yet again, sports).

- News shows, breaking news, current events programs, newsmagazines, financial shows, and other informational shows.

- Big-budget theatrical motion pictures (again, especially if coupled with digital TV's wide screen, surround sound, special effects, expensive locations, and other high production values).

- How-to programming. There's a clear opportunity here for such subjects as home renovation, golf and fishing, travel, automobiles, computers, and so on. Interactivity provides terrific resources to dig deeper and "find out more about it." It also provides great opportunities for direct sales and merchandising and getting information about the viewer back to marketers.

Other potential enhanced programming includes shows that are more interested in how viewers value their programs than in how advertisers value the viewers:

- Educational and public television programming (which are relatively unconcerned about ratings). Public television stations don't need to simulcast their digital and analog channels, because they're not driven by ad revenue. They can use their digital channel for interactive programming, high definition, or multicasting. In their business model, they are more interested in how viewers value the station's programs than in how advertisers value their viewers.

- Subscription television in the form of premium or "pay" cable, as represented by HBO, Showtime, and others.

- Direct broadcast satellite.

Viewers with interactive or digital hardware (or both) are more likely to seek out and buy higher tech programming services such as HBO and DIRECTV.

This type of programming doesn't fit the profile of the early user:

- Prime-time series television and most TV movies, with some exceptions such as *The X-Files* and other high-profile, high-style, young-skewing dramas that might make sense as test beds. Most network series, however, skew female and aim at the broad economic middle. Some shows cut such a wide swath in such huge numbers (*ER*, for example) that they might make interesting candidates for enhancements as well.

- Daytime serials and talk shows, game shows, and court shows. Although game and court shows structurally lend themselves extremely well to interactivity (you play along or you be the jury), the actual audiences watching these shows — older and economically downscale — are not likely to be early users of interactive technology.

What the Major Studios Produce

The main fare is "big ticket" network prime-time series. These generally do not fit the initial demographic profile of potential interactive TV users. All the inherent problems previously mentioned about getting the network to give a studio the ability to add interactive content during a network's broadcast of the show are factors here.

First-run syndicated programming is also a mainstay for many studios. This includes 1-hour action shows (*Xena, Baywatch, Star Trek*) and talk shows, game shows, and court shows. In first-run syndication, the studio is, in essence, the network; consequently, there are far fewer barriers to entry (although there may still be issues with stations and station groups). The 1-hour action shows suggest a particularly good fit. The audience is young males, the subject matter has already shown its adaptability to and acceptance in video and computer gaming, and there's a worldwide reach.

As noted earlier, the syndicated talk shows, game shows, and court shows tend to skew older, female, or lower in education and income. Nonetheless, they might still be of interest, especially as a way to draw other demonstrations to these shows. Early in the growth curve of a new technology, when there's not much software, users of new hardware will sample whatever is out there. It may also prove to be a good place to establish a beachhead, develop expertise, and raise consumer awareness. Why wouldn't a studio jump in right now and add interactivity to programs with the right "profile?" It would ask itself these questions: Do the short-term rewards validate the investment? Will there be a tangible increase in ratings, ad revenue, and license fees? Will there be an increase in intangibles (when it comes to the bottom line) such as publicity, awareness, industry "buzz," and critical attention?

And most studio management, perhaps not demonstrating the boldest vision, will ask, "Can it wait?" After all, interactive enhancements are not now a studio's core business or area of expertise. Large companies believe they can jump in later after the pioneers have perfected the product and grown the market (and often lost their shirts). Even when it comes at a higher price later (such as Disney's purchase of Infoseek), there's a tendency to sit on the sidelines and then buy a successful start-up.

So why would a studio jump in now?

What's My Motivation?

There's no guarantee that a studio will be able to buy its way in later or at a price that makes economic sense. A compelling reason to get in now is to achieve recognition as a leader in new creative techniques in TV development and production, advertising and marketing, merchandising and cross-promotion, financing, coventuring, and revenue generation. Interactive enhanced television provides opportunities to expand franchises and to get the maximum return from the "first exhibition." A studio with early success in interactivity will become more valuable to networks, showing them how it's done by real pros.

Jumping in now means developing expertise in house, before the talented people in interactive TV become very, very expensive. Finally, it looks sexy to shareholders and corporate parents. After all, no guts, no glory. A studio can use enhanced TV to show network buyers that the studio is inventive and forward thinking in its approach to both the business and creative sides. Or it can use enhanced TV to find new ways to reach viewers outside traditional network exhibition. Ultimately, enhanced TV presents new ways to bolster or retain viewership and can augment the bottom line through its transactional capabilities.

Periods of transition are always stressful. This one seems especially so, as both the technological *and* financial models for how television is produced and exhibited are changing drastically. The digitalization of TV presents many opportunities: the interactivity, shared experience, and transactional e-commerce made possible by "enhanced TV"; multicasting enabled by compression; an improved viewing experience through high-definition, as well as time-shifting, video on demand; the "virtual VCR"; and other uses yet to be invented. The digitalization of TV also requires new skills, new models, and new vision.

Is now the time to jump in? That's for your studio to answer.

CHAPTER 6

Baywatch: A Tale of Two Cultures

Kevin Beggs, Producer, *Baywatch*
Tim Millard, Interactive Television Producer, Microsoft Corporation

Tim explains the process that he and Kevin developed for bring-ing a show through development to actual broadcast, while Kevin shares the story from his perspective as a Hollywood insider, one of the producers of Baywatch. *Their different visions will provide you with a greater understanding of the processes —both busi-ness and technical — of creating interactive content.*

Tim and Kevin originally provided me with two separate docu-ments. I brought them together as a script, with acts and scenes. At the end of each act is a chorus section with bullets calling out the key points of the act. By skimming through the key points, you can quickly understand the critical technical and business lessons that emerged from the Baywatch *experience.*

Act I: A Fairy Tale of a Tale

Scene I: Introduction

Chorus This chapter tells the story of two disparate but highly successful com-panies that come together to develop a new technology. The story-like way in which the chapter is presented provides insight into the process by bringing in the per-sonalities, conflicts, and corporate differences that emerged as we were struggling to develop interactive *Baywatch* episodes. Everyone knew that neither company would make a penny and that there was no guarantee of success. Microsoft and *Baywatch* created a partnership that worked, and their story is worth reading.

Kevin At *Baywatch*, our version of enhanced television has more to do with bodies than with bytes. Nonetheless, after telling Tim that I already had a handle on the enhancing process, I sat down with him to learn what it was all about from his perspective. Tim's account explained in detail what Microsoft was exploring in interactive television. After I "got it," I worked with Tim to sell the other producers on the concept. The result was dozens of new possibilities for practical applications of interactive television.

The phrase "interactive television" is bandied about often in the television business. It is a buzzword, thrown into a marketing pitch to convince non–computer-literate executives that their product or sales team is ahead of the curve, up to date, and leading the multimedia charge and is not (as is more likely) about to be swept aside like so many mobile homes in an Arkansas tornado. I was determined, with Tim, to make sure that interactive television would be more than just a buzzword on *Baywatch*. To accomplish that objective, we relied on one time-tested showbiz maxim: "Relationships, baby, are everything."

Chorus

- This chapter introduces interactive *Baywatch* and addresses important business and technical issues.

- "Interactive television" is often used simply as a buzzword to appease non–computer-literate execs. The *Baywatch* story demonstrates that ITV can be much more.

- Showbiz is built on the basis of relationships.

Scene II: Once upon a Time at Microsoft . . .

Tim   In fall 1996, I began contracting at Microsoft in what was known as the MITV, or Microsoft interactive television, team. We worked at the well-known RedWest campus, best known for housing the Microsoft Network (MSN), Microsoft's failed vision for an online entertainment empire. We were so small and inconsequential at that time that, while we called ourselves MITV, we could not legitimately claim the name internally or externally. But first, let's go back, way back.

Kevin   In the 13 years since high school graduation, I had seen Tim Millard once, at our 10-year reunion. It was there that I learned that we were both pursuing careers in entertainment. Tim had become a freelance writer–producer in the Seattle area, and I had started as a production assistant (PA) on *Baywatch* and had worked my way up to producer on that series in addition to two other series and a number of movies of the week (MOWs). While most of our classmates were reminiscing, Tim and I resorted to "talking shop," excited to know that we had each taken a chance in this crazy business. We exchanged phone numbers and promised to keep in touch. And, surprisingly, we did.

Tim sent me some scripts he was writing. I commented on them, suggested a revision here and there, and filled him in on the projects I was developing. When Tim told me he was going to take a contract at Microsoft to work on interactive television, I congratulated him, assuming that his work there would have little to do with producing and lots to do with extending the Microsoft brand into yet another untapped corner of the globe.

For a time, my suspicions proved true. Tim told me that Microsoft was making a significant push to partner with major networks and studios on something called "enhanced television." Before I could even suggest the notion, Tim let me know gently that the powers that be were not interested in working with an independent production company like *Baywatch*. I wished him well and went back to the daily realities of closing deals, developing scripts, and producing episodic television.

Tim   The problem with calling ourselves MITV internally was that several years before, there had been a fairly large and ambitious group that began work on interactive television under that name. This was about the time TCI, AT&T, Time Warner, and others created exciting headlines for what they believed was the potential of interactive TV. It seemed that everyone was talking about the future of video on demand, radio on demand, and pizza on demand, all available through your television set, without addressing the hard issues such as "who wanted these services" or "who would be willing to pay for them." And maybe people forgot that life is really quite convenient enough with video stores, compact discs (CDs), and the telephone. In retrospect, many companies caught up in this technology frenzy are willing to admit that the excitement of this vision of the future clouded their business sense.

We ended up calling ourselves MITV, even when it had such a bad lineage, because Microsoft Interactive Television really was the best name for what we were doing. Some producers, including myself, tried to skirt this issue by saying we were the Microsoft enhanced television group, but this only confused people about what we did, because enhanced television isn't really a widely understood term. So MITV it was, until we were eventually absorbed into the Microsoft digital television group in late 1997.

Externally, we faced a slightly different issue — a growing sense within the Hollywood community that Microsoft was expanding onto their turf through ventures such as MSN. Microsoft's plans to create a television-like online broadcasting network didn't necessarily make sense, but it had the bravado that Hollywood understood is necessary for such a creative endeavor. If it could work, people assumed that Microsoft, with its large bankroll and long line of successes, would be the one to succeed. And this had some people legitimately worried. We were afraid that by giving our directive a name that combined Microsoft and TV in the same sentence, we might scare some potential partners away.

Paul Mitchell, manager of the group, was a castoff from the old Microsoft interactive TV group and had managed to keep himself loosely associated with interactive TV while the rest of the company turned its attention to the Internet. This quick about-face is attributed to Bill Gates' now-famous Pearl Harbor day address that alerted the world that Microsoft would be turning its full attention to a new technology that seemingly had caught the company by surprise: the Internet. Expected to be the online empire for Microsoft, MSN absorbed much of the old interactive TV staff. This was where the company was currently focused, and this was where money was being spent by the bucketloads on such unproven concepts as online soaps, chats, and travel magazines.

The older "interactive TV Titanic" was sinking under broadband expectations, and everyone quickly abandoned it for the vision of a narrowband entertainment speedboat. Whether Paul didn't because he couldn't reach a lifeboat or because he realized the boat wasn't sinking but just taking on a little water, only he knows. In retrospect, he seems like a fairly smart, visionary manager who saw beyond the hype of the moment and stuck with the sinking ship only to right it and make it better than ever. I think the latter. I suspect time will tell how right I am.

Along with Rick Portin, an independent television producer, Paul was developing a business plan for how interactive television could work. For almost 2 years, Paul and Rick worked together in some capacity developing ideas and templates, thinking about the best way to finance the production, developing contacts with Hollywood production companies, and rethinking the interactive television models. Our content development work was in large part a product of their thoughts during that time.

What Paul and Rick came up with was a belief that interactive television would be most compelling by building on what people were already doing: watching TV. The key to this was content. The key to content was Hollywood. When the time for thinking and development was up, there was a need to bring on some staff members for the production of prototypes. As Paul and Rick felt it necessary to work with Hollywood production companies, they began to look for experienced producers who had worked with TV shows, networks, or companies.

Chorus Why choose to work with Hollywood production companies?

Kevin It seemed that the studios and networks, while cautiously interested in "enhanced television" were not altogether committed to working exclusively with Microsoft — or any company, for that matter — until there was a clear revenue stream to be drawn from the venture. NBC, for example, wanted to work with Microsoft and two other interactive television developers simultaneously. Evidently, being one among several didn't appeal to Microsoft. My guess was that Microsoft had hoped to forge high-profile partnerships with successful network series in a fashion similar to the deal they struck with NBC to form MSNBC.

Tim Paul and Rick had met with both network executives and production companies. The problems they encountered at the network level seemed to be twofold. First, other competitors in the development of interactive television were paying large sums of money to get the networks on board, and second, the networks were wary of letting Microsoft have access to their creative content. Because we had no money to pay the networks, we tried to appeal to their desire to test each different interactive technology. This worked about as well as asking a teenager to take advanced calculus just in case they might need it some day in the future. It was a hard sell at best.

We found that much of the network content was also owned by multiple partners, making it even tougher to get any decision making completed in a timely manner. Both Paul and Rick wanted to work with high-profile shows such as *Friends* or *Seinfeld*, but there always seemed to be administrative or financial barriers that made it impossible to create a working partnership. There was some network success in relationships created with both USA Network and TV Food Network, but nothing materialized with the big four networks at that time.

By going to the production companies, we were able to find shows that were wholly owned by the decision makers we were talking to. Starting where content is created is the simplest place, because ownership becomes geometrically more complex once you move up the distribution ladder.

Chorus

- The older "interactive TV Titanic" was sinking under broadband expectations and everyone quickly abandoned it for the vision of a narrowband entertainment speedboat. Microsoft focused on the Internet and MSN, which absorbed much of the Interactive TV staff and technologies.

- The new interactive television group knew it had to build on what people were already doing: watching TV. The key to this was working with Hollywood producers to develop content that enhanced the viewing experience.

- One of Microsoft's goals in working with Hollywood producers was to forge high-profile partnerships with successful television series in the same way it had established MSNBC by partnering with NBC.

Scene III: The Art of Slinking

Tim   The problem was money. Paul had none and wasn't likely to get any. So he did what at Microsoft is a fairly accepted procedure: He "slunk." Slinking is the term I use to describe trying to stay under the corporate "financial radar" to buy time to prove a mission is worthy of financing. Slinking at a major corporation is not uncommon. However, Paul perfected this art at a company that encourages its employees to develop new ideas like a new start-up, fighting tooth and nail for every penny in the effort to stay alive. The thinking is that if you can find a way to justify your existence based on a potential technology or product long enough to create value either internally or externally, then you may just have hit upon something worth corporate dollars in the next fiscal review.

MSN was just hitting a level of maturity that caused executive eyebrows to raise — financial losses were revealed to be around $500 million for fiscal year 1996. While our group was corporately organized in MSN, we didn't fall under the heading of entertainment show, technology, or marketing. So we obviously weren't in MSN's primary areas of interest. Because we didn't generate revenue, we weren't going to be funded in an already tight fiscal atmosphere. If we magically survived, we would need some managerial illusion along with some fiscal sleight of hand. Also, at Microsoft, full-time head count is notoriously hard to come by. Paul therefore slunk and hired contractors slowly, as needed.

Chorus

- Slinking is Tim's description of the time-honored tradition at major corporations of staying under the corporate financial radar, to buy time and prove a mission is worthy of financing.

- By the end of fiscal year 1996, MSN was showing an annual loss of $500 million.

Scene IV: The First Interactive Shows

Tim   In fall 1996, when I began, the MITV team was already seven people strong, with three employees and four vendors or contractors. I had been in contact with Rick Portin over the preceding months about developing interactive show demos. In October, I was brought on to assist producer Kris Evans on a TV Food Network show called *The Essence of Emeril*. Kris had nearly completed our first interactive show, an episode of the USA Network show *Pacific Blue*. The Big Ticket/UPN show *Moesha* was just starting development around that time. With the *Pacific Blue* episode near completion, it didn't make sense to pursue *Baywatch* because there were so many similarities between the shows. Moreover, the goal of our group was to develop as many different genres of demos as possible. Unfortunately, both *Pacific Blue* and *Essence of Emeril* were shown to the executives who commissioned them and then put on the shelf because there really was no way to broadcast or receive the interactive content.

The possibility of creating enhancements for news and sports was discussed early on because of their obvious potential for interactivity. However, it took a long time to develop the relationships with the news organizations (including MSNBC), and working with professional sports involved overcoming significant rights hurdles. Several factors compounded the initial difficulties of finding partners in these fields, including their live nature and the complexity of their production environments. By working with shows that are produced weeks or months in advance, we could mirror their production schedule and create the interactivity necessary to make them compelling. In late 1997, Microsoft began work on tools for producing live interactive shows that should help pave the way for news and sports to excel in the near future.

Moesha made the biggest interactive splash of our early demos. Through showings at the annual UPN executives' meeting and demos to some press members, word quickly spread about the show Microsoft had created. Most of the press was negative, saying that the interactivity was too much, too distracting, and that Microsoft didn't understand how TV shows worked. The press pointed to this being Microsoft's vision so that criticism didn't fall directly on the show or production company itself. This kept the show separated from the interactivity — as if you could critique the one without the other.

Many people thought that the interactivity was too distracting from the show and criticized Microsoft because of this. In truth, the interactivity demanded attention and did detract from the show somewhat. However, I don't ever see where interactive TV won't do this to some extent.

The other problem we had was that we could not demonstrate an ability of the viewers to leave the interactive template if they chose. Either they watched the show only, or they watched the show with interactive elements. There was no easy movement between these two options. These early shows were also created as demos of what interactive TV might look like, and they were therefore loaded with more interactive elements than could normally be digested by a first-time viewer. We thought of them as pilots that would draw optimistic approval from viewers and producers alike.

What some of these naysayers failed to understand is that interactive producer Marie-Rose Phan-Le worked closely with series cocreator and executive producer Ralph Farquhar, and he loved the interactive elements. To counteract this kind of criticism, we had purposely worked with the show producers to create the content, getting their approval throughout the process. Although some of the producers probably defaulted to our ideas, assuming we understood the technology best, they all had final creative approval to ensure that nothing was incorrect and that the interactivity followed the design and feel of the show itself. Regardless of the negative press, *Moesha* caused a significant stir in Hollywood circles, making *Moesha* the most influential and important demo our group ever made. Figure 6.1 shows a screen shot with a "thought bubble" from *Moesha*.

When it came time to produce the *Baywatch* episodes, I tried to counteract some of the criticism we had received by simply doing less interactivity. I also wanted to give viewers greater control over when they accessed the interactive elements, thereby putting the decision about the passive or active viewing experience in the viewers' control.

Figure 6.1   A thought bubble from *Moesha*. (The authors gratefully acknowledge Bill Sanders for his permission to include *Moesha* content.)

Chorus

- The ITV team quickly understood the importance of working closely with the show producers and making the interactivity a complement to the show rather than the focus.

- The ITV team believed it was important to demonstrate interactive TV in a variety of genres that would generate interest in as many production companies as possible.

- Although questioned for its implementation and interface methodology, the UPN show *Moesha* created a significant stir in the entertainment community, making it the most influential and important interactive TV demo made by Microsoft.

Act II: Of Buyouts and Delayed Launches . . .

Scene I: Enter the WebTV

Tim Microsoft's purchase of WebTV in March 1997 caused a stir in our group, although we weren't exactly sure what it meant. It fell in line with the type of work we were doing, and we all hoped that it meant Microsoft was planning on spending more time and money on the convergence of the computer and the TV. However, when we heard in June 1997 that the release of what was then called Windows 97 was being delayed until 1998, our optimism quickly turned to discouragement. This meant that it would be another year before we would receive any assurance of an audience for our interactive elements. For producers Kris Evans and Marie-Rose Phan-Le this was especially disheartening, for the shows they were working on were for the next broadcast season. Nevertheless, both of these announcements turned out to be positive omens for a potential relationship with *Baywatch.*

Initially, I was uncertain whether Microsoft would want to partner with a show that has endured some criticism of its own for the swimsuit-clad beauties that are featured in the now-famous slow-motion montages of running on the beach. And maybe that was a consideration at some point. However, our efforts to work with other high-profile shows such as *Friends* and *Seinfeld* had always run into legal and financial obstacles. The fact that *Baywatch* was easy to work with was a huge plus.

The beginning of the interactive *Baywatch* episodes was based on a relationship, the relationship Kevin and I had as friends from high school, as well as the relationship we had as fellow producers in the TV industry. This solid foundation led to the initial contacts, proposals, and verbal agreement that propelled the project from mere discussion into an active partnership.

Kevin   Quite honestly, by the time Tim received the approval to call *Baywatch*, it was on the heels of disinterest elsewhere, which is fine with me. Partnering with the world's most watched television program might be the kind of interactive gospel that Microsoft needed to jump-start its Windows 98 TV-tuner feature.

Baywatch has always been the little engine that could, canceled after 22 episodes on NBC, scorned for being too gratuitously sexy in a politically correct era, and generally forgotten. Thanks to the determination of four people (Doug Schwartz, Michael Berk, Greg Bonann, and David Hasselhoff), the series breathed life again in first-run syndication, going on to become the most watched show in the history of a television and an immensely profitable franchise. The very air at *Baywatch* exudes a scrappy, come-from-behind attitude, and, when I got Tim's call, I was ready to take a chance. The opportunity to do something first was alluring; the opportunity to work with Tim, inviting; and the challenge of something new, compelling.

Chorus

- The delay of the next Windows release until 1998 and the purchase of WebTV set the stage for the Microsoft–*Baywatch* partnership, a partnership based on a decade-old relationship between two individuals.

- Microsoft's decision to work with *Baywatch* resulted from two situations: the obstacles that Microsoft encountered in trying to partner with shows such as *Seinfeld* and the desire of *Baywatch* producers to work with Microsoft.

Scene II: Initial Obstacles

Kevin   The series business is a strange animal. The overwhelming weight of 22 episodes or more being developed, written, and produced every year on a back-breaking schedule falls squarely on the producers. During development, preproduction, production, and postproduction, most of them are so enmeshed in their work that they lose track of time, family, and life, in short order. Just completing an episode from script to delivery is a major achievement — a mini feature film, if you will. Unless an interactive element is required for delivery, not many producers have time to think about it.

Thus, when the idea of "enhancing" an episode floats across the room from Microsoft or a marketing executive from the studio or network, in most cases, no one's listening. Staff members are wondering how they will finish a rewrite by Monday and a new story outline by Tuesday. And the star isn't coming out of his or her trailer until an espresso machine is installed in the motor home . . . .

It was also clear from my conversations with Tim that most television producers and distribution executives could not see any clear benefit of "enhancing" their programs. Writers and directors wanted audiences glued to one window — their program — not multiple screens. Distribution execs, or "the suits," as we call them, saw no immediate revenue opportunity and thus questioned the value of the technology. Until a clear financial model was established, "enhanced television" was relegated to the lowly status of just another marketing hook. And there are many conventional marketing models from which to choose. I also told Tim that establishing the partnership might involve a battle with our distributor, All American Television (AAT), as they had just lost their new media exec and hadn't replaced him.

Chorus

- A key challenge in jump-starting the production company relationships was gaining the attention of the production staff, from executives to writers, for a new concept that had no proven business model.

- Producers felt threatened by the idea that there would be multiple windows on the screen or content that was different from the core video programming.

Scene III: The Importance of Distributors

Kevin   The distributor in syndication is all important, often providing financing and always serving as the link between the producers and the buyers, the hundreds of independent or semi-independent stations across the country that purchase syndicated programming. The distributor is responsible for "placing" the program with these stations, many of which don't have liquid cash to purchase the product. In those instances, the distributor barters ad time, retaining some for itself, attaching national sponsors (Coke, General Motors, AT&T), and allowing the station to sell the rest locally (car dealer Cal Worthington and his dog "Spot").

LBS Communications was a syndicator that had some success with the 1-hour series *Fame*. This show had begun on network TV and was continued in first-run syndication in the 1980s. The president and chief executive officer of LBS Communications, Henry Siegel, was a pioneer in *barter syndication*, in which syndicators, in lieu of cash from stations, retain advertising time that they sell nationally. A typical split of 14 minutes of advertising per hour is known as "seven–seven," meaning that the local station can sell 7 minutes of ads to car dealers and others while LBS sells 7 minutes to national advertisers. The station doesn't put up cash (few small stations have a lot of money), but it does put up time. On a hit show such as *Hercules* or *Xena: Warrior Princess*, sometimes the split is "nine–five," with the station keeping only 5 minutes of local advertising time.

LBS had fallen upon hard times and was facing bankruptcy. It was desperate for a life preserver, and *Baywatch*, ironically, was it. AAT was not heavily involved in television at the time but agreed to put up some of the money to help LBS with the project. In exchange, AAT would retain a security interest in *Baywatch* and, if LBS went under, would inherit the asset. LBS couldn't survive and ultimately it merged with AAT, which took over *Baywatch*. On the strength of *Baywatch*, AAT became a major player in domestic and international syndication. When AAT took on *Baywatch*, the LBS stock was at $2. In November 1997, Pearson, the British media and publishing giant, paid $565 million for AAT at a stock price of $25.50.

AAT and its subsidiary, LBS Communications, were the only syndicators willing to take a chance on a failed series. Their seed money, along with a substantial foreign contribution from the international distributor Fremantle, ensured that *Baywatch* would get a second chance on television. Getting AAT's approval to move forward with the interactive episodes was essential. It had never done anything like this before, and the fact that no revenue was being generated from the partnership with Microsoft was unattractive, given that *Baywatch* held over 50 licenses around the globe for everything from chewing gum to sunglasses.

AAT certainly couldn't be called "high-tech savvy." Computers, the Internet, and interactive television meant little to the decision makers at the company, so it really boiled down to "why bother?" There was also a great deal of resistance to working with Microsoft, because of its size, rumored business tactics, and wealth. We were able to overcome that reluctance through several meetings and phone calls, but AAT ultimately put the ball back in the producers' court. If we wanted to do this, we would have to contend with the production hassle and see it through to completion. I signed on for that task.

Chorus

- The distributor in syndication is critical, providing program financing and serving as the link between the producers and the buyers at television station groups. The distributor "places" the program with these stations, bartering some ad time, retaining some for itself, attaching national sponsors, and allowing the station to sell some local spots. Getting the OK from AAT, *Baywatch*'s distributor, was a key development.

Scene IV: Previous Interactive Experience

Kevin As television producers, this was actually our second "interactive" partnership. Working with Philips and its subsidiary, POV, we worked on an interactive version of the Rysher Entertainment property *Thunder in Paradise* for the Philips CD-I platform. The concept was to use film elements from the episode throughout the game, including different outcomes and other features, and then to move through levels of 100% game content. This proved a very ambitious undertaking, about a year in the making.

In a similar fashion to today's ITV model, we had a television director and an interactive director. Philips provided all of the financing, including a $600,000 addition to our two-part budget to accommodate the extra days of filming necessary to complete the varying scenarios in the game. In a manner similar to the ITV model, the writer, Tom Greene, moved successfully between episodic requirements and the complexities of the interactive game. In the end, the game turned out to be exceptional, but the limited CD-I market meant the project was judged a commercial failure. Shortly thereafter, Philips did away with CD-I and most of its interactive pursuits as well.[1]

But the Philips interactive game was quite different from what Tim and Microsoft were proposing. In moving away from "interactive" and toward "enhancing," they were making the leap away from the overly ambitious hopes of the early 1990s about a generation of television viewers controlling plots, character responses, and programming in general. Instead, they were offering additional, nonintrusive content that could be accessed via the television signal. A viewer could not change a plot but could access cast biographies, behind-the-scenes video taped on the day of filming, or digital photos of the stars. I would compare it with baseball fans who attend a game and use a radio to hear the play-by-play: They want more out of their entertainment experience. As producers, our job is to give more to them. I definitely saw the potential for a greater audience with Microsoft than with Philips.

---

1. Philips launched CD-I in the United States in 1991 and in Europe in 1992. Estimates are that 200,000 units were shipped in the United States in 5 years (*Wall Street Journal*, June 28, 1996). Philips estimates it sold 4500–5000 units to the education market (*Multimedia Business Report*, July 12, 1996). Philips won't report its losses on the project, but they are estimated at over $1 billion (*Wall Street Journal*, June 28, 1996). In 1996 Philips stopped producing CD-I consumer products and focused on the business market (*Consumer Multimedia Report*, October 14, 1996).

Chorus

- Kevin had helped to create and implement a fully interactive game based on the now-defunct Philips CD-I technology. The relationship model for producing the CD-I content was similar to that for ITV, involving a television director and an interactive director, with separate areas of responsibility. A writer who could move easily between the episodic requirements and the complexities of the interactive game was critical to the production.

In contrast to CD-I, the interactive television model was much more focused on enhancing existing video content. Rather than having the power to control the plot, the viewer could access more information and have a deeper entertainment experience.

Scene V: Finding a Common Language

Kevin   The first hurdle in contemplating the Microsoft project was simply finding a common language. "Microspeak" (the way software people speak) and "TV speak" (the way television people speak) are very different languages, and trying to frame a discussion about enhanced television or WebTV to someone who is still marveling at the miracle of a fax machine isn't easy. We encountered a technology gap.

Among the three executive producers, one had surfed the Internet and two were familiar with word processing. The distribution executives fared no better. Whereas their assistants and midlevel managers got enhanced television immediately, the top brass became glassy eyed almost instantly when presented with even the most rudimentary concepts. However, the power of Microsoft and its coming importance in the television world weren't a complete negative.

I was able to talk AAT's head of production, Syd Vinnedge, into visiting the Redmond, Washington campus of Microsoft for a presentation. We met with Tim, Rick Portin, Paul Mitchell, and several other "Microsofties." They treated us to a video presentation featuring clips from shows that had been "enhanced" and interviews with their producers.

Tim   At Rysher Entertainment's suggestion, our group had partnered with it to enhance its special effects–based show, *F/X: The Series*. An episode completed in the spring by producer Marie-Rose Phan-Le was important because it demonstrated that a high level of interactivity could be created for a plot-based action hour. *Baywatch* is also considered an action-hour drama, and so I decided that *F/X: The Series* would be the best show to demonstrate to Kevin and his associates.

Kevin We viewed about 15 minutes of *F/X: The Series*, a syndicated television series based on the original films. The television show follows the exploits of an ingenious special effects supervisor for films who must use his gadgets, gizmos, and sleight-of-hand trickery to evade bad guys or, better yet, to capture them.

The enhanced show utilized the basic concept of a television field and an L-shaped interactive field. Some interesting graphics, close-ups on key props, and other behind-the-scenes information was available to viewers as they simultaneously watched the television program.

We listened and learned that the concept, as envisioned in Windows 98, was to transmit the enhancements to a viewer's home television by embedding program code into the actual air master of the program. Thus, viewers with television tuner hardware and the television-viewing component of Windows 98 could access the enhancements. Alternatively, the same enhancements could be accessed via WebTV and the Internet, albeit in a less ambitious format.

Syd and I struggled to take it all in, and the phalanx of Microsoft people almost drowned us in their enthusiasm for enhanced television. Consumer Products, MSN, Windows — many Microsoft divisions were represented in the room, and suddenly we both seemed quite insignificant, like titans (on our best days) of an archaic medium. We left chastened and humbled, but we were both excited about the possibility of enhancing 200 episodes of *Baywatch*, all at Microsoft's expense, or so we thought.

In the following weeks, we would learn that Microsoft, while interested in getting the ball rolling, wasn't interested in enhancing an entire library of a series. It was simply too costly, and its goal was to be the catalyst for interactive television rather than the guarantor of it. After many conference calls, memos, and letters, we arrived at a strategy: We would focus on several episodes and enhance them as a beta test. If it went well, we would look to do more together. If it didn't, neither party would be obligated to work together again, and we would each benefit from the potential exposure.

Chorus

- Finding a common language between software people, who use "Micros-peak," and television people, who use "TV speak," is perhaps the most critical nontechnical hurdle in the development of interactive television content.

- The traditional television "L shape" is a good starting point for any enhancement template. Enhancing content wraps around the main video picture.

- The need to give viewers regular enhanced programming (about 22 episodes) must be balanced with budget requirements and the limitations of an emerging technology. It is better to start with a more focused test.

Act III: The Journey Begins

Scene I: Choosing the Episodes

Tim It became apparent that the best compromise would be one or more episodes with a lengthy lead time for development. *Baywatch* had already planned a 2-hour season finale called "White Thunder at Glacier Bay," to be filmed in Alaska aboard the ship *Dawn Princess*.

Kevin Our challenge was choosing episodes that would allow us enough time to implement the enhancements before broadcast. Tim and Microsoft made it very clear that their process would not affect our own. They would not hold up production. They would simply be present, documenting the shoot with state-of-the-art digital video cameras and throwing out ideas to writers, producers, and other staffers. That stated, the enhancements would take time to complete. The executive producers, the lawyers, and I would need to approve the content.

Baywatch distinguishes itself as an efficiently produced series. Each episode is filmed in just under 5 days. In comparison, many network 1-hours are filmed in 8 days or more (*Nash Bridges, Melrose Place, Walker: Texas Ranger*, to name a few). With over 22 episodes, that translates to merely 5 months of production rather than the standard 8 or 9. From the first day of filming to delivery, each episode is completely filmed and put through postproduction in less than 2 months. This leaves little time for the creation of an entirely new enhanced version.

Plans were under way to film a two-part episode in August and September of 1997 that wouldn't air until the May 1998 "sweeps" period.

Tim Kevin quickly recognized the promotional and production possibilities that these episodes offered and suggested that we choose them for our partnership. Paul Mitchell agreed and we began to move ahead into preproduction. Microsoft and *Baywatch* were now working together. Who would have ever thought it could happen?

Sweeps

Sweeps refers to the months of November, February, May, and July, when Nielsen Media Research (formerly A.C. Nielsen) analyzes the performance of television shows for the benefit of advertisers. Networks and studios trot out their most impressive or "stunt" episodes during these time periods to earn high numbers. *ER* went live in November 1997. *Seinfield* aired its last episode in May 1998. Think of a "very special" television episode and it aired either during premiere week in September or during sweeps. To compete in a tough market, *Baywatch* and other syndicated shows do the same. Ironically, this means that all of the shows are doing their best to look great during the sweeps period. Because the size of the viewership pie remains reasonably constant, one "killer" episode (of a show such as *Seinfeld*) can have a detrimental effect on all the others.

Scene II: Of Budgets and Promotions

Tim From the work that had been done on previous shows, our group had come to the belief that the best way to create an enhanced show was for the interactive producer to be included in all phases of the production process. This meant setting up the interactive producer as a separate department, much like the separate departments for props, costume, lighting, camera, script, and promotion. Microsoft paid the interactive producer because of the special development agreement we were working under. Actually, there was no signed agreement as yet, but the verbal understanding was that Microsoft would pay for all production and creation of the interactive elements and *Baywatch* would provide all access necessary between departments and all production information such as scripts, call sheets, and access to dailies.

In the weeks leading up to production, I developed my budget for two episodes, which I estimated at $90,000, made travel plans for production in Los Angeles and Alaska, scheduled what I could, and reviewed the script for interactive ideas. This last area was no easy task, as the current script ended up being scrapped at the last minute. But more on that later.

The episodes that we had chosen to enhance included a number of other partnerships that *Baywatch* had brought together, the biggest of which was Princess Cruises, long known for its connection with the show *The Love Boat*. Princess had offered to cover all of the cruise ship costs for the cast and crew.

Kevin In fact, the White Thunder episodes made the trip even more challenging. The initial proposal to partner with Princess Cruises on a two-part episode similar to *The Love Boat* came to Doug Schwartz in October 1996. From that point forward, Doug and I worked tirelessly to put the entire deal together. That included bringing over 200 cast members, crew, and promotional partners to Alaska, housing them on board the magnificent *Dawn Princess* as it cruised up the Inside Passage for 7 days. We filmed on the ship, from rivers and mountains and the massive Mendenhall glacier, and brought a smaller film crew to Mt. McKinley. Other production challenges, including the filming of a sequence featuring a bear attack, made the work exciting.

Few television shows ever undertake this kind of project. Given our limited budgets in syndication, it was even more foolhardy. To stay within our budget, Doug and I had put together numerous promotional "trade-out" deals with Princess Cruises ($1.2 million), Alaska Airlines ($250,000), Trimark Home Video ($500,000), and others. The total production budget was intended to be $4 million, which included budgets for two episodes plus the amount of trade-out we received from Princess and Alaska Airlines, plus the Trimark Home Video advance. After the single episode became three, that number jumped to $5.2 million.

Chorus If it was so foolhardy, why did you go to Alaska?

Kevin We went to Alaska precisely because no one else would. Doug Schwartz is the "P.T. Barnum" of television, and he knows what audiences want. He relishes a production challenge, and the more people told him that he couldn't do it, the more determined he became. Doug also hails from the same family that brought us *Gilligan's Island* and *The Brady Bunch*. What episodes of *The Brady Bunch* do we all remember? Grand Canyon, Hawaii, and Ghost Town. Doug did the same on *Baywatch*.

Our aim was to make the Alaska episodes the most heavily promoted in our history. Accordingly, we convinced our partners at *Inside Sports* magazine to come on the cruise and to produce its 1998 swimsuit issue with one of our series stars, Carmen Electra. Jerry Croft and Mike Weinstein of *Inside Sports* were happy to do so. They brought their film crew and a dozen breathtaking models that they featured in the magazine and we used as extras on the episodes. *TV Guide* sent feature reporter Mary Murphy on the cruise. *Entertainment Tonight* sent a crew. And now, with the addition of Microsoft, we were really turning up the promotional heat. All we needed was the script. With that in hand, Tim and I could begin work on plotting out the enhancements, and the series production staff could begin working out the logistical nightmare of moving more than 200 people to Vancouver, British Columbia, and from there to Anchorage.

The script, however, was not imminent. Although the story was completed in mid-June, the teleplay didn't come in until the day before we were to leave for Vancouver. As I have learned in television, stars don't like surprises. The teleplay varied dramatically from the original story, and David Hasselhoff hated it. His feet were firmly planted in Los Angeles until a new script was under way.

David Braff, a co–executive producer, came to Vancouver on 2-hours notice, locked himself in a hotel room with a laptop, and fed us new scripts every 6 hours until the first 15 pages were completed. That was enough to get started. David Hasselhoff agreed to fly to Vancouver, and with 1 day of relaxation on board the ship before production commenced, he seemed to like the new direction of the story. However, the production plans made during the 2 months leading up to the departure were completely scrapped, leaving the entire 6-day shoot on board the *Dawn Princess* up in the air. Similarly, the enhancement ideas that Tim and I had developed were no longer relevant to the new story. We knew that we would have to improvise in both camps.

Chorus

- *Baywatch* episodes are filmed in just under 5 days. Each episode requires 2 months to go from filming to completion, including postproduction.

- In choosing your own shows to enhance, look for obvious promotional opportunities as well as for shows that will give you the most lead time.

- To subsidize the tremendous cost of the finale episodes, *Baywatch* worked with large partners and gave them significant promotional opportunities. The same model can work well for enhancements, with several large players helping to foot the bill.

- The actual cost of enhancements relative to the cost of a full-fledged production is relatively low. The budget for the *Baywatch* finale was $5.2 million; the estimated budget for the enhancements was $90,000, or approximately 2% of the actual show cost.

Scene III: North to Alaska

Tim   It was important, from the beginning, that *Baywatch* treat the interactive department as an integral part of the production and not as an afterthought. Television crews are like cliques and notoriously hard to break into. There are the makeup and hairdressing clique, the lighting clique, the camera clique, the cliques for grips, costuming, and so forth. It can be difficult to break down these barriers.

However, with introductions by Kevin and director Doug Schwartz, the cast and crew quickly accepted our two-person interactive crew and made us feel a part of the production team. The staff and stars reacted to us with a combination of humored acceptance and inquisitive suspicion. With our standard camera, several digital video cameras, and our notepads, we seemed more like tourists than film crew.

Kevin   Tim and his assistant, Jeni, got along well with the crew and did not hinder production. In our situation (1 day before leaving, we had no script, no schedule, and no additional money), an outside group piggybacking on our production might have been a major problem. But that was never the case with Microsoft. The type of work they did was unobtrusive, interesting to the crew and cast, and more in keeping with a B-roll beta crew (a crew on the set doing interviews, taking pictures, and filming, but working around the cast of the show) than anything else.

A great deal of cross-pollination occurred between Microsoft, *Inside Sports*, Trimark Pictures, and other promotional partners on board, which resulted in increased cross-promotion for the episode in May 1998. Much of what Tim did was documentary-like — simply using his still or video cameras. Because of our uncertainty about the direction of the script, Tim focused on getting as many images as possible. One enhancement that Tim had planned weeks before we left was to bring in a specialized photographer who would film a 360-degree video image of our film crews working on the glacier. With eight helicopters ferrying the crew from base camp, three film units working in close proximity, and stunt people working on and under ice ledges and caves, we were quite a sight to see on the Mendenhall glacier. Tim's photographer caught all of this for the enhancements, which demonstrated just how rich they could be.

Tim   One of our priorities was to follow the example set by others in our MITV team of low-impact intrusion upon the production process. This meant that we followed all of the production etiquette essential for acceptance by the crew and cast. We were always aware of the needs of the crew to place lights, move the camera, and do the work necessary to prepare a scene for filming. However, filming moves very slowly at best. *Baywatch* is one of the best at keeping the pace of filming moving as rapidly as possible, something they have learned to do as a syndicated show on a limited budget.

Nevertheless, there is a considerable amount of time when crew members are standing around waiting for cast members still in makeup or for directors to make decisions. During this time we often pulled crew members aside for quick interviews on camera or for trivia that we might be able to use somewhere in our enhancements. You'd be amazed at how popular this made us with the crew. A few felt the questions intruded upon their time (keeping them from resting?), but the majority enjoyed the attention paid to their individual tasks that so often go unnoticed. We do not use much of this material, but our actions increased the acceptance we received from the crew and made our work easier.

Chorus

- It is challenging to find a balance between the needs to be both low impact and an integral part of the production. It is important to have the right introductions and the ability to be involved without being intrusive.

- It's critical that the producers and directors integrate the interactive crew as quickly as possible and that the interactive crew understand the production environment.

Scene IV: Alaska Anecdotes

Tim   The biggest obstacle we faced in the production process was the lack of a finished script. The script we had initially received in mid-August was scrapped once David Hasselhoff had a chance to read it. Keep in mind that we left for the cruise August 25, and Hasselhoff didn't read the script until August 23. As an executive producer and the show's star, David had the clout to say he didn't like the script and have it changed, even a day before production was to commence. His negative reaction to the script put the whole production crew in a bind. With all of the preparation to that point, there had to be an Alaska episode of *Baywatch*. The solution was furious rewriting in the week before departure and writing on the ship each day. We knew that most locations would remain the same, so we planned to get coverage of everything and to figure out what to use later. That was the only choice.

Departing for Alaska without a finished script put an extraordinary amount of pressure on Kevin and the entire production crew, because they had to pack everything for shipping a week before departure. For example, the props crew or the costuming crew didn't know what might be written into a scene and could not ensure they had the right items. How do you ensure you have all the details covered for a scene when it hasn't been written yet? You can't. Location scouts studied every possible filming location on the ship. The production manager planned for all possible contingencies. Every department was stretched to the limit of preparation and yet the mood was upbeat and confident. I was amazed.

Aboard a Floating Palace . . .

We boarded the *Dawn Princess* on a Saturday and quickly began the work of shooting the boarding and launch. The next day, at sea, was the only day off for the crew. But with the script being furiously written, this was not a day off for the department heads. In those first few days, an air of controlled hysteria was maintained through the calm confidence of director Doug Schwartz. His firm belief that they would get the script in time to shoot what was necessary for each day proved to be accurate.

While the producers were under a lot of stress, the pressure on the writers loomed as large as the 14-story *Dawn Princess*. Without a script, a TV show production consists of 100 crew people standing around with nothing to do. This was never more evident than on this production. Two writers were splitting the duties because of the last-minute nature of the writing. David Braff, the current story editor for *Baywatch*, was furiously writing the scenes for Ketchikan, the first stop on the voyage, while Deborah Schwartz, Doug's wife and a former story editor, was working on the all-important Wedding Finale between characters Mitch and Neely. David and Deborah were not seen that Sunday except for a quick appearance by David at the production meeting to update the producers on the script. David ran his hands through his rumpled hair, stared at everyone blankly when questioned, and made it clear that the scene wasn't done but would be by morning. No one was confident that it would be a great piece of writing but everyone knew David would have something to shoot.

That is exactly what happened. Each day more and more pages were completed until the script looked like a paint chart with its various hues of blue, red, and yellow for each of the new pages. Often the new script pages would be in my mail slot outside my cabin in the morning along with the crew call sheet for the day. I'd quickly read them at breakfast to see how much was changed and make notes for what props, locations, and references were being made that might be turned into interactive components. I'm sure the actors were going over their lines in makeup at the same time. Although it definitely wasn't the best working scenario, everyone made the best of it. After all, we were on a floating palace with all the food we could eat and gorgeous scenery all around. At least that's the experience I had. David Braff probably had to watch the episodes to see any of it.

Script Overboard

Although this chapter is not meant to be a daily recounting of our production process, there are a few incidents worth pointing out specifically. One hilarious incident involves the delivery of the script pages for the wedding scene the morning we were in Skagway. David Braff had finished another marathon night of writing on the proposal scene and a production assistant quickly grabbed the original out of the printer and ran it straight to David Hasselhoff for review. As the assistant handed one of the script pages to David, a gust of wind blew it overboard. David and the assistant watched it drift down and land on a small iceberg. There it sat and there it may still sit today. Perhaps that iceberg melted and the page drifted to the bottom of the Gulf of Alaska. Or maybe the iceberg joined with other icebergs, sealing the page inside so that in some future age an explorer may find it and gain insight into life in the 20th century, when lifeguards were celebrated heroes who earned free cruises on luxury liners. The assistant ran back to David Braff and had him print another page. And this time they made a copy before delivering it to David Hasselhoff.

Fire and Ice . . .

Another funny incident includes Carmen Electra, who played Lani, and a 3-foot-tall swan carved out of ice. It was a frigid, windy morning in Glacier Bay and everybody was wearing winter clothes, except Carmen, who wore only a black bikini with a sheer black scarf. She was to do a dance appropriately called "Fire and Ice," where (you guessed it) she provided the fire and the glaciers and frozen swan provided the ice. When Carmen sat on the ship's frigid steel railing and began her contorted dance, the temperature was in the 30s with the wind chill 15 to 20 degrees below that. Within minutes, the upper deck was packed as word of Carmen's dance spread among the shipload of male sailors used to a mostly elderly passenger list. The sailors weren't going to miss this once-in-a-lifetime opportunity.

None of this was funny, although it was uniquely *Baywatch*. The humor was brought by second unit director Lewis Stout, who alternately ran his hands down his own body and shouted out directions to Carmen about the swan: "Embrace it . . . touch it . . . make it breathe." Carmen did her best to resuscitate the swan with her sensual contortions and velvet touch, but there's only so much you can do with an ice swan. Appropriately, this section was deemed too steamy and was cut from the TV version. You can watch it if you rent the "too-hot-for-TV" video version. And when you see Carmen reach out for the swan, remember Lewis' words: "Embrace it . . . touch it . . . make it breathe."

To Film on the Glacier or Not to Film on the Glacier

The most stunning example of the production team's daring was not the script, which everyone knew must be finished to some degree, but the journey of a three-camera film crew onto the Mendenhall glacier for the climax to the plot line about the jewel thief. The difficulties of shooting on a glacier and the stunning visuals it promised compelled director Doug Schwartz to make this location central to all the Alaska episodes. Doug's decision caused tremendous concern and many headaches for members of the crew, but it also points out the courage and vision necessary to create compelling television.

On a Tuesday morning, when I first looked outside and saw the fog hanging like a curtain within 3 feet of the ship, I was certain there would be no glacier filming. The producers told me that they were going to try to salvage the day by filming on board ship and in Juneau, where we were currently docked. Then, on the outside chance that the fog would lift and the weather on the glacier would improve, they could still try to make the glacier. By 8:00 A.M., the fog was back from the ship about 20 feet. By 9:00 A.M., when the second unit was filming on the Mt. Roberts tram, the fog was patchy but still strong. And then the wind must have picked up because within an hour the fog had retreated to the top of the hills. Word from the glacier was that it was good enough to film.

Suddenly, everybody switched gears and all the preparation that had been put in for the glacier scene allowed the crew to load up the trucks quickly with equipment and film. By noon, everyone was at the staging area for a briefing about helicopter and glacier safety. Then the shuttling of equipment and crew began. Approximately 60 cast and crew members, three camera systems, and hundreds of boxes and bags were weighed, labeled, and loaded for the 15-minute helicopter trip to the glacier. The helicopters had originally been reserved for the morning, so we had to wait for helicopters to finish giving tourists "flightseeing" tours. At approximately 1:30 p.m., I boarded one of the last helicopters going up to the glacier.

I had previously scheduled Duncan, a photographer, to join me in Juneau to take several surround videos for possible use in our enhancements. Duncan left on an earlier helicopter flight and was already stationed to shoot the first of two surrounds on the glacier. My preparation for the glacier paid off in what turned out to be truly compelling interactive content that can't be done with traditional TV. Unfortunately, bandwidth restrictions would leave me unable to broadcast the surrounds with the show.

The late start to the day meant everyone was working furiously to set up the stunts and various scenes before we lost daylight behind one of the large mountains to the west. Amazingly, all the necessary footage was shot and the weather couldn't have been any better. Doug's faith and vision were richly rewarded, and I feel the glacier scenes are the most exciting of the Alaska episodes.

Chorus

- Enhancing a show when you have the script and understand the flow of the episode is challenging — enhancing a show without the script is truly difficult. To overcome the hurdles presented, grab as much content as possible for later use — video, photos, and interviews can all be assembled in a postproduction process to offer a compelling experience.

- The interactive producer on the set must make decisions about what content to gather for each day, reacting to any last-minute changes to the script.

- Every production has funny behind-the-scenes stories, which you should record because you may be able to use them in the enhancements. These weren't used in the *Baywatch* episodes, but they ended up in this book.

- Vision and courage make for more compelling content, whether in the show or in the interactive elements. Push yourself to try what seems impossible, because if you pull it off you've really done something worthwhile.

Act IV: Creating the Enhancements

Scene I: Back at the Studios

Tim   Once we finished the production on the Alaska episodes, I returned to Seattle to design the interactive environment. The environment is the template for the integrated TV and interactive experience and includes the properly sized video window, graphical background, navigational structure, and branding. It really is the first phase of production design, even before storyboarding.

Here's a quick overview of the design process:

- Decide on initial ideas and the amount of interactivity desired for your audience.

- Gather materials from production: photos, video clips, behind-the-scenes information, and other elements.

- Create the template.

- Storyboard interactive elements, based on materials gathered.

- Produce interactive elements, create art, and code the elements.

- Encode interactive elements onto show tape.

During the summer, Microsoft had released version 4 of Internet Explorer (IE4), and our group was making the technical transition, from version 3 and frames to dynamic hypertext markup language (HTML). What this technological advance meant to producers was that we no longer had to adhere to our old formula of breaking the page into a set of frames. Usability and entertainment became the primary design motivators instead of technology alone.

Kevin and I had discussed this new freedom and thought seriously about using transparent overlays on the video to indicate different interactive elements available to the user. Our initial thoughts revolved around enhancements concerning video and sound downloads, script references, and behind-the-scenes photos and information. We left the meeting very excited about the possibilities and felt that we had found a fairly compelling angle for the interactive *Baywatch* episode.

Within a week of returning to Redmond and discussing some of these ideas with the MITV team, I realized that the technical limitations were still significant relative to our plans. When we actually tested the overlays, we found that they left a lot to be desired. There was a sharp degradation of art caused by the transparency and there was a lingering pink background that followed the size changes of the video. We determined that the use of transparent overlays was still too unpredictable and primitive.

I rethought our overlay ideas and decided instead to create a thin border area for navigation that required the video area to be reduced by only about 10%. This would then show navigation without any ugly overlays. I decided to put the navigation on the right-hand side of the screen and use the bottom area like a ticker with textual information. This is a look that people are used to seeing in news and sports graphics, where the bottom is used for tickers, so I believed it would be fairly unobtrusive. I planned this as my first interactive template. Then I planned a second template that would reduce the video so that the interactive elements could be prominent. This was important if we were to make the interactivity important enough to interest the viewer.

Use of Text in an Interactive Show

Text provides the most information, uses the smallest bandwidth, and does all this with low impact. However, because TV is a visual medium, text takes the viewers' full attention away from the picture. I had noticed in our previous demos that many of the enhancements were pictures with accompanying text. This meant that the viewer had to look at three different things at once (TV picture, static images, and text) every time a new enhancement was received. If a lot of the information was textual, why not put all of this text in one definitive area and save the bandwidth for pictures and information of a more important nature? That was my reasoning.

Although text is not interactive, it can work as an enhancement to the show by providing information and directions pertinent to the interactivity. I think this is more important in the early stages of interactive television than it will be when certain functions become default standards in the interactive environment of the future. But while people are learning how to use interactive TV, and as long as there is a large variety of different templates, text will be a valuable tool for communicating information to the viewer, much as it is on the Web today.

Text becomes even more of a tool for shows featuring "how-to," news, sports, or a magazine format, because information is most easily relayed by text. The long-term benefits to a dramatic show may be primarily in alerting the viewer when the interactivity is available.

After I decided against transparent overlays and moved to a graphical template, we created a design. We spent several days developing a background, the navigation area, and the two templates that I wanted.

Figure 6.2 and Figure 6.3 show some screen shots from the interactive version of *Baywatch.*

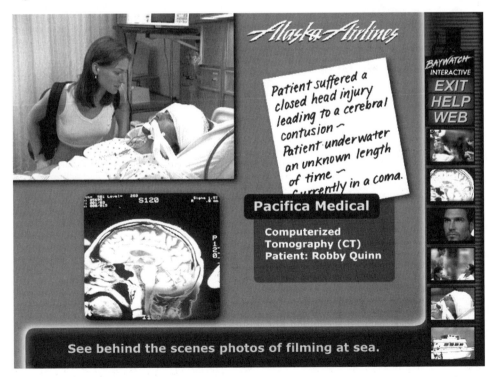

Figure 6.2 Screen shot with *Baywatch* enhancements showing additional information on the patient. (Copyright Pearson Television.)

The crew films boat to boat as Leslie (Heather Stevens) prepares to use a scuba tank wrench to knock out her boyfriend.

DIVE BOAT

See behind the scenes photos of filming at sea.

Figure 6.3 Screen shot with *Baywatch* behind-the-scenes photos. (Copyright Pearson Television.)

Chorus

- Dynamic HTML, a key part of IE4, offers a significant advance over traditional frame-based authoring.

- Use of translucent overlays offers the potential to show video full screen while still providing additional information. The technology for doing overlays is still developing, so significant testing is required before implementing overlays for a production service or enhancement.

- Text formatted like a ticker can offer very useful information to the consumer without detracting from the core viewing experience.

Scene II: Return to Reality

Tim   There were a number of problems with our initial creative discussion that revolved around both technical and usability issues. While we were relying on the Vertical Blanking Interval (VBI) as the backbone for our transmission, we were finding that our original demos required many more lines of the VBI than were normally available. The Microsoft technical team released a new specification that recommended we limit our content to three VBI lines. At a transmission rate of about 9600 bauds per line, we planned for download speeds equivalent to a 28.8-kilobit-per-second (Kbps) modem.

I wanted to make the enhanced *Baywatch* episodes appealing while remaining within the bandwidth requirements. The limitations of modem-like speeds did not permit downloading video clips. Moreover, sending video and audio clips wasn't necessarily the best idea, as competing video and audio is not an ideal usability scenario. However, the idea of sending down clips for viewing after the show was compelling. The bandwidth limitation meant that even this was somewhat unrealistic. Kevin and I wanted much more.

Building the Interactive Show . . .

Once we had the templates designed, I created storyboards of the ideas I had developed during the production phase. I had from 35 to 40 enhancement ideas that I quickly reduced to 10. Many of the enhancements I had envisioned either required too much bandwidth (such as the glacier surround video) or could simply be reduced to text only (such as a reference to the value of some emeralds). To fit the enhancements into the three lines of the VBI, I was forced to discard these high-bandwidth ideas and convert all the others into low-bandwidth functionality. I hated to let go of the most compelling ideas I had envisioned, but that was the current nature of the technology.

Baywatch has always been a show strong in promotional partnerships and with a highly recognizable cast of characters. This led us to orient the enhancements more toward promotion and cast and less toward the plot. We didn't abandon plot information, but we did direct more of the enhancements toward transactions and promotions by linking them with the show's partners.

We spent a lot of time creating behind-the-scenes enhancements so that the interactive viewer would receive inside knowledge not available to a casual viewer. Giving the interactive consumer "more" than traditional consumers was key. "More" meant more on the story, the cast, and the show production process or access to special promotions and transactions not readily available anywhere else. We included information on the ship, exclusive photos from the *Inside Sports* swimsuit shoot (Figure 6.4), and a limited online ordering opportunity for a video release of

Figure 6.4 Screen shot with photos from *Inside Sports* video shoot.
(Copyright Pearson Television.)

the special Alaska episode (Figure 6.5). It's this use of exclusivity or immediacy that makes interactive television most compelling.

Advertising within the enhancements was another element that we wanted to include in these episodes. Advertising will surely play a significant role in the interactive television business model. Thus, the enhancement template included an animated banner ad linked to the enhancement, visible to anyone accessing the enhancement but not visible when the video was shown full screen. The ads were linked to the Web page of each advertiser, making it possible for the viewer to bring up a browser on top of the enhancements.

Kevin   After I reviewed Tim's storyboards, we collaborated on text for the enhancements. Some involved the history of the series, and some of involved the script for "White Thunder at Glacier Bay." The day-by-day evolution of the script and the vast amount of film that we shot in Alaska and in Los Angeles resulted in a three-part Alaska episode instead of the planned two episodes. This affected our agreement with Microsoft, for now there were three episodes to enhance in the time originally projected for two.

Figure 6.5   Screen shot showing how the user can order the Alaska episode video. (Copyright Pearson Television.)

The Creation of the Content

Tim   During November, we made conference calls, reviewed storyboards, and collaborated on text for the show "Bon Voyage," the first of the three episodes. Art production began in December. The idea was to do one entire episode before continuing with the next two episodes. We knew that most of the work that needs to be done is for the pilot episode. The creation of the graphical template, style, and the code template is the bulk of the work in creating interactive episodes. Once this design is finished, all shows after that can work within the template. That's why we called the first shows pilots, for this is where all of the time and effort to create the unique look, voice, and feel of the show are spent.

Baywatch also presented some unique challenges, such as creating navigation icons on the initial template that worked in a queue. To let the viewers decide when to access the interactive elements, I wanted to take advantage of the information that was living in the computer's cache and let the viewers access the information at their discretion. By having graphical representations of what was in this queue, or cache, we had to create some code unique to this show. By making sure we worked all of the bugs out of the first episode, we knew that we wouldn't be creating art for something that would have to be modified later.

Once we were ready to create our art, I gathered all the elements — including key photographs, logos, and props — and delivered them to my artist, David Yaw. David then took these elements and created the art for each page based upon my storyboard design. After a review, revision, and approval process, David compressed the images so that each individual page was no larger than 50 kilobytes (KB). This was a preset size limit the production team had agreed upon to ensure transmission over three lines of the VBI. The developers built the enhancement stream file and underlying HTML, tested the enhancements, and encoded them onto beta tape.

There was a certain amount of trial and error and some pieces of art were redone multiple times, primarily because of our uncertainty about the time to broadcast the pages, including the retransmission of the background and navigational elements every few minutes. We changed our large-size water background into a tiled solid image to conserve space. We made our navigational buttons easier to see. And we moved some art around the screen for better placement. The art process was overall quite simple, limited mainly by bandwidth restrictions. New tools should make the process of scheduling, layout, and content transmission much more straightforward.

Chorus

- Be aware of bandwidth constraints in designing your enhancement content. Both the VBI and digital TV will require trade-offs between video quality and data bandwidth.

- Enhancements should provide "more" to the viewer, meaning more on the story, the cast, the show production process, or access to special promotions and transactions not readily available anywhere else. It's this use of exclusivity or immediacy that makes interactive television most compelling.

- Model your enhancement postproduction process after the television postproduction process: gather all your content, create models of your content, determine the technical limitations, revise your prototypes, and utilize tools to facilitate the process as much as possible.

Scene III: The Crossover Link Compromise

Tim The original idea for broadcast of the *Baywatch* episodes revolved around the VBI transmission. As spring approached and we began to face deadlines, we realized that there were some inherent difficulties in broadcasting a syndicated show on the VBI. The biggest obstacle to using the VBI for transmission of a syndicated show is the absence of guidelines about the ownership of the VBI for a television show.

Some stations have designated certain lines for internal use, others have sold certain lines, and others don't pass the lines that aren't being used. The only line guaranteed to be passed through all the way to the consumer is line 21, used for closed captioning, which is why WebTV chose it for embedding Crossover Links. Crossover Links allow a show producer to embed Web addresses (also known as uniform resource locators, or URLs) on line 21 that are presented to the user during the TV program via a clickable, translucent, interactive logo. Often, a successful VBI transmission may simply be a matter of educating stations about the content and requesting that they pass the interactive content associated with a show. I realized that to extend my potential audience for the broadcasts and to ensure that my broadcast was nationwide, I could simply add Crossover Links to the *Baywatch* episodes. This helped remove some of the uncertainty caused by the still unresolved VBI issues.

At the National Association of Television Production Executives (NATPE) conference in January 1998, it was clear that WebTV was actively pushing Crossover Links to the Hollywood production community. Given our time frame, using Crossover Links seemed like a good option.

Kevin Windows 98 was due out in summer 1998, and thus our May 1998 enhancement airing would be seen only by beta users, as WebTV did not yet include enhancement display capabilities. Tim's group decided to leverage both technologies and create enhancements using Crossover Links while simultaneously creating an "enhanced" version for Windows 98. Later, that turned into only one episode of "enhancements" but three episodes enabled with Crossover Links. I was disappointed because I was more interested in the potential of the "enhancements," but nonetheless using a technology available on both platforms meant that actual people would see our work.

Tim At a meeting I set up at AAT to show them the Crossover Link technology, we discussed the ease and certainty of going forward with Crossover Links. It was an easy decision, because all *Baywatch* needed to provide was room on their server for new pages related to the current episodes and a commitment from their closed captioning service to embed the appropriate URLs when they encoded the closed captioning to the master tape.

Crossover Links are indicated to the viewer by an interactive "I" logo placed translucently over the video as shown in Figure 6.6.

The Caption Center, which *Baywatch* used for captioning, was terrific in responding to our request quickly, and we soon had all the pieces in place for Crossover Links. Immediately, I began to convert the art I had created for the VBI transmission into Web pages. This was a fairly simple process of resizing the art and meeting the layout requirements for WebTV Plus. The artwork and HTML scripting were also fairly simple after we selected the content and chose URL names.

Kevin   Crossover Links are significantly more limiting than enhancements. Long before airing the episodes, we had to agree on distinct URLs that we could tie to particular parts of the show. The promotional aspect was the driving force behind the entire venture, and so we approached Princess Cruises, *Inside Sports*, and Trimark Pictures about links to their respective Web sites. Other links were specific to each of the three episodes.

Meanwhile, Tim and his team were working on the first enhanced episode, "Bon Voyage," as more of a beta test than anything else. In Los Angeles, we were deep

Figure 6.6   The interactive "I" logo as used in *Baywatch*. (Copyright Pearson Television.)

into development for the next season of *Baywatch* in addition to preparing to shoot a movie of the week for TNT in Vancouver during May. Tim continued to send me drafts of links and enhancements, made changes where necessary, and kept the ball rolling.

The Crossover Links were completed by April 9 for the first episode and I began to press in earnest for a draft agreement from Microsoft. Pearson was also showing some interest in the Microsoft venture, and I was asked to send a videotape of the enhancements to Paul Pavlis, their in-house attorney, and their chief executive officer, Tony Cohen. I struggled to explain to them that the enhanced episode couldn't be sent to them on videotape. The content was broadcast specific or could be accessed via the Web, I told them. Eventually, I asked Tim for a list of the URLs to forward to Pearson. However, because Paul didn't have Internet access, that proved cumbersome. Eventually, Paul asked me to send a WebTV box to Tony Cohen so that he could watch other enhanced shows, try out the product, and see the initial episode when it aired. Later, Tony sent me a personal note describing how much he liked the WebTV box and the first enhanced *Baywatch* episode.

Tim   The biggest argument that I had about the Crossover Links was an internal one. The Crossover Links are simply a URL. Consequently, the design emphasis returns to the Web site and doesn't rely at all upon the broadcast of the VBI information. This reality seemed to make some of our scriptors treat the Crossover Links as if they were a backward step in our evolution of interactive television. In reality, they were. However, I saw the Crossover Links as a safety net, a way to ensure that we met a least common denominator in terms of interactivity and audience.

Figure 6.7 shows the Web page associated with one of the *Baywatch* Crossover Links.

The fact that Crossover Links necessitate a back channel isn't a problem for WebTV Plus users, as they basically bought the box for Internet access. On a computer, there is a chance that someone might not have an Internet connection. However, a back channel is a reasonable requirement in the future. As the WebTV Plus box improves and as the content and business models evolve, I believe that Crossover Links will have a practical interim value for both producers and consumers. In the near future, the computer and WebTV Plus environments will have similar capabilities, but for now it is important to understand their subtle differences.

Chorus

- Crossover Links are Web addresses (URLs) embedded in line 21 of the VBI (also used for closed captioning) that are presented to the user during the

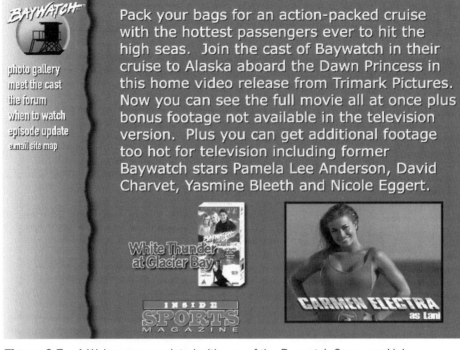

Figure 6.7 A Web page associated with one of the *Baywatch* Crossover Links. (Copyright Pearson Television.)

TV program via a clickable, translucent, interactive logo. Line 21 is guaranteed by law to be passed through all levels of the broadcast infrastructure, ensuring that Crossover Links will reach the consumer.

- Crossover Links are a good interim technology and helpful for associating a Web site with a particular part of a show. However, they don't provide seamless, synchronized integration of interactive content.

- Clear business rules need to be worked out to determine ownership of bandwidth for enhancement transmission. Without such rules, it will be difficult to ensure that enhanced content will make it all the way through the production and transmission path. Content producers must educate stations and networks about the VBI.

- Business relationships for Crossover Links and enhancing content must be defined so that links provided by networks or stations are complementary to those that production companies provide. Without such relationships, production companies run the risk that someone will replace their links later in the food chain.

- In today's analog world, Crossover Links are an implementation-specific detail. In the future digital era, the distinction between content that accompanies the video signal and content that is received via some other method (high-speed dial-up, for example) will become less clear.

Act V: Getting Down to Business

Scene I: Contract Issues

Kevin While the technical changes were taking place, Tim and I negotiated a formal contract between AAT and Microsoft. We had relied on a letter of intent drafted before leaving for Alaska, but everyone knew we had to get a final agreement finished before broadcast. A complication was AAT's acquisition by Pearson, in November 1997. The acquisition itself went smoothly, but the change in management relegated the Microsoft agreement to the back burner.

I was also concerned about Pearson's desire to continue with the agreement. In the entertainment world, new management usually means that anything associated with the old regime is suspect and often eliminated. Our saving grace was that Pearson had bought AAT primarily to acquire *Baywatch*. The series itself was safe. If we "flew under the radar" with the Microsoft deal, quietly gathering support from the new team, it might still hold together. In February, we met with Pearson and the Microsoft creative team. The meeting went well, and although we still didn't have a contract, I was no longer worried about the entire project going south.

Tim Kevin and I talked frequently about finalizing the contract and we both pressed on our respective ends for a quick resolution. I'm not sure what took so long in the early months, but I believe that some of the difficulty was in finding legal counsel available to work with our group. Our group was dealing with number of legal issues, and finalizing a verbal partnership that seemed to be moving along fairly smoothly didn't jump to the front of anyone's action pile. I was at the mercy of corporate timing and tried not to worry about it. It was only as the broadcast date loomed on the horizon that I could finally get a contract to Kevin for review.

Kevin Around May 1, we received the draft agreement from Microsoft. Paul Pavlis sent it to outside counsel to review. With the broadcast date fast approaching, we worked hard with Microsoft's counsel to close things up. Perhaps the most difficult part of the entire process was the actual contract. An issue was the definition of "the work." Pearson defined "the work" as the episodic television elements. Microsoft defined "the work" as the enhanced episode. Pearson could not grant

Microsoft broad rights to the episode that might later complicate a sale of the entire series. Microsoft could not be in a position to create the enhancements but control only the enhancements and not the episode. In a marathon week of conference call negotiations, we sought a consensus that allowed Microsoft to publicize and promote the enhanced episodes without compromising Pearson's ownership of the television product.

Tim and I, as the creative people, worked on keeping the project alive, but several times it nearly died over language and control issues. In one final conference call on a Friday afternoon before a Monday airing, we were able to achieve enough agreement from all sides to go forward with the broadcast. Within days of that critical date, all parties signed the agreement.

Tim The last-minute agreement was very frustrating for both Kevin and I. However, Kevin's calm explanation of the terms in our phone conversations with the lawyers provided the catalyst to get the action completed. While Kevin's unerring belief in the partnership and his firm commitment to spending his time on all the issues made the partnership possible in the first place, his follow-through to the final contract issues truly exemplifies his importance in this relationship. For anyone who has ever wondered what it a producer does, this is it: the producer makes sure the deal, including every detail from start to finish, gets done.

Chorus

- Legal agreements, not technology, are often the hardest part of creating enhanced television, especially when one partner (Microsoft) provides underlying technology while another partner (*Baywatch*) provides content. To overcome this hurdle, draft a simple letter up front that states each partner's goals and objectives, sets expectations on both sides, and establishes a schedule for the project.

- In legal negotiations, always have the company representatives involved. Do not simply have the legal counsel negotiate alone. You will end up both poor and with an unsatisfactory relationship, if you have any relationship at all. The time that the company representatives save by not negotiating alongside the legal counsel will be costly in the long run.

- One person on each side must completely believe in the process and must make sure the deal gets done.

Scene II: Publicity and Testing

Kevin The enhanced episodes aired in May. We expected, and received, a substantial amount of press coverage on the partnership. Executives at Pearson/AAT, *Baywatch*, and Microsoft were pleased, and we made a little history.

Tim I hadn't completely abandoned our original VBI application for Crossover Links. Instead, we decided to choose one episode, "Bon Voyage," for the VBI broadcast on one TV station as a test. I met with the Seattle station that broadcasts *Baywatch*, KCPQ, and discussed the possibility. KCPQ agreed to a test broadcast as long as it didn't interfere with its normal broadcast, which I assured them it wouldn't. Once their engineer told us which lines of the VBI were available, we proceeded to encode a beta air master of the episode I received from AAT. The station then tested all of the equipment and the tape one final time before broadcast.

Unfortunately, the actual broadcast of the enhancements revealed a potential weak link in creating interactive shows — the enhancements were stripped before ever going onto the airwaves. KCPQ, in checking the machines, forgot one machine at their transmission tower. That machine stripped the data we were sending and we never received it. This mistake was unfortunate but it emphasizes the need for close partnerships between the content creators and the broadcasters. This is especially important for syndicated shows and their relationship with individual TV stations. In a second test, we encoded the last episode of the season and again sent the tape to KCPQ for broadcast. This broadcast was not flawless, but the Windows 98 client machines received the interactive content.

Chorus

- In doing the VBI transmission, it is critical to test all elements of the network path. The VBI data transmission has been successful at a number of stations and across a number of networks.

- Syndicated shows introduce some additional complications when trying to ensure that data will be transmitted.

- Successful broadcasts in the future will require both business and technical coordination across all parts of the television food chain.

Act VI: The Future

Kevin Our goal now is to develop a business model that will make the Web TV–WebTV for Windows links and enhancements self-sufficient components within the production process. Without an economic benefit to enhancing episodes, distributors will not be interested in spending their time on the process. Conversely, Microsoft doesn't want to be in the content business. We are meeting with various companies and discussing more interactive *Baywatch* episodes.

Tim Evaluating the process now, I am glad that we decided to do both a Crossover Link version and a VBI version of the episodes. In the future, some shows will decide to go with the Crossover Links as a safe option of interactivity for their viewers. Some will be inspired to tackle the more complicated issues revolving around the VBI transmission of enhancements, believing that the greater interactivity and better integration are worth the risk of using emerging technology. Others might emulate *Baywatch* and use both.

Currently, *Baywatch* and Microsoft continue to work together, although no longer in a content partnership for additional episodes. Microsoft continues to support *Baywatch* through technology development and advice about future interactive episodes.

I have been asked how our new method for interactive TV works any better than some of the old broadband techniques of the early 1990s. My answer is that our ideas are not necessarily better, but I believe they are more realistic. Interactive TV, as represented by the enhanced *Baywatch* episodes, doesn't cost millions of dollars to produce or require users to spend thousands of dollars. Through the use of WebTV Plus at a cost of around $200, viewers can use Crossover Links today to enhance their TV experience. Or with the purchase of Windows 98 and a compatible TV tuner in their computer, viewers can receive both Crossover Links and the VBI enhancements that provide for interactivity on their desktop. Soon, set-top boxes will expand these options for even more viewers by integrating these interactive TV capabilities. These are models that work today, as exemplified by *Baywatch*. And these models will act as the foundation for the fabulous interactivity that others will develop as the technology evolves over the next few years.

The MITV group wants to talk about what you can do today, not next year or the next 5 years. We always ask these key questions:

- How can you build upon current products to create interactivity that will expand in the future?

- How can TV shows get in on the ground floor of this opportunity to tell stories or provide information?

I hope answers to these questions have appeared through this chapter.

Of course, there are still questions without answers. How can we find business models to pay for even these entry-level costs of production? Advertising is important, but how will it integrate with the interactivity? How long will it take for users to become comfortable with interactivity? How will the availability of transactions affect interactive TV? Which shows will most benefit from interactivity?

The real question is how we can make interactive TV the embodiment of everything we've envisioned for television and the Internet. The very fact that you are reading this means that you have an interest in the possibilities offered by the coming convergence era. I challenge you to take what we learned in creating interactive episodes of *Baywatch* and use that knowledge to better your shows, your software, and your own ideas for interactive television.

Chorus

- Using both simple and interim technologies, such as Crossover Links, while also building more complex and emerging technologies, such as detailed interactive content, will enable you to both reach the broadest audience and learn the most about content and business models.

- Material used for enhancements and Crossover Links can be essentially the same. If you design with both models in mind, you will be able to leverage your content easily.

- Use the processes, lessons, and models that emerged from *Baywatch*, *Moesha*, and other shows when designing your own content and business strategies.

The Brand Dialogue

Mike Samet, Chairman, Brand Dialogue
h t t p : / / y r . c o m

Brand Dialogue is the interactive communications practice of Young & Rubicam (Y&R) Inc. Y&R is one of the world's preeminent global communications networks, offering clients fully integrated marketing solutions from advertising and public relations to direct marketing and design consultancy. Brand Dialogue creates online presences and digital solutions for many of Y&R's key corporate clients. In this chapter, Mike speaks to the increased relevance of branding in a converged marketplace. He also introduces what might be the most technically accurate term for the subject of this book: IPeT (Internet Protocol enhanced TV).

We are about to enter a new age of television. For the first time, the content of television (and therefore the way it is produced, viewed, and used as a marketing tool) will undergo a fundamental change. The medium of television will be able to become truly interactive.

This is exciting because everyone wins — the broadcaster, the viewing public, and the advertiser — as each is offered new arenas in which to engage the others, in ways only previously imagined. At the heart of this new technology will be the ability to merge Internet, computers, and classic TV broadcasting in real time, with the look and feel of an Internet home page or even a Web site. Let's call this new creature Internet Protocol enhanced TV (IPeT).

The Role of Broadcasters and Content Producers

For nearly half a century, since the 1950s, TV has been the largest tool for mass communications in the world. Since its earliest days, this medium of "sight, sound, and motion" has captivated millions of viewers through its ability to explore real and imaginary worlds. Through TV, we have visited other people and cultures, watched the first moon landing, and witnessed the scourge of war. Television viewing was measured and analyzed by the A.C. Nielsen Company (now Nielsen Media

Research), whose rating system has been the deciding factor in the life of many television shows.

In the last 20 years, the huge market share held by NBC, CBS, and ABC has been eroded by cable television, a significant industry that has attracted many television viewers. But television still attracts the world to its shows each night.

Technology is constantly changing and new techniques replace old methods. Businesses that depend on those technologies must often "reengineer." The latest technical advance is IPeT. Today, both the major broadcast and cable networks have embraced the Web, using it both as a tool to enhance the viewing experience of their programs and as a place for advertisers to extend their messages to their audiences.

IPeT will offer broadcasters vast new opportunities, challenges, and questions:

- How can this new technology be used?
- What kinds of programs will be best suited to its use?
- What are the business and economic models?
- How can it be used to competitive advantage?
- Can it stop the loss of network television viewers to cable?
- Can it win back some of those viewers who have moved over to the Web as a source of information and even entertainment?

The answers to these questions will come only through experimentation on the part of broadcasters and content producers and through the evolution of the new technology.

But we can do a little hypothesizing.

Putting Technology to Use

Internet users more often choose utility over entertainment when using the Web. (For example, note the popularity of news.com, investment sites, portals, sites such as Expedia, and communities such as iVillage.) It makes sense that some of the first IPeT simulcasts should focus on delivery of information.

Both sporting events (such as the Olympic Games) and news lend themselves to this technology. Sports offer the opportunity to review information, such as the life of a participant, while watching the event. IPeT can personalize an event. Or consider the news. It can be much richer with additional information or graphics such as maps. I believe IPeT will revolutionize the reporting of elections.

But let's not simply dismiss entertainment. It would be interesting to "watch" a character's thoughts "off screen" as that character is really thinking them. More interesting is the production of programs in which IPeT plays a real role, with the IPeT being created as part of the original formulation of the show. For example, certain critical subplots might be created to appear only on the IPeT simulcast.

I foresee mysteries filled with "missing information," known only to the IPeT viewer. Documentaries might have critical maps and statistical data appended via IPeT. The IPeT section could provide early clues to the outcome of a movie or simply provide a richer context for viewing.

Another interesting feature is the creation of IPeT data that can be downloaded to a computer for later analysis. This would be particularly attractive to viewers of weekly programs who could analyze and engage the data between programs, not during the program. The viewer might be challenged to engage in a puzzle, a subplot mystery, or even crack a secret code. This approach brings continuity to a miniseries or adds significant content to weekly shows that currently have little continuity of plot. This approach creates a significantly enriched and interactive viewing experience, one that would be particularly attractive to advertisers.

Another possibility is instantaneous feedback. Viewers could change the outcome of a story, participate in game shows from home, compete with other viewers, and win prizes. The developers of a new show could allow viewers to "test" the show, casting votes for both the show and its characters. It's clear that this new technology holds many opportunities for broadcasters and content producers. Likewise, it holds significant opportunities for advertisers.

The Role of Advertisers

Many marketing professionals have called television the most influential force in marketing in the past 50 years. For example, television has allowed successful mass marketing, which in turn has supported billions of dollars of television production annually.

But now the rules of marketing are changing. At one time, awareness of a product would be sufficient to generate sales. Cars, refrigerators, washing machines — even homes — were easily sold. (The primary challenge was in finding consumers who had enough money to purchase them.) Marketing strategies were governed by "overdemand and undersupply," with many companies and products effectively monopolizing their markets.

But today's marketplaces are driven by oversupply. Consider the number of personal computers, consumer electronics, automobiles, telecommunications, over-the-counter pharmaceuticals, and packaged goods brands. Brand marketers today face strong competition from generic products and so-called store brands. U.S. marketers face effective competition from foreign manufacturers — competitors that did not exist 20 years ago. Advertisers have learned that in the battle for market share, advertising to create simple awareness is just not enough: "Brand building" has become a necessity. My parent company, Young & Rubicam Inc., has been conducting the largest ongoing study of how brands are built. Y&R's Brand Asset Valuator has studied over 95,000 people and over 13,000 brands worldwide. (For a complete description, visit *http://yr.com/bav.*) Today we know that there are four fundamental elements to building a brand, and that these elements are formed sequentially in the consumer's mind:

- Differentiation
- Relevance
- Esteem
- Knowledge

These elements (shown in Figure 7.1) are created both by the messages that consumers receive and by brand "experiences" (for example, at events, on the Internet,

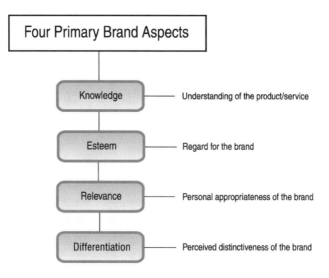

Figure 7.1 The four fundamental elements needed to build a brand.

or through telemarketing and other so-called direct experiences of the company or brand).

Brand Management in a Convergent World

Today, the management of the "experience" promised by the brand goes hand in hand with the promise itself: Successful brands build strong relationships with consumers, continually defining and reinforcing the brand's differentiation and enabling the consumer to establish and confirm the brand's relevance. Such relationships address the consumers' needs and build real trust over the long term. Such relationships endure beyond product and economic cycles.

One hallmark of a strong relationship is the degree to which the consumer "collaborates" with the brand to help the marketer provide or create a superior product or service. Today's media providers fall short in their ability to deliver that experiential conversation, primarily because current media are one way and nonparticipatory. But modern consumers have learned — and marketers are now learning — that Web-enabled businesses can forge stronger ties with consumers than businesses that are not Web enabled. Therefore, IPeT can become an important part of a Web-enabled brand's strategy. What it does is bring "experience" to the commercial message, thus becoming a tool that enables the creating and managing of the consumer relationship.

How Might Advertisers Employ This New Technology?

IPeT's potential for increased (i.e., differentiating) information content offers exciting opportunities for information-rich categories such as automobiles, computers, food (in the form of recipes), hard goods, consumer electronics, and finance.

IPeT's ability to provide immediate interaction with the consumer adds new possibilities to the practices of promotion and telemarketing. For example, based upon the consumer's activity with the streamed hypertext markup language (HTML), the consumer might be prompted to call a toll-free telemarketing number immediately for an "Instant Win." Of course, much work remains to be done between the advertiser and the broadcaster. Creating and agreeing on such details as ad formats and measurement systems (space and time) will require dedication, shared vision, and attention to a number of key questions:

- What constitutes an ad?
- Will it be a banner-like presentation, similar to that used on the Web today?
- How long will the ad stay in view?

- Can it be reloaded?

- Can it be downloaded?

- How will viewership be measured?

- What constitutes a view or, indeed, a viewer?

Conclusion

Finally, there is the great unknown — the consumer's reaction to the possibilities posed by IPeT:

- How important is IPeT to a viewer who is mainly concerned with entertainment?

- Will IPeT enhance or detract from the viewing experience?

- Will viewers become more involved? Will they pay more attention to the program? Will they stay tuned to the same network for longer periods of time?

- Will age materially affect a viewer's ability or desire to engage effectively with the new process?

- Which programming categories are most easily "digestible?"

The answers to these questions will depend on the ingenuity of the programmer and, possibly, the advertiser.

But one thing is clear: Today, we find consumers embracing choice, vitality, innovation, and, yes, even technology. And although not all consumers and TV viewers embrace change easily, a fair number of early adopters will always seek approaches that offer new experiences and visions.

IPeT technology and products such as WebTV for Windows expand our boundaries and engage us with rich capabilities and possibilities. As these technologies spread to other media beyond the computer, new paths to the consumer will be found. The success of these ventures will depend on their practicality, their novelty, their economic value, and upon the visionary collaboration between advertiser and media. IPeT technology may well revolutionize the television industry. When it does, we will all be richer for it.

CHAPTER 8

The Message Is Not the Medium

Doc Searls, President, The Searls Group

www . s e a r l s . c o m

*I was first introduced to Doc Searls' writings when a friend for-
warded me an essay Doc wrote for David Strom's electronic
newsletter,* The Web Informant.[1] *Over the ensuing weeks and
months, Doc and I traded comments and thoughts on numerous
drafts of his writings, which resulted in this — one of the most
thought-provoking chapters of the book.*

*As with the other chapters, this one will help you ask the right
questions as you approach the digital television era. But if you
read what follows here with an open mind, you will find much
more than just the right questions.*

*Writing in the late 1960s, Marshall McLuhan, noted communica-
tions theorist, declared that the medium — the way of communicating information — is often more important than the message
— the information itself. Use Doc's writing to help you reevaluate
the Web and television metaphors and models you're used to, as
you begin to explore the new medium of interactive television.*

The future has arrived. It is just not evenly distributed.

— *William Gibson*

Convergence

A key difference between a dialogue and an ordinary discussion is that,
within the latter people usually hold relatively fixed positions and argue in
favor of their views as they try to convince others to change. At best this
may produce agreement or compromise, but it does not give rise to anything
creative .... What is essential here is the presence of the spirit of dialogue,

---

1. Doc Searls, "There is no demand for messages," *Web Informant,* May 26, 1998, p. 26. See *http://www.strom.
com/awards/112.html.*

which is in short, the ability to hold many points of view in suspension, along with a primary interest in the creation of common meaning.

— David Bohm and F. David Peat[2]

The resemblance between TV and the Web is only screen deep, yet their convergence is inevitable. Television has been the most pervasive and powerful social influence through the whole second half of the 20th century and an enormous economic influence as well: a $45 billion industry in the United States alone. The Web is the most personal and interactive medium since the telephone, as well as the first in a position to facilitate direct commercial relationships between vendors and customers, producers and consumers, up and down countless value chains.

Both technologies lend themselves to projection, so it's easy for us to project the assets of one across the liabilities of the other. Coming from TV, it's easy to see a huge advertising market on the Web, just from TV's spillover. Coming from the Web, it's easy to see TV's channels and program sources as links suitable for browsing and as content ready for downloading on an as-wanted basis, preferably for free.

But fixed positions have two problems here. First, the Web is growing and changing *way* too fast for easy characterization — and is changing the world along with it. Second, the terms in which we understand familiar media — especially television — limit our understanding of the Web's potential, especially as it converges with those media.

These problems argue for the kind of dialog Bohm and Peat suggest: one that holds open any number of viewpoints, looking for a common meaning that isn't here yet.

So if you're open to real dialog, this is your chapter. You'll read things here that you won't find anywhere else, and your views will be challenged by them. I know, because I've held many — perhaps all — of the same views. My own career path has wandered from writing to publishing to radio to advertising to marketing, while staying involved in all those professions.

What I'm looking for, and want to share, are not self-evident truths for all of us to hold but rather truths that will become evident as convergence proceeds. This chapter suggests a few candidates. It will succeed if it gets us thinking and talking about them.

---

2. David Bohm (1917–1992) was a quantum physicist and one of the 20th century's great thinkers. David Peat was coauthor with Bohm of *Science, Order & Creativity* and the author of a new biography of Bohm, *Infinite Potential: The Life and Times of David Bohm.*

Market Conversations

Conversation is the socializing instrument par excellence.

— *Ortega y Gasset*

Business is social. We can't do it without other people.

Markets are the societies of business. Every market, from the streets of Tashkent to the Web pages of Amazon.com,[3] is a bustle of social activity. It might not be live talk, but if the market is alive, people are talking. And if it's growing, people are talking a lot. That's what "buzz" is all about. Hot markets buzz with both talk and business. The buzz around Amazon.com is huge right now, even though almost nobody says a word when they buy a book from the company's Web site. The buzz happens inside Amazon and inside the bookselling market that Amazon radically changes. Amazon isn't changing that market just by adding a new channel but by adding a new and interesting subject to the bookselling *conversation* — and by facilitating much of that conversation on the Web, which is the most conversational medium since the telephone.

Today Amazon sells $400 million worth of books per year on the Web. Barnes & Noble sells $100 million. That's a $500 million business where 4 years ago there was nothing.[4] So the bookselling market grows along with the bookselling conversation. The growth is positive sum and is accelerating with the new sales channel.

A similar thing happened to the bookselling conversation a few years earlier, when Barnes & Noble rolled out its superstores. The business changed radically, almost overnight. Independent bookstores were hurt in some cases, but on the whole the market not only grew but became much more active and interesting and far less hidebound. Yet the press treats the bookselling business as a battlefield — which it is. Between Barnes & Noble, Borders, the warehouse stores, and the countless independent bookstores, competition is fierce. Tempers boil over into lawsuits. Right now the American Booksellers Association, representing independent bookstores, is suing Barnes & Noble for allegedly predatory business practices. It all makes great copy.

So what we have here are two metaphors for a marketplace: a conversation and a battlefield. Which is the better metaphor for the Web market? One is positive sum and the other is zero sum. One is virtual and the other is physical. One uses AND logic, and the other uses OR logic.

---

3. The formal name of the company is Amazon.com. It is commonly referred to as "Amazon," which is what I am doing here.

4. "The baron of books," *Business Week*, June 29, 1998.

It's no contest. The battlefield metaphor insults that world by denying those sums. It works fine when we're talking about battles for shelf space in grocery stores, but when we're talking about the Web, battlefield metaphors ignore the most important developments. But the conversation metaphor describes a world exploding with positive new sums.

There are two other advantages to the conversation metaphor. First, it works as a synonym. Substitute the word "conversation" for "market" and this fact becomes clear. The bookselling conversation and the bookselling market are the same. Second, conversations are the fundamental connections human beings make with each other. We may love or hate one another but, unless we're in conversation, not much happens between us. Societies grow around conversations. That includes the business societies we call markets.

Reese Jones, the brain researcher who founded Farallon Computing (now Netopia), believes that conversation is the fundamental basis of all social interaction — that people are built to talk one to one, not many to many. The human brain can pay close attention only to what one person says at a time. Even when one person speaks to a large group, the relationship is always one to one, speaker to listener. For that speaker and each listener, it's half of a personal conversation.

That's why Jones wanted to make "software for telephones." He thought the telephone was a much better platform than the computer for the social activity we call business. Saying this in 1989, he was way ahead of his time, because now we do have software for telephones. It's called the Web.

The Web as Conversation Hub

The Web is growing at an explosive rate: from zero to 50 million domestic users in just 4 years. It took television 13 years to reach the same number of viewers. And it took radio 40 years to reach that many listeners.[5] Business growth projections are even more wild. The U.S. Commerce Department expects business on the Internet to grow from $8 billion this year to $327 billion by 2002.[6] It was approximately zero in 1994.

The Web is not a market. It is a new technological development that expands the conversations in existing markets and — in some cases — adds a new sales and distribution channel. So the Web is not one conversation but a place that invites *many* conversations, each with its own vocabularies, interests, prejudices, and standards.

5. *Time*, July 27, 1998, p. 19.

6. *The Emerging Digital Economy*, U.S. Department of Commerce, 1998. See *http://www.ecommerce.gov/emerging.htm*.

The Role of Standards

In every business that relies on technologies, there are endless arguments about standards. The Web is no different. But the standards that matter most are the ones we talk least about, because we don't even know they are there. Network guru Craig Burton says, "There are three kinds of standards: *de facto*, *de jure*, and *de rigueur*. But the third is the one that really matters, because it's the hardest to change — and therefore the most standard. *De rigueur* standards are the habits of societies and industries. They are so ingrained that almost nobody can even imagine any other way."[7] And what makes them so is their common sense.

"Common sense has a conceptual structure that is usually unconscious,"[8] says George Lakoff, who is professor of linguistics and cognitive science at the University of California, Berkeley, and the leading thinker in both fields. "We are even less conscious of the components of thoughts — concepts." And all our concepts are metaphorical.[9] Thanks to metaphor, we understand everything in terms of something else.

Life, for example. We talk about life all the time. But do we bother to see *how* we talk about it? Almost never. Life is a matter of common sense. Yet our most common conceptual metaphor for life is *a journey*. This is why we speak about life — unconsciously, of course — with travel metaphors. Birth is "arrival." Death is "departure." Choices are "crossroads." Purposes are "destinations." We get "sidetracked" or "lose our way" if we don't "know where we're going." Our counselors give us "guidance." We say "he has a long way to go" or "she's come quite a way." We could fill this whole book with examples of travel metaphors, just for the subject of life.

So the *de rigeur* standard conceptual metaphor for life is *a journey*. Without even thinking about it, we all agree.

---

7. Craig Burton and his wife Judith Clarke Burton changed *de rigueur* network thinking in the eighties, when they developed and implemented Novell's strategy for changing the networking business from a hardware to a software conversation — from one about "pipes and protocols" to one about Network Operating Systems and the software that worked with those operating systems. After leaving Novell, they founded The Burton Group, which got the industry to talk about networks as sets of services, rather than as platforms.

8. George Lakoff, *Moral Politics: What Conservatives Know That Liberals Don't*. Chicago: University of Chicago Press, 1995, p. 4.

9. The most accessible book on this subject is George Lakoff and Mark Johnson, *Metaphors We Live By*. Chicago: University of Chicago Press, 1980.

We don't all agree about the Web. Right now we understand the Web in terms of at least five different conceptual metaphors. Each of these constitutes a different market conversation. Let's look at each of those conversations and their underlying conceptual metaphors. None yet are "common sense," yet all of them would like to be. As convergence progresses, one or two will emerge as the common sense (and therefore *de rigeur* standard) understanding of the Web. The conversations it supports should define and limit the markets that emerge there as well.

The Publishing Conversation

Publishing is the original Web metaphor — the one used more than any other by the thinkers and developers who created the Web. Here we "write" or "author" "hypertext" "documents," "content," "pages," and "files" for "visitors" to "browse," occasionally marking locations with "bookmarks." The publishing business is quick to adopt this vocabulary, of course, and to publish its own work extensively on the Web. Newspapers and magazines are published whole on the Web, complete with "sections," "stories," "features," "letters to the editor," and the rest of it. There is also an *art topic* within this conversation. Here we "design" pages "creatively," with "graphical elements" and "high production values."[10] Still, we're publishing pages. So, by this conceptual metaphor, *the Web is a publication.*

The Real Estate Conversation

The creators of the Web also borrowed heavily from the real estate vocabulary. Thus, everything on the Web is a "site," a "home," or a "location" with an "address," which we "build," perhaps with the help of a "developer." By this conceptual metaphor, *the Web is a development.*

Ironically the real estate trade has been slow to adopt the Web. Unlike publishing, retailing, advertising, and entertainment, it contributes little to the overall Web conversation, in spite of the Web's adoption of real estate metaphors.

The Retail Conversation

Unlike the real estate industry, lots of existing retail businesses have embraced the Web and contributed to its vocabulary. Amazon.com, for example, presents itself as a "store" where you can "browse" through "subjects" organized to resemble "aisles." You can also visit the "gift center" while loading up your "shopping cart"

10. See David Siegel, *Creating Killer Web Sites: The Art of Third-Generation Site Design*, 2d ed. Indianapolis: Hayden Books, 1997, pp. 12–15.

before "proceeding to "check-out." Onsale (*www.onsale.com*), although an "auction supersite," calls itself "the smarter way to shop," posts sale "specials," and features a "bazaar" section. By this conceptual metaphor, *the Web is a marketplace.*[11]

The Advertising Conversation

The Web is a communications medium that will potentially reach billions of people. This immediately invited occupation by the advertising conversation, which largely employs freight transport metaphors. We "put out," "send," or "push" an "inventory" of "products" or "messages" that we "target" over "signals," through "portals" and "channels," or on "vehicles" directed toward "eyeballs." We hope to "capture" some percentage of those eyeballs through "branding," "exposure," and other advertising practices, nearly all of which move goods in a one-way fashion, from advertisers to consumers. By this conceptual metaphor, *the Web is a delivery service.*[12]

The Entertainment Conversation

The entertainment business is interested in the Web for the same reasons as its broadcasting and publishing companion, the advertising business: the prospect of reaching and serving billions of people. But as an entertainment medium the Web has been "a costly and vexing flop," says *The Wall Street Journal.*[13] "It's a mistake to treat the Internet as an entertainment medium," says Ed Bennett in the same article. Bennett was president of VH-1 for 5 years and was hired by Prodigy in 1995 to bring TV savvy to that online service. He failed.

With the exception of erotica and multiplayer games (which have simply expanded what happens behind the screen to include players and programs elsewhere on the Internet), entertainment-related sites on the Web are accessories to other media. Most of the listings under Yahoo's entertainment heading lead to publishing or retail conversations by entertainment companies or individuals with entertainment interests. Even the TV networks now use the Web mostly as a publishing medium where they can promote their shows or add value to those shows by providing, say, live traffic and weather reports. And while many radio stations now broadcast on the Web, nothing in their use of the Web contributes to a new Web market conversation.

11. We might say *the Web is a mall* or . . . *a Main Street*. But the original and most well-conceived understanding of *a place where many vendors sell many things* is a marketplace, not a mall or a street — although those *are* conceptual metaphors we often employ.

12. Or we might say *the Web is a vehicle*. "Conveyance," however, suggests one-way delivery, while "vehicle" does not.

13. Jared Sandberg, "It isn't entertainment that makes the Web shine; It's dull data — sex aside, sites that offer consumers convenience prove to be the big hits," *The Wall Street Journal*, July 20, 1998.

It's just another topic in the existing radio conversation. So we don't find conceptual metaphors such as *the Web is a theater* or *the Web is a TV set*. Not yet, anyway.

So far, the only entertainment conversation that works with the Web is the one concerned with the fashion and cosmetics end of Web site design. Here we find talk about "exciting," "cool," "killer," "attractive," and "stimulating" designs that "enhance the image" of a site by "developing a story," "framing a narrative," or "creating a sense" of something or other. By this conceptual metaphor, *the Web is a stimulant*.

Facilitating Conversations as Markets

Now let's look at how well these conceptual metaphors map to the Web and how well the Web *facilitates* these conversations *as markets*.

The *publishing* metaphor describes the Web well; but it does not follow that publishing — as we have understood it since Gutenberg — is a good way to make money on the Web. As John Perry Barlow puts it, "Protecting physical expression had the force of convenience on its side. Copyright worked well because, Gutenberg notwithstanding, it was hard to make a book."[14] So, while the physical nature of ink on paper made publishing hard to do and easy to protect (and therefore a good business to be in), the virtual nature of the Web makes publishing easy to do and hard to protect (and therefore a bad business to be in).

Publishing, however, is the Web's original metaphor and the one we still use more than any other. So there is a market for it. But that market is like the one for telephony: a necessary convenience and a welcome cost. Not a way to make money.

Bottom line: Publishing is a great way to make money *with* the Web, not *on* it.

The *retail* metaphor is another matter. As Amazon.com, CDnow.com, and many others demonstrate, the Web is a terrific place to sell stuff. But its virtual nature also makes it a poor place to sell perfumes or even shoes. Still, it's a fabulous new sales channel and one that works both ways, allowing vendors and customers to engage in all kinds of new (and far more direct) conversations than were possible in the past.

The *real estate* metaphor is extremely popular and equally misleading. That's because the real estate trade's most important cliché — "Only three things matter:

14. John Perry Barlow, "The economy of ideas," *Wired*, issue 2.03. See *http://www.wired.com/wired/2.03/features/economy.ideas.html*.

location, location and location" — has only transitory relevance on the Web. Short uniform resource locators (URLs) may be preferable to long ones, and ".com" domain names may have "brand" qualities, but any location is still just one click away from any other location. And the time will come (as we'll see later) when we won't need search engines to find exactly what we want. That will reduce the brand value of Yahoo and other "portals." You can put together your own damn portals, right on your desktop.

The *advertising* metaphor works, but only so far as advertising remains acceptable in the Web environment. As with the real estate metaphor, advertising will be undermined — in this case by the opportunities the Web provides for direct conversations between vendors and customers, producers and consumers. We'll go more deeply into this in the next section.

The *entertainment* metaphor is the weakest of all. The entertainment conversation around the Web is primarily about two things:

- Web site design (landscaping and interior decorating for the real estate metaphor)
- What will happen when the Internet's capacity grows to accommodate the entire entertainment industry (radio, TV, movies, audio recordings)

Entertainment is not a great way to make money on the Web, even though the Web is a great way for entertainment companies to enlarge their existing market conversations.

So at this early stage, a few things are clear:

- Publishing, retailing, and real estate are proven metaphorical concepts that should support rich and substantial market conversations.
- Advertising metaphors are a success to the degree that they work on the Web as they work in other media.
- A substantial entertainment market conversation (one more about reality than promise) awaits the bandwidth required to support distribution and exchange of entertainment products.

So, in simple terms, the Web efficiently serves two fundamental human needs: the need to *know* and the need to *buy*.

A Historical Legacy

As we contemplate convergence, what can we learn from the history of the Web?

Publishing came first. The thinkers and inventors who developed hypertext theory,[15] including Vannevar Bush,[16] Ted Nelson,[17] Marshall McLuhan,[18] and Doug Englebart,[19] all used publishing concepts and terms. The metaphor was later expanded by the people who put hypertext theory to work, including Tim Berners-Lee,[20] Marc Andreessen,[21] and the original Internet community of scientists, hackers, and academics. Today the Web remains an extraordinarily useful way to publish, archive, research, and connect all kinds of information. No medium better serves curious or inventive minds.

And although commerce wasn't a primary focus of the initial Web developers, no more commercial medium has ever been created. The Web invites every business in the yellow pages either to sell on the Web or to support existing business by using the Web to publish useful information and invite dialog with customers and other involved parties. In fact, by serving as both an ultimate yellow page directory *and* an endless spread of real estate for stores and businesses, the Web demonstrates extreme synergy between the publishing and retailing metaphors, along with their underlying conceptual systems.

---

15. The whole Web is a hypertext construction. You can see it at the front of every address. "http" stands for "hypertext transfer protocol."

16. Vannevar Bush foresaw countless developments in his landmark essay, "As we may think," published in 1945 in *The Atlantic* magazine. Chief among these was the explosion of knowledge enabled by developments in technology. He foresaw compression of computer processing to cheap and tiny forms, ubiquitous communication, and the critical need to share and navigate the explosion of knowledge that would result. His notions on navigating that knowledge were the first hypertext theories. See *http://www.theatlantic.com/unbound/flashbks/computer/bushf.htm*

17. Ted Nelson coined the term "hypertext" in 1965. While he is credited as the foremost thinker on the subject, Nelson also holds the world record for development time on an unreleased product — Xanadu — which is still in the works after decades of effort by Nelson and others. See *http://www.xanadu.com.*

18. Marshall McLuhan is famous for his radical thinking on media, plus a raft of other subjects. His ideas about the relationship of individuals and society to their media was merely quotable when McLuhan was alive (he died on the last day of 1980); but with the arrival of the Internet those ideas are increasingly germane and useful. See *http://www. mcluhan.utoronto.ca/mm.html.*

19. Doug Englebart is the "Thomas Edison" of the Web. Most famous for inventing the mouse (and with it the whole notion of pointing and clicking), Englebart has countless other inventions to his credit.

20. Tim Berners-Lee created the Web. His paper describing that work is at *http://www.w3.org/People/Berners-Lee/1996/ppf.html.*

21. Marc Andreessen led a team at the University of Illinois that developed the first Web browser, Mosaic. Andreessen then started Netscape and developed the Navigator browser.

Although the Web also serves as a fine way to ship messages to eyeballs, we should pause to observe that the message market is a conversation that takes place entirely on the supply side of TV's shipping system. In that market — advertising market — media sell space or time to companies that advertise. Not to consumers. The consumers get messages for free, whether they want them or not.

What happens when consumers can speak back — not just to the media, but to the companies who pay for the media? In the past we never faced that question. Now we do. And the Web will answer with a new division of labor between advertising and the rest of commerce. That division will further expose the limits of both the advertising and entertainment metaphors.

Dividing Labors

> Advertising is what you do when you can't go see somebody. That's all it is.
>
> *—Fairfax Cone*

Fairfax "Fax" Cone founded one of the world's top advertising agencies, Foote, Cone & Belding, and ran it for 40 years. A no-nonsense guy from Chicago, Cone knew exactly what advertising was and wasn't about. With this simple definition — *what you do when you can't go see somebody* — he drew a clear line between advertising and sales. Today, 30 years after he retired, we can draw the same line between TV and the Web and divide the labors accordingly.

On one side we have television, the best medium ever created for advertising. On the other side we have the Web, the best medium ever created for sales.

The Web, like the telephone, is a much better tool for sales than for promotion. It's what you do when you *can* go see somebody: a way to inform customers and for them to inform you. The range of benefits is incalculable. You can learn from each other, confer in groups, have visually informed phone conversations, or sell directly with no salespeople at all.

In other words, you can do business. All kinds of business. As with the phone, it's hard to imagine any business you can't do, or can't help do, with the Web.

So we have a choice. See or be seen: See with the Web, or be seen on TV. Talk *with* people or talk *at* them. Converse with them, or send them messages.

Once we divide these labors, advertising on the Web will make no more sense than advertising on the phone does today. It will be just as unwelcome, just as intrusive, just as rude, and just as useless.

The Web will call forth — from both vendors and customers — a new kind of marketing that seeks to enlarge the conversations we call business, not to assault potential customers with messages they don't want. Web advertising — and most other advertising — will be exposed as the spam it is, and new opportunities for fulfilling supply (without insulting demand) will rise from the remains. This new marketing conversation will embrace what Rob McDaniel[22] calls a "divine awful truth,"[23] a truth whose veracity is exceeded only by its deniability:

There is no demand for messages. And there never was.[24]

And when this truth becomes clear, we will recognize most advertising as an ugly art form[25] that only dumb funding can justify and damn it for the sin of unwelcome supply in the absence of demand.

The Divine Awful Truth, Part II

In fact, most advertising has *negative* demand, especially on TV. It actually *subtracts* value from programming. To weigh the value of TV advertising, imagine what would happen if the mute buttons on remote controls delivered we-don't-want-to-hear-this messages back to advertisers. When that feedback finally gets through (and someday it will), the $180 billion annual advertising market will fall like a bad soufflé.

It will fall because the Web will bring two developments advertising has never seen before and has always feared:[26] direct feedback and accountability. These will expose another divine awful truth:

22. Rob McDaniel is a screenwriter currently working on a new book, *The Mind of the Species*, which he hopes to have out before the end of 1998. He is a partner in Technorganic, a retailer of T-shirts and other goods on the Web. Both the site and its goods contain McDaniel's provocative and quotable "trance codes." See *http://www.technorganic.com*.

23. The notion of a "divine awful truth" is one of McDaniel's "trance codes."

24. I will admit to a little hyperbole here. Many people watch the Superbowl game to see the ads, and there is clearly demand for the kinds of messages Nike and other powerful "branding" companies put out. But I maintain that advertising in these cases works like television at its metaphorical best: as a source of stimulation, not information. In other words, it succeeds as programming. But if you ask people if they demand messages, the answer is usually no.

25. Ever the contrarian, Marshall McLuhan said, "Advertising is the greatest art form of the twentieth century." *Advertising Age*, September 3, 1976.

26. With the notable exception of David Ogilvy, the greatest ad man of all time. Ogilvy inveighed constantly against advertising that failed to respect its consumers and was a tireless advocate of research. In this mission, Ogilvy considered himself a voice in the desert. "Most people," he said, "use research the way a drunk uses a lamppost: more for support than illumination." Ogilvy has written a number of books, but the best is *Ogilvy on Advertising* (New York: Random House, 1987). This book does for advertising what Strunk and White's *The Elements of Style* does for writing. It vividly clarifies a very foggy subject.

Most advertising doesn't work.

In the safety of absent alternatives, advertising people have always admitted as much. There's an old expression in the business that goes, "I know half my advertising is wasted. I just don't know which half." (And let's face it, "half" is exceedingly generous.)

With the Web, you *can* know. Add the Web to TV, and you can measure waste on the tube, too.

Use the Web wisely, and you don't have to settle for any waste at all.

Good-bye Consumers, Hello Customers

> Consumption is the sole end and purpose of production; and the interest of the producer ought to be attended to only so far as it may be necessary for promoting that of the consumer.
>
> — *Adam Smith*

It's easy to confuse consumers with customers and producers with vendors. Adam Smith didn't make those distinctions when he wrote *Wealth of Nations*. In 1776 there was no need to. Now there is. The customers of TV's entertainment product are not its consumers. Nor are the customers of its advertising product. These splits between customers and consumers create both communication gaps and market misperceptions that become costly errors when TV's business model is applied to the Web.

To make sense of the differences between TV and the Web, let's explore market relationships between these five roles in different market conversations, both within the TV business and on the Web:

- Producers
- Consumers
- Vendors
- Customers
- Distributors

The Roles and Rules of Television

Television comprises two businesses that carry on two different conversations: an entertainment delivery service and an advertising delivery service. The first is huge and includes everybody. The second is narrow and includes only advertisers and broadcasters.

Entertainment Delivery

TV's entertainment *producers* are program sources such as production companies, network entertainment divisions, and the programming sides of TV stations. These are also the *vendors* of the programs they produce. Their *customers* and *distributors* are the networks and TV stations, which give away the product to their *consumers*, the viewers.

Advertising Delivery

TV's advertising *producers* are the advertisers themselves (or their agencies). But in this market conversation, advertisers also play the *customer* role. They buy time from the networks and the stations, which serve as both *vendors* and *distributors*. Again, viewers *consume* the product for free.

In the past, the difference between these conversations didn't matter much, because consumers were not part of TV's money-for-goods market conversation.[27] Instead, consumers were part of the conversation around the product TV gives away: programming. See Figures 8.1 and 8.2.

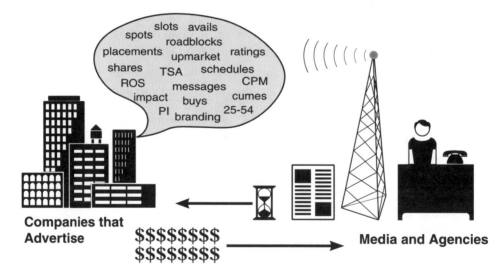

The advertising market exists largely between the media and the companies that advertise on them. Media and agencies sell time and space to advertisers, and the whole market conversation takes place largely between these two groups.

Figure 8.1   The advertising market.

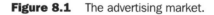

27. "Product placement," while promotional in nature, is not a form of advertising. It is a promotional sales or barter arrangement worked out between the TV show's creators and the companies placing the products.

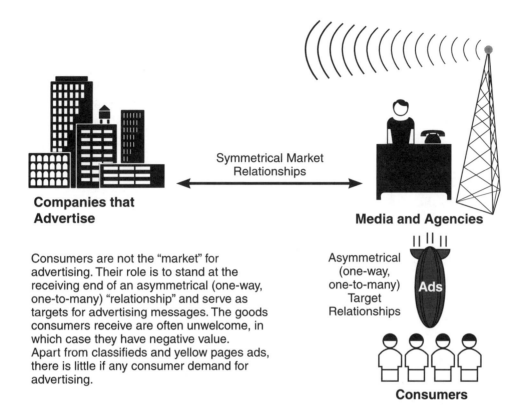

Companies that Advertise

Symmetrical Market Relationships

Media and Agencies

Consumers are not the "market" for advertising. Their role is to stand at the receiving end of an asymmetrical (one-way, one-to-many) "relationship" and serve as targets for advertising messages. The goods consumers receive are often unwelcome, in which case they have negative value. Apart from classifieds and yellow pages ads, there is little if any consumer demand for advertising.

Asymmetrical (one-way, one-to-many) Target Relationships

Ads

Consumers

Figure 8.2   Consumers and advertising.

In the economics of television, however, programming is just bait. It's attractive bait, of course, but it's on the cost side of the balance sheet, not the revenue side. TV's $45 billion in revenues come from advertising, not programming. And the sources of programming make most of their money from *their* customers — networks, syndicators, and stations —*not* from viewers.

Broadcasters, however, are accustomed to believing that their audience is deeply involved in their business and often speak of demographics (such as "men age 25 to 54") as "markets." But there is no market conversation here, because the relationship — such as it is — is restricted to terms set by what the supply side requires, which are ratings numbers and impersonal information such as demographic breakouts and lifestyle characterizations. This may be useful information, but it lacks the authenticity of real market demand, expressed in hard cash. In fact, few viewers are engaged in conversations with the stations and networks they watch. It's a one-way, one-to-many distribution system. TV's consumers are important only in aggregate, not as individuals. They are many, not one. And, as Reese Jones told us earlier, there is no such thing as a many-to-one conversation. At best there is only a perception of one. Big difference.

So, without a cash voice, audience members can only consume. Their role is to take the bait. If the advertisements work, of course, they'll take the hook as well. But the advertising business is still a conversation that does not include its consumers. So we get supply without demand, which isn't a bad definition of advertising.

The Roles and Rules of the Web

On the Web, the *customer* is the *consumer*. He or she can buy the *advertisers'* goods directly and enjoy two-way, one-to-one market conversations without a TV intermediary and without encountering one-way messages (bait). He or she can also buy entertainment directly from program sources (which serve as both *vendors* and *producers*). The distribution role of TV stations and networks is unnecessary, or at least peripheral. In other words, the Web disintermediates TV. See Figure 8.3.

So the real threat to TV isn't just that the Web makes advertising accountable. It's that it makes business more efficient. In fact, the Web serves as both a medium for business and a necessary accessory to it, much like the telephone. No medium since the telephone has done a better job of getting vendors and customers together and of fostering the word of mouth that even advertisers admit is the best advertising. The Web is an unprecedented clue exchange system. And when companies get enough clues about how poorly their advertising actually works, they'll drop it like a bad transmission, or change it so much that we'll no longer call it advertising.

What about other kinds of advertising? Well, print ads are tolerable and often welcome, because the reader has some choice about them. They actually compete with editorial for the reader's attention. Junk mail is 98% waste, by its own admission. Banner ads on the Web are in the same range. Most surfers consider them low-impact spam: rarely useful and never welcome. Yahoo and some other Web services already charge only for click-throughs (and this has actually contributed to Yahoo's modest profitability). But add a little more accountability (what happens *after* the click-through) and advertisers might not even pay for that.

Of course, there will still be demand for television programs. Just expect consumers be more involved in the market conversation — in other words, to pay for some of it, to become customers.

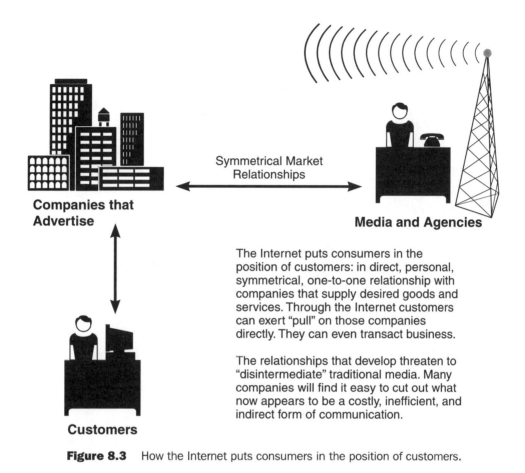

Companies that Advertise

Symmetrical Market Relationships

Media and Agencies

The Internet puts consumers in the position of customers: in direct, personal, symmetrical, one-to-one relationship with companies that supply desired goods and services. Through the Internet customers can exert "pull" on those companies directly. They can even transact business.

The relationships that develop threaten to "disintermediate" traditional media. Many companies will find it easy to cut out what now appears to be a costly, inefficient, and indirect form of communication.

Customers

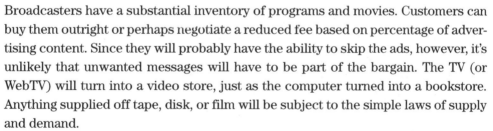

Figure 8.3 How the Internet puts consumers in the position of customers.

Broadcasters have a substantial inventory of programs and movies. Customers can buy them outright or perhaps negotiate a reduced fee based on percentage of advertising content. Since they will probably have the ability to skip the ads, however, it's unlikely that unwanted messages will have to be part of the bargain. The TV (or WebTV) will turn into a video store, just as the computer turned into a bookstore. Anything supplied off tape, disk, or film will be subject to the simple laws of supply and demand.

Live TV will be a bit safer for traditional TV advertising. Real time will always be scarce, and so will the kind of content that's best provided by live TV: news, weather, and sports. The question of who will pay for it will still be open, however, because today's advertisers may still find more efficient ways to spend their marketing money in a Web-mediated business world.

Funding Illusions

Words Are Nutrition. Images Are Drugs.

— *Rob McDaniel*

I recently asked an executive with one of the Web's most popular sites if his enterprise was making money yet. "No," he said. "But that's okay. We just got $27 million in our latest round of funding."

Form follows funding, Stewart Brand says.[28] The story of the Web's development is primarily a story told by those who funded it. These fall into two groups. One is the entertainment and media moguls. These guys look at the Web the way Bugsy Siegel looked at the Nevada desert: as a perfect place to build attractions where people will spend money or where their eyeballs will pause long enough for ads to capture them. The other is the venture capitalists, who seem willing to fund lavishly just about anything with a plan to replicate TV's product, market model, or both, on the Web — in spite of the Web's obvious deficiencies as a big-time advertising medium.

Why? Are they all on drugs?

Field of Drugs

Well . . . yes. All of us are. Because all of us are in the entertainment conversation, with an endless supply of topics from television. We're in Oz. It doesn't matter that it's not real. We're all on the yellow brick road together, and hey, those bricks are gold. Why else would the venture capitalists and entertainment moguls pay so much for them? This Oz is another Field of Dreams. They're building it, and most of us are coming right along. So what if we're not paying for it? Hell, *they are*.

Entertainment is a form that also follows fashion. This year, the most fashionable sites are dressed as "portals," advertising-gilded openings to a space that was never closed. They're as absurd as a dancing scarecrow and as necessary as a door to the sky. But, surreal as they are, the concept sells. Excite, an ordinary portal company with 1997 sales of $53 million and losses a third that large, today has a market value of more than $2 billion[29] Yahoo!, a company with similar sales and a marginally positive balance sheet, is valued at more than $9 billion.

Not bad for a total illusion.

Last year's Oz fashion was "push." For a while push was so hot that *Wired*, the computer industry's utopian fashion monthly, declared the death of browsing and its

28. Stewart Brand, *How Buildings Learn*. New York: Viking Books, 1995.

29. July 7, 1998.

replacement by TV-like "immersive" media that offered "a zillion nonpage items of information and entertainment."[30] At PC Forum in March 1997, I asked the gathering — about 500 industry figures, including many of the most fashionable push designers — to raise their hands if they really wanted content pushed at them over the Web. None did. Many laughed. It made no difference. It was a fashion, so it ran its course, as fashions do.

Why are these fashions so compelling? Because this conversation is about entertainment, not truth.

TV Trivia

Consider the following statistics provided by the group TV-Free America:[31]

- Most Americans divide their time between three kinds of activities: work, sleep, and watching TV. The average American watches more than 4 hours of TV every day. That's 28 hours per week, 2 months per year, 9 years of life.

- Advertisers spent more than $45 billion on TV advertising in 1997 in the United States. That's more than one-quarter of all advertising expenditures.

- Over a year, kids spend 1600 hours watching TV. That's nearly twice the 900 hours they spend in school. They also spend 38.5 minutes per week in meaningful conversation with their families. That's a ratio of 436 to 1.

- Ninety-nine percent of American households have at least one TV. On the average, those TVs are on nearly 7 hours a day.

- Two-thirds of us watch TV while we eat dinner. One in four of us often fall asleep while watching TV, too.

- The average kid sees 20,000 thirty-second TV commercials per year. By the time he or she reaches 65, the number will reach 2 million.

30. Kevin Kelly and Gary Wolf, "PUSH! Kiss your browser good-bye: The radical future of media beyond the Web." *Wired*, issue 5.03, March 1997. See *http://www.wired.com/wired/5.03/push/*.

31. TV-Free America has abundant statistics at its site (*http://prince.essential.org/tvfa/*), mostly on its statistics page (*http://prince.essential.org/tvfa/stats.html*), which cites the A.C. Nielsen Company (1996) plus other sources, footnoted on that page.

As Howard Beale put it in the movie *Network*, "Television is not the truth. Television is a goddamn amusement park. Television is a circus, a carnival, a traveling troupe of acrobats, storytellers, dancers, singers, jugglers, sideshow freaks, lion tamers and football players. We're in the boredom-killing business."[32]

Few would argue that TV is a good thing. Hand wringing over TV's awfulness is a huge nonbusiness. TV-Free America (TVFA) counts 4000 studies of TV's effects on children. TVFA also says 49% of Americans think they watch too much TV, and 73% of American parents think they should limit what their children watch.

And, as the tobacco industry will tell you, smoking is an "adult custom" and "a simple matter of personal choice."

Then let's admit it: TV is a drug. So why do we take it when we clearly know it's bad for our brains?

Six reasons: (1) because it's free, (2) because it's everywhere, (3) because it's narcotic, (4) because we enjoy it, (5) because it's the one thing we can all talk about without getting too personal, and (6) because it's been with us for half a century.

Television isn't just part of our culture; it *is* our culture. As Howard Beale tells his audience, "You dress like the tube, you eat like the tube, you raise your children like the tube." And we do business like the tube, too. It's standard.

If We Hurt Them, They Will Come

Howard Beale had it right: *television is a tube.* Let's look at it one more time, from *our* point of view.

What we see is a one-way freight forwarding system, from producers to consumers. Networks and stations "put out," "send out," and "deliver" programs through "channels" on "signals" that an "audience" of "viewers" "receive," or "get" through this "tube." We "consume" those products by "watching" them, often intending to "vege out" in the process.

Note that this activity is bovine at best, vegetative at worst, and narcotic in any case. To put it mildly, *there is no room in this metaphor for interactivity.* And let's face it, when most people watch TV, the only thing they want to interact with is the refrigerator.[33]

---

32. *http://www.filmsite.org/netw.html.*

33. I'd like to credit somebody with this, because it's a great line. But I don't remember where I got it.

Metaphorically speaking, it doesn't matter that TV contains plenty of engaging and stimulating content, any more than it matters that life in many ways isn't a journey. TV is a tube. It goes from them to us. We just sit here and consume it like fish in a tank, staring at glass.

Of course *we're* not really like that. *We're* conscious when *we* watch TV.

Well, of course we are. So are lots of people. But that's not how the concept works, and it's not what the system values. TV's delivery system metaphors reduce viewing to an effect — a noise at the end of the trough. And they reduce programming to container cargo. "Content," for example, is a tubular noun that comes straight out of the TV conversation. What retailers would demean their goods with such a value-subtracting label?[34] Does Macy's sell "content?" With TV, the label is accurate. The product is value free, because consumers don't pay a damn thing for it.[35]

There is a positive side to the entertainment conversation, of course. Writers, producers, directors, and stars all put out "shows" to entertain an "audience." Here the underlying metaphor is theater. By this conceptual metaphor, *TV is a stage*. But the negotiable market value of this conversation is provided entirely by its customers: the TV stations and networks. The audience, however, pays nothing for the product. Its customers use it as advertising bait. This isolates the show biz conversation and its value. You might say that TV actually *subtracts* value from its own product by giving it away.

Another conceptual problem appears when we look at the conceptual metaphor for advertising messages: *messages are weapons*. Advertising talk is full of military language, and not just in the TV business. Ads everywhere are "deployed" in "flights" that are "positioned" or "aimed" to "deliver impact" against "targets." Thick ad schedules get nicknames such as "carpet bombing" and "roadblocks." Would we talk to (or about) *customers* this way? Of course not. Customers are involved. They pay us for our goods. We have relationships with them. We're in a conversation together. *We wouldn't want to hurt them.* When we conceive of marketing in military terms, hurting people is a virtue.

---

34. "Content" also comes from the publishing conversation, where it serves as a synonym for meaning. In all of today's Web conversations, however — including the publishing conversation — "content" is a synonym for cargo.

35. There are four exceptions: (1) noncommercial TV, which customers buy directly from stations; (2) pay TV, including premium and pay-per-view channels; (3) home shopping channels, which are retailers and distributors; and (4) cable, which is a passive signal distribution system.

But hey, these metaphors are just figures of speech, right? We don't really want to bomb people. We just want to get messages across. This is just the way we talk about it.

Wrong. *We understand advertising as a delivery service, and we dramatize it with military metaphors.* But whereas TV works *only* as a delivery service, the Web works as much, much more. Understanding the Web primarily as a delivery service denies the power it gives to the human beings in the bomb sights, whose psyches have been cratered by a lifetime of advertising. Now they don't have to hold still for it. And they can strike back.

Tales of Two Metaphors

As we said earlier, the Web is understood by a variety of terms: delivery service, marketplace, retail store, publication, art project, and real estate development, among others. Often we mix these metaphors, especially when we try to understand or explain the conflicting interests of different professions that need to cooperate. Take this paragraph, for example, from a recent *Computerworld* article: "As the industry works to hammer out new types of Internet ads, a basic tension is emerging: Advertisers want larger, more complex spots to grab viewers' attention. Web site publishers don't."[36]

In the traditional publishing business, there is little distance between publishing and advertising. For example, advertising account executives work on the "publishing side" (rather than the "editorial side") of the business. In the Web world, publishers and advertisers are far apart because they conceive the Web in very different terms.

To show just *how* vast those differences are, Table 8.1 compares roughly equivalent terms, based on the very different conceptual metaphors: TV and advertising on one side and the Web and publishing on the other (along with other nondelivery metaphors). Note that what matters here isn't that we use different terms for the same thing but that the underlying conceptual metaphors are radically different — and might never meet.

In the long run (which might not be very long), the Web conversation will win because it supports and nurtures direct conversations and therefore grows business at a much faster rate. It also has conceptual metaphors that do a better job of supporting commerce.

36. "New ads: 'Rich concepts, not rich media'" by Sharon Machlis, *Computerworld*, August 31, 1998, p. 40.

Table 8.1 Mediums and Metaphors

TV	Web
Watch, receive, surf, tune, select	Visit
Channel, signal, station	Home page, site, presence, location
Present, broadcast, transmit, deliver	Publish
Tube	Display, screen, monitor
Tune, channel surf	Link, navigate, explore, surf, search
Network	Space, Net, Web, server, map, domain
Station	Home
Create	Write
Receive	Visit
Signal	Hypertext
Hook up, cable	Connect, connection
Remote	Mouse
Select, choose	Choose, link
Experience	Activity
Time	Space
Schedule	Location
Look	Search
Listings	Findings
Eyeballs, viewers, consumers, audience	Visitors, users
Productions, programs, shows, content	Content, pages, sites
Favorites	Bookmarks
Audience, reach, penetration	Visitor count

Drugs have their uses. But it's better to bet on the nurtured market than on the drugged one.

Trees don't grow to the sky. TV's $45 billion business may be the biggest redwood in the advertising forest, but in a few more years we'll be counting its rings. "Propaganda ends where dialog begins," Jacques Ellul says.[37]

37. Regis McKenna credits this quotation to Marshall McLuhan, as do some others, but Nelson Thall, the McLuhan Archivist of the McLuhan Program for Culture & Technology at the University of Toronto (*http://www.mcluhan. utoronto.ca/mm.html*) and former president of the Marshall McLuhan Center for Global Communications, credits Jacque Ellul. See *http://www.mediaguru.org/Post23.html*.

The Web is about dialog. The fact that it supports entertainment, and does a great job of it, does nothing to change that. What the Web brings to the entertainment business (and every business), for the first time, is dialog like nobody has ever seen before. Now everybody can get into the entertainment conversation (or the conversations for any other market you can name). Embracing *that* is the safest bet in the world. Betting on the old illusion machine, however popular it may be at the moment, is risky to say the least.

The truth is, we never left Kansas. And that's not such a bad thing. Because thanks to the Web, Kansas will be a much better place to do business.

Marketing Returns

> There can be no effective corporate strategy that is not marketing oriented, that does not in the end follow this unyielding prescript: The purpose of a business is to create and keep a customer. To do that, you have to do those things that will make people want to do business with you. All other truths on this subject are merely derivative.
>
> — *Theodore Levitt*

More than 35 years have passed since Theodore Levitt gave substance to the word "marketing." In his 1960 manifesto *Marketing Myopia*,[38] Levitt defined marketing's job as "satisfying the customer, no matter what." Unfortunately, marketing was much more successful as a buzzword than as a discipline, but this kept Levitt busy, serving with thought what too many others served only with words.

In *The Marketing Mode*,[39] Levitt heaped coals on companies "whose policies are geared totally and obsessively to their own convenience at the total expense of the customer." Finally, in *The Marketing Imagination*, Levitt summarized his thinking with the preceding quotation.[40]

When those words were published, marketing was still understood in what we might call "broadcast" terms. Even for companies that met face to face with large numbers of customers, such as McDonald's and Sears, marketing was a top-down, one-way effort aimed at large numbers of people from whom little direct feedback (in forms other than cash) was expected. Or wanted.

The Web changes all that.

---

38. Theodore Levitt, "Marketing myopia," *Harvard Business Review*, July/August 1960.

39. Theodore Levitt, *The Marketing Mode*, 1969.

40. Theodore Levitt, *The Marketing Imagination*. New York: Free Press, 1984, p. 19.

The Web does not work like an 800 number, a mail-back card, or any other "direct response" medium. It can't be controlled and managed by customer service or an order fulfillment office, because it's too open and too interactive. Anybody outside the company can reach anybody inside the company whose e-mail address can be found. And with so many employees participating in newsgroups and other Internet activities, finding and making contact with those people is not difficult.

For companies with fortress mentalities, the Web is a scary development. It lets the rabble in the gates and turns them loose in the ivory towers. In fact, fortress-minded companies are often so Web blind that they hardly see the rabble penetration that does occur. Webmasters at these companies find themselves in the interesting position of knowing far more about what's going on than the guys upstairs.

But for companies with frontier mentalities, the Web is a wide-open galaxy of *Star Trek*–grade opportunities (with new places "to boldly go" exploring new worlds and splitting new infinitives). These companies see the Web as a rich new medium through which customers — and everybody else — can participate in the marketing process. To them, the Web is nothing less than the best medium ever developed for marketing as Levitt defined it: something that will make people want to do business with you.

In *Relationship Marketing*, Regis McKenna insists that marketing is entirely about relationships: "dialogue, not monologue."[41] But by 1984 Levitt already saw the growing importance of relationships in marketing and used relationships to differentiate between "old" and "new" styles of selling. In the old style, "the seller, living at a distance from the buyer, reaches out with his sales department to unload onto the buyer what the seller has decided to make." With the new style, "the seller, living closer to the buyer, penetrates the buyer's domain to learn about his needs, desires, fears and the like, and then designs and supplies the product in all its forms."

"The future," Levitt summarized, "will be one of more and more intensified relationships." The Web takes "more and more" and pushes that slope straight up at the sky. Already it threatens to make relationships more numerous and intense than most companies can stand. Even Microsoft strips its gears trying to manage countless customer relationships over both the Web and the phone.

This makes relationship management perhaps the most important work a webmaster faces. And the ever-prescient Levitt provides us with a few very helpful suggestions:

---

41. Regis McKenna, *Relationship Marketing: Successful Strategies for the Age of the Customer*. Menlo Park, CA: Addison Wesley, 1991, pp. 14, 18, 119–31.

- Recognize relationships as the most precious assets a company has, and invest in them.

- Foster actual or felt dependences between buyers and sellers.

- Establish direct links between buyers and sellers, and use them.

- Recognize that it is the seller's responsibility to create and nurture these relationships.

- Help the buyer understand the long-term costs and benefits of these relationships.

- Prefer to humanize, rather than institutionalize, relationships.

- Use your imagination, and start by getting down the "the simple essence in things" — in other words, don't BS.

The Web does all those things. It's as if it were made to fill Levitt's order. Television doesn't do any of them.

The Killer Service

Our ineptitude in getting at the record is largely caused by the artificiality of systems of indexing.

— Vannevar Bush, 1945

We're still at the end of the Middle Ages, and the renaissance won't get here until we solve the directory problem. And we won't solve that problem without metadirectory.

— Craig Burton, 1998

The Web is a wonderful thing, but it isn't organized. Nor, for that matter, is television. Worse, our only concepts for organizing either are the index or catalog (Yahoo!) and the search engine (Excite, Infoseek, and the rest of them). Despite their high regard by Wall Street, these services are woefully inadequate, given their failure to address reliably the simple *need to find*. Mostly these services only *narrow down*. Few customers go to any directory only to have choices narrowed down.

In computers and networks, the organizing work belongs to a *directory* of one kind or another. There are many kinds of directories, each designed to serve the arcane needs of an operating system or an application. This is little different from the directories in our daily lives, which include maps, channel listings, book indexes, and floor numbers in elevators. The difference is — these directories get along in the real world. In the networked world, they don't.

Craig Burton defines a directory as "*a way to manage identities, locations and relationships that change over time.*" We can do that in our daily lives, with calendars, address books, and the other directories that fill the social spaces around us: white and yellow pages, maps, restaurant menus . . . . The presence of one does not exclude another. They get along.

The directory chaos in computing produces both schizophrenia and Alzheimer's disease. Look at search engine findings. How often does a search produce different versions of the same document, plus links to pages that have moved? Too often.

A real directory would comprehend all the constantly changing contents of the Web — or at least of the parts of the Web we want to know about. We wouldn't need search engines that merely narrow down. We could go straight to what we want.

The Web does have a minimal directory called the Domain Name Service, or DNS. But the DNS defines only the domain level, or top level, of the Web — what comes between the double forward slash (//) and the first forward slash (/) (for example, *www.microsoft.com*). To the right of the first forward slash (/), however, the Web is all haystack. It has never been organized in any way, nor has anybody attempted to organize it.

Search engines might find needles in that haystack or at least reduce the big haystack to a smaller one that *might* include the needle you're looking for. But no improvement to any search engine will deny the haystack nature of the Web. It isn't organized. And it won't be organized until two fundamental network services are applied to it: *directory* and *security*.

The Need for Directory and Security

Every serious private network provides both a directory and security. That goes for Microsoft Exchange, Lotus Notes, Novell NetWare, IBM SNA networks, and so on. Differences between directories are political as well as technological, for vendors as well as users. Directories tend to be exclusive. They lock in customers and lock out competitors.

Complicating things is the matter of security. Our security metaphors favor locks and vaults, but in fact security is mostly a matter of record keeping. (Think of it as a very private form of publishing.) When you authorize a purchase with a credit card, for example, the record of your account number is compared against a list of revoked numbers.

Security on the Web doesn't currently extend far beyond what you get just from your own credit card. And without first-class security, it'll be a long time before we see the promise of electronic commerce truly fulfilled.

The final complication is the matter of distributed or object-oriented computing. Everybody agrees that the whole computing world will evolve into a vast collection of "objects": building blocks of data and code that can be assembled on an as-needed basis into applications, files, and so on. This world, however, requires a complete and coherent directory and security infrastructure. But we don't have it, and we won't have it as long as the world is also filled with exclusive directories.

This is why, when the Web was built as a wide-open space, directory and security services were left out. It's also why progress has been slow.

The Metadirectory Solution

There have been positive steps. One is Lightweight Directory Access Protocol (LDAP), which allows directories to exchange information. But LDAP doesn't organize the Web or (more appropriately to the Web's design) allow it to organize itself.

Analysts agree that the only technology that will solve this issue in the long run is *metadirectory*. A metadirectory joins the contents of multiple directories in a way that maintains each directory's autonomy but allows them all to work together as a functional whole. It also provides a kind of social space where both political and technological issues can be resolved.

Think of metadirectory as the computing equivalent of the real-world space where countless different directories, few with any awareness of the rest, coexist in your own life. We have nothing like that today in computing — even on our own computers, where our list of fax numbers doesn't know about our lists of e-mail, snail mail, and phone numbers. Products such as Microsoft's Outlook Express do a good job of embracing and extending many of those directories, but often at the expense of displacing other systems the customer might want to keep. Multiple directories won't go away, because directories tend only to proliferate. Netscape's new browser (version 4.05), for example, introduced features that require two or three entirely new directory "name spaces" in a server, each of which acts as an alternative to DNS. The only way truly to embrace and extend them is with metadirectory.

The Metadirectory and Convergence

On the Web of today, *buying* is easier than *finding*. But with a functional directory infrastructure, *both* will be far more easy and efficient. For example, imagine how

Some Rules

I have no use for rules. They only rule out the possibility of brilliant exceptions.

— Ed McCabe[42]

Don't think of the Web just as a new way to make money. Think of it as a way to make more money doing what you're already doing.

Do we think of the telephone as a source of revenue? Or as a business necessity it would be suicidal to do without? At the very least, Web sites are brochures or yellow page ads with no printing and minimal placement costs. At most they are ways to enjoy the fruits of what Bill Gates calls "frictionless capitalism" in his book, *The Road Ahead.*

Think usability.

Read Jakob Nielsen,[43] whom Jesse Berst of *PC Week*'s Anchordesk calls "the smartest person on the Web."[44] Nielsen's obsession is usability, not "coolness" or "killer" design.

Embrace Web-initiated conversations of all kinds.

This won't be easy for any broadcasters, except perhaps for QVC and other shopping channels, which really *do* have direct vendor–customer relationships with their viewers. On the whole, broadcasters would rather not talk with all the "eyeballs" out there. Meanwhile, the sources of funding — the advertisers — are quickly becoming well equipped to converse directly with their customers.

Hate regulation.

"Any content-based regulation of the Internet, no matter how benign the purpose, could burn the global village to roast the pig," *Time* magazine said on June 24, 1996. Regulation is competitive friction and a conversational distraction. It's a useless conversation that displaces useful ones. The computer industry is lightly regulated, while the broadcast industry is highly regulated (as are the cable and telephone industries).

Continues

---

42. Ed McCabe is the founder and namesake of McCabe & Co., a New York advertising agency. He is also a legend in his field. A founder of the great agency Scali, McCabe, Sloves, McCabe has given the world many of advertising's most memorable messages.

43. *http://www.useit.com/.*

44. *http://www.zdnet.com/anchordesk/story/story_1822.html.*

Some Rules (Continued)

Credit everything wonderful about the Web to the absence of regulations that would have made most of those things difficult or impossible.

Crave conversation.

The biggest uncredited reason for Microsoft's success is the conversation it craves with all the parties in all its markets — especially the people who use its products. One Microsoft official once told me, "there isn't a feature in Word that some user didn't ask for."

This stuff is Marketing 101. But most computer companies never took the course, because for too long they were too busy selling ice in the desert (or selling their promises on the promise market, to venture capitalists). And few in the broadcasting business took the course because the consumers paid nothing and they were in a well-regulated seller's market with their customers. Microsoft could teach the course. In fact, it's doing that right here.

If the prospect of conversations with "too many" prospects dims your ambitions, you'll lose to competitors who crave contact with the same prospects. That's the plain truth.

Use your webmasters.

They are in the best position to understand what it takes to make conversations happen. If they're not interested in making conversations happen, or if all they care about is decorating their sites with fashionable features, replace them.

---

easy life would be if you didn't have to keep track of every user ID and password that different Web sites require or if you could log just one time into multiple e-mail systems. *That* is what metadirectory does. And "single login" is just one of its obvious benefits.

Its biggest benefit in terms of TV/Web convergence is *closure*. When metadirectory comes along and provides a coherent directory and security infrastructure, the difference between the Web and TV becomes largely a matter of display. Whether you want to research a paper, download a movie, or book a flight, directory and security marshal the resources you require, given your available technologies.

Exactly one company offers a metadirectory product today: a small Canadian company called Zoomit.[45] The product is VIA. Watch for it. *Somebody* is going to make this thing happen.

A Choice, Not an Addiction

> TV is just chewing gum for the eyes.
>
> — *Fred Allen*

This might look like a long shot, but I'm going to bet that the first 50 years of TV will be the *only* 50 years. We'll look back on it the way we now look back on radio's golden age. It was something communal and friendly that brought the family together. It was a way we could be silent together. Something of complete unimportance we could all talk about.

And, to be fair, TV has always had a high quantity of good stuff. But it also had a much higher quantity of drugs. Fred Allen was being kind when he called it "chewing gum for the eyes." It was much worse. It made us stupid. It started us on real drugs such as cannabis and cocaine. It taught us that guns are the best way to solve problems and that violence is ordinary. It disconnected us from our families and communities and plugged us into a system that treated us as a product to be fattened and led around blind, like cattle.

Convergence of the Web and TV is inevitable. But it will happen on the terms of the metaphors that make sense of it, such as publishing and retailing. There is plenty of room in these metaphors — especially retailing — for ordering and shipping entertainment freight. The Web is a perfect way to enable the direct-demand market for video goods that the television industry was never equipped to provide, because it could never embrace the concept. They were in the eyeballs-for-advertisers business. Their job was to give away entertainment, not to charge for it.So what will we get? Gum on the computer screen, or choice on the tube?

It'll be no contest, especially when the form starts funding itself.

Bet on Web/TV, not TV/Web.

---

45. See *http://www.zoomit.com*

CHAPTER 9

The Coming Convergence: Implications for Audience Measurement and the Media Industries

Manish Bhatia, Vice President,
Interactive Services, Nielsen Media Research
www.nielsenmedia.com

Just 40 years ago, television was considered a "new medium," and it had to fight print publications and radio broadcasting to earn its spot in the media plan. Fifteen years ago, it was cable's turn, and now the Internet is in the limelight. This chapter describes the convergence of technologies that is poised to change the face of television as we know it and describes the implications of these changes for a variety of media industries, including the field of audience measurement and research.

The Historical Role of Media

An Internet Advertising Bureau publication observes: "Television's recent history has demonstrated that media budgets ultimately are pragmatic. As audiences migrate, media plans follow, acknowledging that the ultimate goal of any brand is to reach its target audience effectively and efficiently."

The advertising industry — including those of us who specialize in audience measurement — is in a continual process of reinvention as it adapts itself to any vehicle that delivers audience traffic. With each reinvention comes new business models, new types of ad creativity and format, and new techniques for ad distribution, ad insertion, and auditing.

Television is by far the most popular electronic medium. It is in 98% of U.S. households and is in use for more than 7 hours a day, every day of the year. By comparison, only 40 to 45% of U.S. homes have a computer and, of these, about 50% have Internet access.

Recognizing the high penetration and usage of television, various Internet companies have begun to develop technologies and content that would allow the delivery of the Web on TVs and also enable the linking of TV content (programming and advertising) with related Internet content, in a process called *convergence.*

Convergence: What Is It?

The physical distinctions between computers and televisions are increasingly blurred. Numerous companies are working hard to integrate these devices into a *converged environment* consisting of the computer, digital set-top boxes, and digital TVs. Digital streams of information will come to these devices and be made available to the consumer as audio, video, or data:

- Intel's Intercast system already delivers digital information along with analog TV on TV-ready computers. WebTV for Windows includes Intercast support.

- The Fantastic Corporation delivers multimedia content (voice, data, video) through a satellite in an environment known as "data broadcasting." Content producers using the system can offer enhanced programming to viewers.

- WorldGate plans to deliver the Internet to a TV by encoding the Internet information on the Vertical Blanking Interval (VBI) of a traditional TV signal. It also offers the ability to link TV programs and commercials to related Web-based content with a technology called *channel hyperlinking.* WorldGate is currently field testing the technology with large cable operators and broadcasters in the United States and Europe. In the WorldGate model, Internet access would become an add-on to the cable service.

- Microsoft's Windows 98 operating system features a built-in TV tuner (WebTV for Windows) that allows a computer with a TV tuner card to receive televised content. Viewers can watch television from their desktops. Computer manufacturers plan to include the tuner card as a built-in option, thereby eliminating the need to buy a separate card.

- Microsoft's WebTV Plus boxes allow users to connect to the Internet and browse the Web using standard TV sets. The company has recently introduced a technology called *TV Crossover Links* that allows broadcasters to take viewers easily from a segment of a TV program (or a commercial) to related Web content at the click of a button. The broadcaster can maintain the televised image while the viewer–surfer is on the related Web site.

It's easy to see why so many companies are working on making convergence a reality:

- The Internet has demonstrated a compelling advertising and direct marketing model for various companies.

- Users have found value in the services the Internet provides, from stock quotes to product information to travel reservations.

- Connecting TV and the Internet offers the opportunity to combine the mass reach of TV with the interactivity offered by the Internet, along with the back-end efficiencies offered by Internet-based fulfillment systems.

Advertisers will be able to unleash the power of targeting and interactivity on a larger scale than ever before. Convergence is not only about Web site surfing — it is about interactivity. QVC and the Home Shopping Network (HSN) have a combined market capitalization of approximately $10 billion — this from a model in which viewers must call an 800 number to place an order. Imagine the potential when orders can be placed with a simple click of a remote.

Adopting the New Technology: Measuring Audience Trends

As one prominent cable executive pointed out, about 25 years ago, surveys that asked people if they would ever pay for TV yielded an overwhelming "no" from respondents. Yet today, more people pay for TV than don't pay. So it's obvious that although opinion-based research is a reliable method for predicting adoption of new products or ideas, it can be misleading or miss important developments. For example, the Internet came virtually out of nowhere about 5 years ago to become the fastest growing medium in history. A Morgan Stanley Technology research paper outlines the adoption curves of various technologies (Table 9.1):

Table 9.1 Years for Various Technologies to Reach 50 Million Users

Technology	Years
Radio	38
TV	13
Cable	10
Internet	5

Defining Digital TV

With digital TV (DTV), information is passed digitally — in bits and bytes — rather than by frequencies and waveforms. Digital transmission is efficient, allowing saved bandwidth to be used for such improvements as better quality pictures (high-definition television or HDTV), more channels, on-demand programming, and data.

To handle digital signals, reception devices must have the components necessary to receive and display this information. These include a central processing unit (CPU), an operating system, storage, and a display device. A collection of these elements, in essence, represents a computer. It could come as a digital TV or a $300 set-top box that has a processor, operating system, and storage but uses the current analog TV as a display device.

Large amounts of research and a number of trials have studied the consumer's preference for high-definition television (HDTV) and on-demand programming as well as the technical issues related to delivering digital television. Although surveys indicate that people would like HDTV and on-demand programming, such studies could be erroneous for a few reasons:

- *Survey results can be extremely sensitive to questionnaire design.*
  Depending on how a question is asked, respondents can give very different responses. For example, the question, "Would you prefer better-quality pictures?" would invariably result in a "yes" answer. The question, "Would you be willing to spend $2000 on a TV set that displays better-quality pictures" would probably get a different — and negative — response from many. Similarly, although almost everyone would like to have access to programming on demand, their positive responses might vary if the question contained actual price points.

- *Respondents have difficulty imagining a platform that is still evolving.*
  Most surveys about peoples' desire to get the Internet on a TV suffer from two limitations:

  > The difficulty of explaining the concept of the Internet on TV to respondents.

  > Explanations that are based on the current perception of the Internet — which don't necessarily reflect the future reality. For example, many

users might perceive the opportunity to visit a Web site as an interruption of their television viewing and therefore respond negatively — not realizing that future technology will minimize the interruption.

Implications for the Media Industry

Convergence has serious implications for members of the media industry:

Advertisers

Despite its effectiveness as an advertising medium, television's one-way nature has prevented advertisers from directly attributing and quantifying viewer response and behavior. The closest that TV has come to completing the loop between advertising and sales is through paid programming, in which viewers call an 800 number in response to a product promotion.

But the convergence of technologies will allow complete interaction — from brand awareness to purchase — between the viewer and the marketer, all from one platform, all in a single interactive session. A car manufacturer might point a viewer to the nearest dealer or offer an on-the-spot cash rebate for the purchase of a vehicle. McDonald's restaurants could offer cents-off coupons. How will different types of advertisers increase brand awareness?

Advertising Agencies

Because traditional marketing functions will be available on television, media plans will become increasingly integrated with overall marketing plans. Accordingly, the share of the budget assigned to media advertising will probably increase to reflect the expanding power of television as a marketing and fulfillment vehicle.

But whereas today's viewers have a limited number of available responses (change the channel or shut off the set), the new world of digital TV will broaden those options, allowing viewers to watch TV while sending e-mail or surfing the Web. In fact, the TV program (and therefore the commercial in it) might be reduced to a small, stamp-sized window. In this new world of enhanced viewer control, how does a creative agency ensure that it (1) conveys its message and (2) obtains the desired result?

Content Producers–Broadcasters

Content producers will be confronted with both a great opportunity and a creative challenge. How might they offer enhanced programming and value-added services to increase viewer loyalty? Some possibilities already exist today:

- Additional information (tickers, scores, headlines) delivered in conjunction with existing broadcasts

- Chat rooms that let viewers of a particular show talk to each other

- Game shows that allow viewers to play along and win prizes

- Talk shows that allow viewers to ask questions of the host or the guests via e-mail or phone, right from their interactive TV

The enhanced advertising–marketing opportunities are also significant. Historically, program development has been paid for by advertising revenue, with the size and demographic composition of the delivered audience dictating the value. The larger and more desirable the audience (from an advertiser's perspective), the more a content producer–broadcaster can charge in terms of the common currency — the cost per thousand impressions (CPM). This CPM model is based on the only activity that can happen on TV — the viewer's exposure to the message.

But with the enhanced interaction made possible by the changing technology, viewers won't be limited to viewing — they'll be participating and possibly even purchasing. Should the content producer–broadcaster who enables this potentially lucrative interaction demand a higher price? Should a broadcaster charge the advertiser more money for actually delivering the buyer?

Research Solutions for the New Age

Any measurement solution that aims to provide the industry with complete viewer behavior must consider this diverse viewing–surfing landscape:

- It must have the tracking technology to collect information from the new platforms.

- It must determine which behaviors are important to capture.

- It must assign value to these different behaviors.

Nielsen Media Research is leading the development of measurement methods that will enable us to continue to assist our clients as they work through this media transformation:

- Our new active/passive (A/P) meter allows us to capture audio and video embedded codes from the content itself and to capture passive signatures of nonencoded content. We can match these signatures with a reference library at our processing center, providing a complete view.

- We have developed software that will allow us to track Internet and TV activity on computers as well as TVs. One software meter tracks TV viewing within the Intel Intercast system and extracts and interprets the supplemental information sent through the Vertical Blanking Interval (VBI). Another tracks TV viewing within the Windows 98 platform. Using this technology, we can determine (1) when a TV tuner application is activated, (2) which channels are watched, and (3) for what duration. The meter also tracks whether users connect to the Internet or perform another on-screen activity while watching TV on a computer. We are also working with WorldGate Communications to provide research solutions to its clients.

- On the Internet, we track every Web site and Web page a user visits and measure the time spent at each.

- Our software is compatible with different Windows platforms, including Windows CE (an operating system for consumer devices including set-top boxes). In addition, we have strong relationships with key industry players including Sun Microsystems (developers of the Java programming language), Scientific Atlanta, Next Level, and others that are developing systems and platforms to enable interactivity and convergence.

Nielsen Media Research is ready to capture user behaviors on platforms and operating environments not yet released. We will stay on top of the rapidly changing landscape and continue to develop collective measurement solutions that enable our customers to make the right decisions for their respective businesses.

CHAPTER 10

Digital Renaissance and T.A.G.: You Have a Story to Tell. So Do We.

Digital Renaissance

www.digital-ren.com

At Digital Renaissance, storytelling is about the power of one great idea — that "my way" is as valid as anyone else's way. In the Digital Renaissance view, the audience doesn't just sit back and listen to what is being said but is allowed to recreate as the audience member sees fit. Based on the recognition that we can all be storytellers, T.A.G.'s architecture helps authors extend the resonance of the story by allowing a two-way exchange between author and audience.

Once upon a Time . . .

. . . there was a 20-something guy named Keith. As the founder and figurehead of Digital Renaissance, all he had at that time was a bedroom and a computer. But more than that, Keith had a vision. He envisioned a change in the way we communicate using platform-independent computing.

From its inception, Digital Renaissance developed custom software for some of North America's largest organizations. As Digital Renaissance grew, it was dubbed a new-media *wunderkind* for its ability to make a statement by building network-centric solutions. It became a leading contender in the new-media software and systems race. From electronic commerce–enabled Internet sites to next–generation media-on-demand broadband architecture, Digital Renaissance garnered international acclaim for award-winning business-to-business and business-to-consumer solutions.

Digital Renaissance now applies its experience to forge a different philosophy concerning new media and human communications by using storytelling as a foundation. It was under this philosophy of storytelling that the Temporal Annotation

Generator — T.A.G — was developed and ultimately launched. The T.A.G. editor is shown in Figure 10.1.

The Digital Renaissance History

Digital Renaissance embraced the storytelling philosophy for one simple reason: People make sense of the world by creating and repeating stories. Consider cultural fables, myths, and fairy tales. Look at how easily they are understood. Look at how often they're repeated. More important, look at how long they've lasted.

In an effort to translate the traditional storytelling model to the new technologies, Digital Renaissance came up with a series of goals that would direct the development of a new tool. Digital Renaissance wanted to

- Create the models and platforms that allow businesses to utilize stories to capture knowledge, increase efficiency, and conduct commerce.

- Create new classes of tools that enable today's master storytellers to engage tomorrow's audiences.

- Join the ranks of the storytellers by driving the forefront of the new form, the new story, to extend the power of your own story.

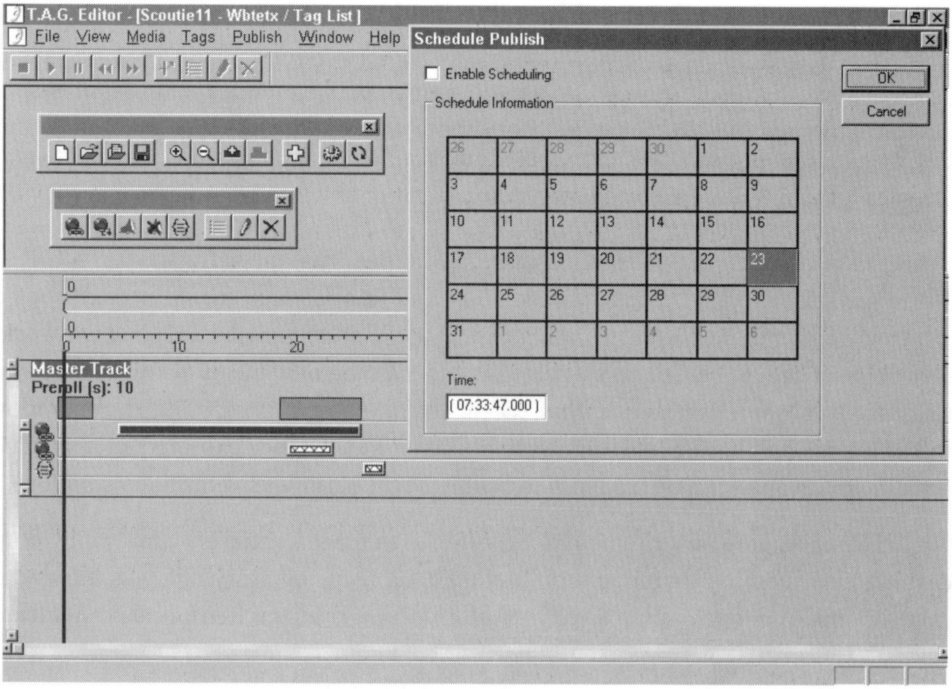

Figure 10.1 The T.A.G. editor.

- Pursue the development of technologies and the stories that empower the storyteller in all of us by making the exchange two way.

T.A.G., You're It

By 1995, Digital Renaissance was developing solutions for synchronizing Web content with media, regardless of the format of the media. A mandate for a product called the T.A.G. Editor was formalized:

- Capture the author's audience with the power of interactive media using stories — whether the story is an infomercial, a news clip, a nature documentary, or a music video.

- Provide authors the ultimate flexibility when designing their interactive stories by supporting media independence without sacrificing artistic license.

- Remove the scripting chaff from the development wheat by giving less technical authors the ability to create without knowing Visual Basic, Java, or any other scripting languages.

In 1997, Digital Renaissance introduced T.A.G. Editor 1, which focused on content synchronization[1] with standard video types such as AVI[2] or MOV.[3] The software was extended to support streaming media such as Microsoft's NetShow and RealNetworks' RealAudio and RealVideo.

As WebTV became a reality, Digital Renaissance extended T.A.G. Editor, which became the first integrated authoring platform that supported both hypertext markup language (HTML) (including ASF[4]) *and* WebTV for Windows components (or, to put it another way, both streaming *and* broadcast functionality).

By improving T.A.G. Editor to support Broadcast Architecture, Digital Renaissance found the missing link for enhanced show creation. A prototype, T.A.G. Editor 1.5, Broadcast Special Edition, was quietly introduced in November 1997. Lauded for its simplicity, it provided a clean graphical user interface that was dedicated to event

---

1. The uniform resource locators (URLs), graphics, textual content, or media coordinated with the television program.

2. AVI is an acronym for Audio Video Interleaved. AVI is a Windows multimedia video file format developed by Microsoft.

3. MOV is an acronym for Macintosh QuickTime MOVie file format.

4. ASF is an acronym for Active Streaming Format, Microsoft's streaming media format used in NetShow.

and content synchronization, asset collection,[5] and bandwidth usage. These features automated the authoring of interactive stories. This ingenuity allowed both developers *and* designers to author interactive stories for both TV and the Web.

Redefining the Art of Storytelling

With tools such as T.A.G., authors are able to create comprehensive stories that are, in essence, coauthored by the user and the user's interactions with them. How? By adding new elements called *tags* that provide additional information that users can access as desired.

The Medium-Tag Dynamic

Authors must create a cohesive content structure that unifies the medium and its tags:

- The *medium* is the primary story line. Ultimately, the measure of a good medium is how it engages its audience. It should lure the audience in with a specific emotion, piece of information, or message. The medium also needs an underlying element to act as the trigger point for additional details. These trigger points will be used by the audience as a way of raising issues or formulating questions.

- *Tags* are trigger events associated with a frame in the medium's linear time line. They make a story interactive. Each tag has a name, a description to help identify it, and a start and finish time. A tag can be one of the following types: a URL flip,[6] Script flip,[7] Hotspot,[8] Marker,[9] Caption,[10] Ticker Tape,[11] or Marquee.[12]

---

5. In T.A.G. Editor 1.5 assets synchronized with the television show could be stored in a resource palette, a method of collecting and housing assets until they were needed.

6. A URL flip automatically launches an HTML page at a specific time to an audience.

7. A script flip tag automatically launches a Visual Basic script or Java applet at a specific time.

8. A hotspot tag causes a specific event (such as a URL flip) to occur when a clickable rectangle on the video is activated by the audience. A hotspot can be visible or invisible.

9. A marker tag identifies a specified point in your medium so your audience can scan for it, as done with a bookmark.

10. A caption tag flashes a string of text in a separate window at a specific time for a specific duration.

11. A ticker tape tag adds text to a project that crawls from the right side of the player window to the left for a specific duration. It looks different from a marquee tag in that it has two lines to the text string: the top text string is white and the bottom text string is green.

12. A marquee tag adds text to a project that crawls from the right side of the player window to the left for a specific duration.

The content structure must be mapped out before the media and tags are authored in the T.A.G. Editor.

Content Mapping

The goal of content mapping is to track the logic flow and to locate gaps or context flaws within the story. The following steps outline a typical content-mapping process:

1. Scope all parts and details of the story. Select all details that must be included in the story and that will make it a cohesive unit.

2. Determine what authors believe the audience must know (as opposed to what content the audience would like to have). Then map which parts and details should be broadcast or which are better singlecast.

3. Create or locate a broadcast medium that best captures the details that authors have earmarked.

4. Create or locate the resources that match the story's trigger points so they seem like a natural fit to the story. A resource could be a URL, a document, an executable program, or even another media file.

5. Test and evaluate what cause-and-effect relationship the story line and tagged resources will have. Ensure that the tags support the media and don't distract from them.

This targeting of details within an interactive story is what makes authoring in the T.A.G. Editor so revolutionary: T.A.G. technology allows the author to manipulate the strengths of each medium in the design of the interactive story. To do so effectively, the author must know the strengths and weaknesses of the story.

Casting a Larger Net: Broadcast, Multicast, and Singlecast Content

As part of the content-mapping process, authors must distinguish between two content types: content that the entire audience must know versus content that a few individuals in the audience might desire. To communicate various pieces of the story to specific users in specific ways, the author uses T.A.G. to choose between broadcasting, multicasting, and singlecasting methods:

- Broadcast transmits content to all audience members.
- Multicast transmits content to a subset of the audience.
- Singlecast offers content individually to whoever requests it.

Identifying Push versus Pull Interaction Techniques

T.A.G. gives authors the ability to target and capture different audiences within one interactive story by using casting tactics and push–pull strategies:

- Push tags are automatically launched and broadcast to the audience without an audience member making a request, with tags such as URL flip, marquee, ticker tape, or caption.

- Pull tags let audience members request a resource by actively clicking URL buttons or hotspots. Often, pull tags are content that allows the author to pad the main story with additional content.

Because T.A.G. is a revolutionary technology, viewers might benefit from a push strategy that coaxes them to interact with the story:

- Authors writing for a passive audience[13] should use a pure push strategy initially — especially for interactive stories that are designed for advertising and training purposes. Push strategies will educate the audience about T.A.G. technology's interaction patterns. Audiences that become accustomed to this interaction level will eventually become comfortable with a pull strategy.

- Authors who must ensure the audience's awareness of specific issues should use a push tag. Push tags are an excellent way of making certain content known to users, because they don't have to search for it to launch the tag. Push strategies are also invaluable when adding content to the story that must be clarified further, particularly with captions or marquee tags.

Multicast Tags

Multicast tags are resources such as URLs, ticker tape messages, and captions that are targeted toward an audience subgroup. Although multicast tags can be still media, they also have time-based elements if authors add ticker tapes, captions, or marquees.

Multicast tags pinpoint the type of content the subgroup requires and allow authors to tailor messages, content, and information for them, presented in a timely syn-

---

13. People unaccustomed or unwilling to use interactive elements.

Content Caveats

The following list outlines some issues that will help you create and map the content for an interactive story:

- Understand and respect the limits of user comprehension. A story might be dense with content, but if the audience isn't assimilating that knowledge or is completely missing the point of the story, additional content is irrelevant.

- Use interaction to enhance a story, not disrupt it.

- Test the interactive story before a sample audience.

- Ensure that the amount of extra content reflects the complexity of the subject.

chronized fashion. For example, a story has its audio in English but also has a button for a user to identify himself or herself as a French speaker. That audio track would then be translated into French as a series of captions flashed on screen to only the French speakers in the audience.

Singlecast Tags

Singlecast tags consist largely of still media. Because still media are constant, they do not change over time. In many cases, singlecast tags will be resources such as URLs and graphics (such as charts and graphs). Occasionally, they will be executable or even additional media — for example, a piece of content designed to allow one or more individuals in an audience to click actively on a notification object (such as a button) to gain access to it.

These characteristics of still media serve as a pleasant contrast to the time-based media the author uses to tell a story. Time-based media entice an audience with a broadcast message that might appeal to the emotional side of the audience; however, still media are some of the singlecast messages that might appeal to the intellectual, adventurous, or curious nature of the audience.

For T.A.G. interactive stories, still media can support the time-based media by either developing, defining, or explaining the content they contain. For example, imagine an individual watching a story on the construction of the Great Wall of China. The viewer wants more information, such as the impact of the climate on the wall, the historical economics surrounding its construction, and the soldiers who were stationed in its towers.

If all of this extra content were included in the documentary, it would probably overwhelm the viewers. But if the story of the Great Wall were given to the user as tagged textual resources, the 2-hour documentary would be "padded" with other pieces that would be the equivalent of an extra 18 hours of content — pieces that are optional to pursue.

After the authors have analyzed the entire story for its broadcast, multicast, and singlecast content requirements, they'll be able to decide on a push–pull interaction strategy.[14]

Mirror, Mirror on the Wall: When to Use the Fairest Authoring Tool of Them All

Three or more "yes" answers to the following questions indicate that T.A.G. is a viable solution for a story concept:

1. Could the content be aided by a story line, case study, theme, or vision? Any subject matter that can be related over a sequence of time is a candidate for creation of a T.A.G. interactive story.

2. Does the content require a minimum of interaction and user involvement?

3. Does the content need to be communicated by a subject matter expert with various levels of knowledge?

4. Does the content have enough depth to capture the interest of an audience who will ask different questions on a given subject?

5. Does the content have a strong relationship between a main story line and additional resources that complete the story?

6. Does the story concept show something in live action but still require added content to support or explain the live action being shown?

7. Does the story concept teach something that would be too expensive to experience in a real-world situation?

8. Is the story concept trying to foster a sense of community spirit? Is the broadcast medium the entry point to other fun, community-building experiences such as chat rooms, discussion groups, and network games?

---

14. The process by which information is automatically launched or actively pursued by an audience.

A Tale of Two Technologies (NetShow and WebTV for Windows)

T.A.G. provides a common development interface for both NetShow 3 and WebTV for Windows architectures. Authors do not need intimate knowledge of the two formats: T.A.G. automatically generates the necessary script files for both.

- Microsoft NetShow 3 allows stories to be told on the Internet, an intranet, or a CD-ROM, using a digitized video and synchronizing it with browser commands or HTML pages. This technology allows the user to access both the video and its synchronized content via modem or Ethernet connection. NetShow requires that the video be compressed. This compression ensures that the best quality is delivered for any given bandwidth.

- Although similar stories with similar videos can be created with WebTV for Windows, the technology is quite different. In this environment, the video is standard NTSC television broadcast format.[15] Unlike NetShow videos, it does not have to be digitized.

The synchronized content is then added to a one-way bandwidth path using the Vertical Banding Interval (VBI). All HTML pages, images, and commands are incorporated into the analog television signal. Unlike NetShow, the viewer does not need a modem — all data is transmitted through the television signal.

Conclusion

A story — any story — is a reflection of our experiences, fears, and imaginations. Whether through television, literature, film, or theater, we gain a larger-than-life window on our collective experience. But the one-way delivery inherent in these media limits the possibility of true "exchange" in storytelling. Of course, you're rarely expected to "change" these stories. After all, they're designed and developed in the traditional context of an author–reader relationship: the audience members experience the work of the author and derive meaning from the extent to which they identify with the work.

But if something wants to survive, it needs to evolve. It needs a rebirth. For storytelling, that Renaissance is Digital.

15. NTSC stands for the National Television System Committee of the Electronics Industries Association and is the standard format adopted by the Federal Communications Commission for broadcast television in the United States. NTSC is also the standard used in Japan, Canada, and Mexico.

With the introduction of interactive technologies such as T.A.G., a new type of viewer is being created: a viewer who doesn't just initiate participation but demands it. This is an active viewer, one no longer satisfied with simply being told a story. This viewer wants in on the action. How might the demands of the new interactive viewer affect these tenets? There is no question that they will have a dramatic effect (pardon the pun) but a question is, How? Another question is, Why? Perhaps a better question is, Why not?

Therefore, the way the audience digests the interactive story created with T.A.G. isn't defined by how much of the narrative they retain but by how they choose to navigate the connections between the story and the tagged content to design their own personalized story. The interaction that authors create must reinforce the relationship between the two.

Data Broadcasting

High-bandwidth data broadcasting (datacasting) will play a critical role in the digital TV era. Direct broadcast satellite (DBS) networks already use their bandwidth to deliver high-value content — from software to corporate manuals and documentation. The advantage of a broadcast model for data delivery is its ability to send the same content to large numbers of people. Transmitting content once and reaching many people (à la television) is more cost effective than establishing millions of point-to-point connections (as is done with the Web today, where users individually connect to servers). In addition, the increased size and reduced cost of today's hard drives, along with Internet connection and access costs having reached a plateau, make the delivery and storage of data over high-speed broadcast networks extremely compelling.

Existing broadcast networks already reach an enormous national and international audience. *Digital Household Report* of August 31, 1996 projected that 96.9 million households in the United States would receive analog and digital broadcast transmissions by the end of 1996. Broadcasts also reach a growing number of households internationally as broadcast satellite networks continue to proliferate.

The high bandwidth of many broadcast networks makes them ideal for transmission of not only audio and video data but also computing data such as high-resolution images, large aggregated blocks of Web pages, databases, and software. (Such data is generally too large to send or receive over telephone connections, even with the fastest modems.) And because modular components are used to receive, process, and present this data, developers can create applications without regard for the underlying technology. Hardware vendors can provide drivers to make their devices compatible with other broadcast client components.

The combination of a true push model and high-bandwidth networks allows the *Broadcast Architecture* delivered with WebTV for Windows to deliver large quantities of data to customers conveniently. The Broadcast Architecture, which refers to the underlying data delivery components that are part of WebTV for Windows, can

Pulling and Pushing: Delivery Models

Computer networks, including the Internet, generally use a *pull model* for transmitting data: A client requests specific data from a server and the server processes the request and responds (Figure 11.1). Even the most powerful servers can handle only a limited number of requests at a time, and bandwidth limitations restrict how much data can be transferred.

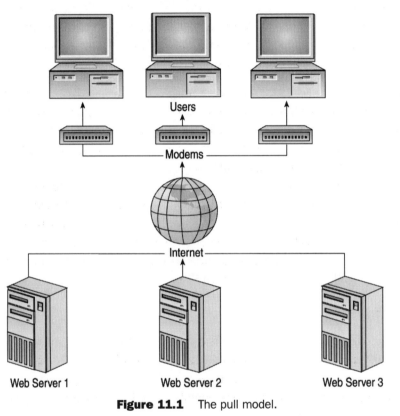

Figure 11.1   The pull model.

Television uses the push model of data transmission: information is supplied without waiting for requests, in a one-to-many fashion. (Alternatively, clients can request data, but the data is transmitted only after a significant number of clients have requested the same information. Some television networks have recently used this model to determine which movies to show.) In the push model, one server transmission can service an unlimited number of clients at time — there is no significant increase in cost to the content provider if a new receiver is added to the network.

deliver this data to a client automatically, in the background, without the customer having to dial in, tune in, or download anything.

New Kinds of Data

Data can be sent over digital networks and can be incorporated into analog television signals in the Vertical Blanking Interval (VBI). (An example is the program guide data provided by Gemstar and other companies.) Because of its ability to broadcast a variety of data efficiently, a digital datacast is ideal for delivering information such as stock prices, local news and weather, product catalogs, software updates, and other information provided by subscription services.

For example, frequently visited Internet sites can be broadcast, cached on a hard drive, and instantly available in an up-to-date form when a viewer wants them (perhaps in conjunction with an associated show or advertisement). Caching such sites eliminates frustrating busy signals, slow server response, and long download times caused by use of a modem. Digital information previously difficult or time consuming to acquire (background images, video, and music) can be made immediately available. For example, games or courseware might be regularly updated with new scenarios, information, or backgrounds that provide users a constantly changing landscape of interactivity. Software users would receive upgrades automatically, especially with the right purchase and subscription mechanisms in place. The types of new data services possible are shown in Figure 11.2.

Web Content and Files

On low-bandwidth networks, such as the VBI of existing television signals, delivery of very select pieces of Web content can be effective. On high-bandwidth networks, delivery of massive amounts of data to proxy and file servers provides, in the short term, a way to reduce network costs significantly. In the long run, it provides significant new revenue streams.

In targeted delivery, Web pages are sent to and stored in a user's Internet browser cache. The user is directed to the pages through mechanisms such as TV Crossover Links. Targeted delivery can be extremely successful with limited bandwidth. However, because the VBI supports transmission of approximately 100 megabytes per line per day, it is relatively limited in its ability to deliver enough general content to reduce connection-based download times sufficiently.

Delivery of large numbers of files — such as software packages and file server replication — is effective only in a high-bandwidth environment. By stuffing proxy servers

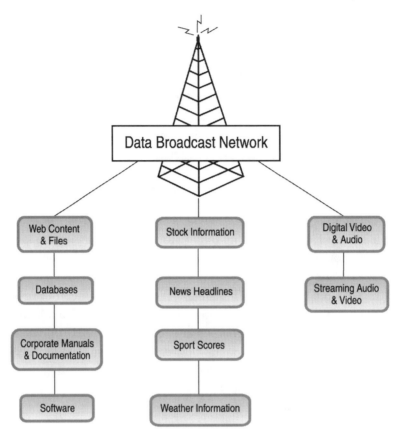

Figure 11.2   A data broadcast network.

or by replicating large file servers, delivery of Web content and files can solve the data-center-to-distribution-hub problem that plagues businesses, Internet service providers, and others. With high-bandwidth broadcast networks, corporations don't need to develop their own network; they can contract with companies that already own and operate high-bandwidth networks.

Today, stations should leverage webcasting and file delivery capabilities by referencing particular pieces of content as part of their interactive programming and storing the referenced content in the user's local cache. The simplest example of this is the use of a TV Crossover Link, specifying a uniform resource locator (URL) that the user can jump to. Because the URL is already stored in the user's cache, Internet dial-up is unnecessary. Today's broadcast stations, for example, should focus on using stand-alone Web delivery capabilities as a way to learn about the technology. However, they should also realize that stand-alone delivery of files or Web content, for example, will not be truly feasible without increased bandwidth.

Streaming Audio and Video

Streaming audio and video can be delivered over both low-bandwidth and high-bandwidth broadcast networks. Although three VBI lines (equivalent to a 28.8 kilobits-per-second modem) will probably be sufficient for only audio streaming, five VBI lines offer sufficient bandwidth to stream low-resolution video.

Providers with access to higher bandwidth networks can effectively use streaming video via IP multicast to deliver broadcast quality audio–video feeds to locations where they do not have landing rights. Streaming video can be used to offer a number of intriguing viewing experiences, such as the delivery of additional camera angles. Streaming video can also display teasers for other channels that may be associated with the actual video channel (for example, C-SPAN, C-SPAN 2, USA, and the Sci-Fi Channel).

The differences between the streaming video of today and the digital broadcasting of tomorrow will eventually disappear (as all transmissions become digital). In the short term, streaming audio and video may provide an interesting area for experimentation.

Tickers

Tickers are perhaps the easiest type of data feed to provide. They can be viewed in association with the TV picture, or they can be viewed using stand-alone applications (as long as the computer or viewing device is tuned to the right channel to receive the data). With Windows 98, a stand-alone ticker running off the task bar can be a compelling way for a station or network to attract viewers to its video feeds. Moreover, a station or network could offer additional opportunities to its advertising partners even when viewers aren't watching the TV signal.

As hard as the concept may be for producers to accept, viewers might not always want to watch their television programming. On the other hand, due to network constraints (such as dial-up access), the viewer might want to receive a ticker feed with current news, sports, and weather information. (A ticker server or script can also transmit advertisements, branding, and information about upcoming shows.) These types of information can be delivered in an automated fashion, without requiring any additional personnel to change or update the content during the day. Most stations and networks already provide this sort of information during their newscast or on their Web sites. Some simple development work might be required to take data in its current form and transmit it as a ticker feed.

Existing Satellite Datacasts

Satellite-broadcast digital data streams with capacities in the megabits are already available on broadcast clients. At 1.2 megabits per second, a channel can transfer over 10 gigabytes every 24 hours, and 6 megabits per second translates into more than 60 gigabytes of information per day. By contrast, a compact disc today holds about two-thirds of a gigabyte, which means that 6 megabits per second of data is equivalent to just under 100 CDs worth of data per day.

Technology Considerations

Before establishing a data service using the Broadcast Architecture, a content provider must create or acquire computer software to manage the delivery of the data from its source to its audience. Of course, the best programming strategy depends to some extent on exactly what kind of data is involved.

Where appropriate, a content provider must establish an online server for managing viewer subscriptions, purchases, and responses. Although the needs of such a server should be taken into account during development, the specific functions of any particular server are beyond the scope of this chapter.

Three key pieces of technology are required for datacasting (Figure 11.3):

- File delivery. The underlying mechanisms for delivering files must be reliable and easily used by application developers.

- Scheduling. Servers must be able to allocate bandwidth effectively and schedule data transmissions. Clients must receive the data and provide users with information about schedules for data transmissions.

- Subscription and security. Client devices must provide a way to manage incoming data and a way to subscribe to content of interest. For corporations, mechanisms must be available for securely transmitting and receiving content. For commercial services content — from software to video clips to digitized music files — there must be a way to encrypt data packages until users purchase them.

In many cases, existing technologies (such as those built into WebTV for Windows, the Broadcast Server, and the Broadcast Architecture) can help meet technology needs. In some cases, of course, "glue" software — software that takes existing pieces and builds them together to meet your requirements exactly — might also be

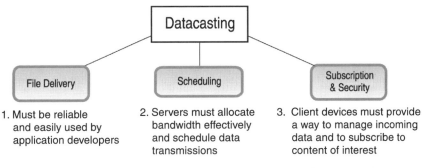

Figure 11.3 The three key technologies required for datacasting.

required. Keeping the preceding technology pieces in mind will help you determine the types of software and the network infrastructure that best suit your needs.

Broadcast Data Characteristics

Data suitable for broadcast falls into many different categories and can have a variety of formats. The following general characteristics have important implications for the software needed to generate, transmit, and receive the corresponding broadcast streams:

- *Value.* How much is the data worth? A high value probably justifies better encryption, more error correction, and more frequent transmission. Low value might allow higher compression and less frequent transmission.

- *Precision.* How much of the data's value depends on its complete and accurate transmission? When a software program is transmitted, for example, every bit must be correctly received and verified or the data is useless. When streaming video is transmitted, on the other hand, a good deal of data can usually be lost without compromising the value of the image. Note that because a broadcast client cannot notify the server of lost data, the Broadcast Architecture file transfer service (FTS) discards incomplete or damaged files. Data packets that are only partially complete or that contain errors are also discarded at lower levels of the operating system.

- *Transience.* Some data —such as stock prices or enhancements to a television show —loses its value soon after it is transmitted. Other data — such as a software program or reference work —loses value slowly.

- *Urgency.* How important is it that viewers receive the data within a given time frame? Urgency can be understood as a function of value and transience, but it also has a psychological component derived from viewers' perceptions. For example, a user purchasing a new software program expects it to come shortly after paying for it. On the other hand, a user purchasing regular updates to encyclopedia articles does not expect an immediate response.

- *Expiration.* How long can a viewer keep the data? Highly transient data is often used immediately upon reception and discarded, but other data might be kept indefinitely. The viewer's right to store and use data is often limited by licensing agreements, as in the case of software rentals, pay-per-view programs, or limited subscriptions.

- *Segmentation.* How is the data divided, particularly from a subscription standpoint? A viewer might sign up for a persistent stream of information (stock tickers), for individual files (downloaded software), or perhaps for filtered subsets of a complex data stream.

- *Homogeneity.* How homogeneous is the data? Stock price data, at one extreme, usually consists of small, uniform data objects that all have exactly the same size and format. A news stream, at the other extreme, might consist of many different types of data objects of radically different sizes and formats.

Analyzing a data service in terms of these characteristics is useful in determining what software is needed in the content provider's studio, at the broadcast head end, and on the receiving device to manage the data most effectively.

Conclusion

Like interactive television, data broadcasting is still in its infancy. From the delivery of Web content to streaming audio and video, data broadcasting offers a number of intriguing opportunities. With refinement of the appropriate business models, data broadcasting is set to reduce network infrastructure costs and perhaps ultimately reduce the cost of access to the Internet itself.

Engineering and Technologies: The Broadcast Architecture

It was around one in the morning — the time when most good engineering projects get started — when we pulled the 22-foot camper out of the parking lot and made our first wide turn onto the main street in front of the Microsoft campus. Inside, we had packed two computers, with monitors, keyboards, and mouse devices, along with two VCRs and miles of cables. In typical Microsoft tradition, we had a variety of soft drinks in the refrigerator. And as with most engineering projects, our first setup was a real mess. We had tape all over the place to hold the equipment down. We looked back to make sure nothing had broken or fallen over, and we wondered if we had remembered to put down the critical roof-top antenna after running our initial tests. After each bump in the road, we silently prayed that the hard disks and the software on them would be all right. This was our first attempt at capturing data samples. We were traveling the long road to refining our decoding algorithms for reception of data in the Vertical Blanking Interval (VBI), a non-viewable portion of the analog television signal.

The team originally formed to write the software code-named "Burbank" (later known as the Information Highway PC and even later as the Broadcast PC) had been formed over 2 years earlier, with two primary goals:

- To provide consumers with a compelling entertainment device that could display high-quality video on high-quality display surfaces

- To enable reception of high-speed data delivery services in the home, delivering such capabilities without expensive infrastructure costs

Like many software projects at Microsoft, the Broadcast PC effort started out as one thing and ended up as something very different. But along the way, one goal remained constant: our mission to build a foundation for digital television and broadcast data transmission and reception that would endure into the future.

The chapters in this section describe

- The standards and technologies that make possible the delivery and reception of interactive content and broadcast data services, including the Advanced Television Enhancement Forum (ATVEF) specification

- The Broadcast Architecture as implemented for Windows 98

- The detailed processes involved in the reception, display, and synchronization of interactive content in association with a television signal

- The similarities and differences between the Windows 98 implementation of interactive content and that specified by the ATVEF (a second edition of Windows 98, due out around the time this book went to press, is expected to include full ATVEF support)

CHAPTER 12

The ATVEF Specification and the Broadcast Architecture

Broadcast Architecture is the underlying set of technologies, components, and standards that make it possible to display television, receive broadcast data feeds, provide interactive services, and display enhanced content. A critical part of Windows 98, it is the foundation for WebTV for Windows. Although Broadcast Architecture will eventually be replaced by industry-wide common content specifications, an understanding of it will enable you utilize future standards, such as those in the ATVEF specification, quickly and easily.

On July 28, 1998, Microsoft and a number of other companies — including Cable-Labs, CNN, DIRECTV, Discovery, Disney, Intel, NBC, NDTC Technology, NCI, PBS, Sony, Tribune, and Warner Brothers — formed an alliance called the Advanced Television Enhancement Forum (ATVEF). The ATVEF advocates an open Web-based specification for creating, transmitting, receiving, and viewing interactive television programs.

The Broadcast Architecture, as shipped in Windows 98, does not implement the exact specification proposed by the ATVEF. However, many of the standards and protocols it *does* use are also used by the ATVEF specification. And although the Broadcast Architecture implementation varies from one device to another and from one platform to another, the standards, principles, and capabilities of the architecture remain the same.

Common Standards: One Architecture, Many Platforms

The Broadcast Architecture relies, to the greatest extent possible, on standard procedures that are widely accepted, understood, and supported in the industry. This ensures that data can be sent from a wide variety of servers to a wide variety of clients that support the common standards.

The following existing standards are used to deliver and display interactive content:

- Internet Protocol (IP), which is used for delivery of data. IP Multicast, in particular, is used to transmit data over unidirectional (broadcast) networks. A key advantage of multicasting is that it enables clients to filter data easily by receiving data only on specific addresses, while ignoring data on other addresses.

- Hypertext markup language (HTML)[1] and dynamic HTML (DHTML), which are already used to specify the display of text, graphics, and other content on the Web.

- Session Announcement Protocol and Session Description Protocol (SAP/SDP), which are used to announce data and interactive content streams.

- ECMAScript and the Document Object Model (DOM), which together form Microsoft JScript 1.1, implemented in many of today's Web browsers.[2] Together, these technologies are used to synchronize interactive content with television programming.

The following technologies are used to implement interactive television:

- Internet Explorer (IE). By incorporating IE technology, the broadcast client can take advantage of all the latest Internet and Web enhancements, including DHTML and style sheets.

- Windows Sockets (WinSock) version 2. This application programming interface (API) provides a network abstraction layer that allows applications to receive and send network data without needing any information about the network involved. WinSock provides access to IP Multicast data.

- Network Driver Interface Specification (NDIS). NDIS provides a low-level abstraction layer between data reception hardware and the higher level parts of the operating system. It allows hardware device drivers to be written independently of the target operating system.

- CryptoAPI. This API provides an abstraction layer for encryption and decryption services so that applications can use different encryption methods without requiring any information about the hardware or software involved.

---

1. For the specification, see *www.w3.org/TR/REC-html40/*.

2. See *www.ecma.ch/stand/ecma-262.htm* for the complete specification.

- Component object model (COM). This open standard allows different software modules, written without information about the other module(s), to work together as if they were part of the same program.

- DirectShow (formerly called ActiveMovie). This ActiveX technology provides an extremely flexible and capable architecture for managing and playing interrelated multimedia streams, which the broadcast client relies on. The key function of the DirectShow API is to connect many independent filter programs together. Each filter participates in the overall process of receiving, decoding, transforming, scheduling, and displaying interdependent video, audio, and data streams.

Internet Protocol

Perhaps the most critical aspect of the Broadcast Architecture is that it uses the existing standard IP for delivery of data and interactive content. Over the Internet and other computer networks that make use of IP, broadcasts take the form of IP multicasts sent to many recipients at once (in contrast to typical unicasts, which are directed to a single recipient). One of the great benefits of using IP Multicast is that both server and client applications can be tested and used on any network that supports IP — from a simple local area network (LAN) to a high-bandwidth broadcast satellite network.

The Broadcast Architecture, as shipped in Windows 98, enables you to receive data over the VBI, over traditional two-way networks, and over other unidirectional networks such as satellite networks. For each network, the underlying method of carrying IP data might differ. (For example, over the VBI, IP packets are placed inside NABTS[3] packets; for DVB,[4] IP packets are placed inside DVB MPEG[5] packets.) Because IP is used across all of these networks, server and client applications (such as tickers and enhancement tools) can be written independently of the underlying transport. The only major difference apparent to the applications and their users will be an increase or decrease in the amount of bandwidth available for data transmission.

3. North American Basic Teletext Standard.

4. Digital Video Broadcast, a standard used for high-power satellite transmission.

5. Moving Pictures Experts Group, a set of standards for video and audio compression.

The IP Addressing Scheme

IP includes an addressing scheme that allows multiple data feeds to be sent over different addresses but with all feeds sent in a single actual data signal. This enables, for example, ticker data and enhancements to be transmitted over the same portion of the television signal but be received by different client applications. In addition, the addressing scheme enables easy scheduling of different data feeds at different times.

The addressing scheme can be used to differentiate between different data providers. If a particular broadcaster has an agreement with multiple providers (a stock quote provider and a software delivery service, for example), the broadcaster can monitor given addresses to make sure that a particular service does not exceed its bandwidth or data capacity over the course of a day.

When used over a broadcast chain, IP addresses from different parts of the chain might conflict with each other. For example, when transmitting data over the VBI, content providers such as a show producer, a network, a television station, and a cable channel could all attempt to insert data. Different providers using the same addresses could result in loss of data. The various providers must make appropriate business (not technical) arrangements to make sure that the addresses used do not conflict with each other. From a technical standpoint, address reservation software could be used to help automate the process of allocating and reserving addresses.

Data Transmission and Announcements

Some applications use *announcements*, which allow a server application to tell broadcast receivers on a common address about other addresses that will be used for actual data transmission. Announcements operate like a ship-to-ship radio: one or more fixed channels are used for transmitting your name and boat identifier as well as a description of whom you want to speak with and the channel on which you want to communicate. Actual communication then commences on the specified channel. Similarly, a server application sends an announcement on one of a set of common announcement addresses describing the type of content and the address that will be used for actual data transmission.

For example, the server might send an announcement telling the client that interactive content will be arriving on a given IP address and port; the client application can then listen on that address for the actual data. An announcement consists of a simple set of line-separated strings that are described later.

Other applications rely on a fixed or a default address for data transmission or require the address and port for data reception to be configured on the client.

WebTV for Windows Components

The Broadcast Architecture provides a number of components that are used in the presentation of video, audio, interactive content, and data to the user. The most visible use of these components is WebTV for Windows. However, many Broadcast Architecture components can be used separately in Web pages or in other applications. The components are implemented as ActiveX controls, which are simply reusable software objects that can add specialized functionality to Web sites, applications, tools, and interactive programs. Under this definition, WebTV for Windows qualifies as an ActiveX container because it contains a number of other components implemented as part of the Broadcast Architecture:

- The video control, which tunes television channels and displays them. The video control can also be used in a Web page to add television functionality to a Web site. This control can display video on the entire screen or in separate windows.

- The program guide control, a highly visible part of WebTV for Windows, which uses a grid to display information on all broadcast programming available to the user over various time periods. With this control, the user can search for favorite shows, keep track of episodes, set up reminders to watch or record shows, and watch previews. This control is updated with Electronic Program Guide information from various providers.

- Announcement listener, an operating system service that receives announcements of upcoming data. Announcement listener filters each announcement and hands it off to an appropriate announcement listener filter. The enhancement filter is part of the Broadcast Architecture; developers can add additional filters, utilizing an open architecture, to support other types of data.

- The enhancement control, which receives enhancement content (in the form of files) and triggers (which use scripting) and therefore synchronizes interactive content with video.

From Components to Display

The display of television video and interactive programming in WebTV for Windows includes these key aspects:

- Each channel in the guide is associated with a Web page that is stored locally on the user's hard disk. A default page is used if no other page is specified. Alternative pages can be specified in the underlying database from which the guide retrieves the programming information (guide data) that it displays to the user.

- WebTV for Windows uses the Internet Explorer MSHTML control to display the Web page itself. This control is the underlying engine used in Internet Explorer to parse and display HTML. Thus, all of the functionality available through pages displayed in Internet Explorer is available in WebTV for Windows through this control. In other words, any multimedia capabilities, scripting capabilities, and other functionality available to Web developers is also available to developers of interactive programs. Moreover, existing tools can be used for quickly designing and creating interactive content without a significant effort to develop software.

- The Web page contains the video control and the enhancement control, permitting the display of video, delivery of audio, and presentation of interactive content.

- After the associated Web page is displayed, the enhancement control receives the interactive content and triggers, which are used to synchronize the content to the video. A content producer can use triggers to synchronize the display of HTML material with television programming and can add, update, or remove HTML material without any intervention on the viewer's part.

Furthermore, through scripts and ActiveX controls included with HTML pages, broadcasters and independent software vendors can take full advantage of the broadcast client's computing capabilities to enhance a show in new ways, to provide complex interactivity with viewers, and to deliver valuable services.

System Software Extensions

Although the operating system software that forms part of the Broadcast Architecture is intentionally based on industry standards, some software extensions have been required in order to perform specific tasks:

- Accommodate the large bandwidth occupied by high-quality digital audio and video streams and provide for flexible control over these streams. These extensions are special filters based on the DirectShow API.

- Support interactions with users. Broadcast clients use specialized software to control, process, and display high-bandwidth broadcast streams. Some of this software, such as the guide database system, also handles user interactions. The guide database provides a single secure repository for program data. At the same time, any service provider can deliver program guide information to the database by writing a simple loader.

- Support Television System Services (TSS), which allow applications to tune to, schedule, and control available broadcasts.

Architecture and Implications

The architecture of the broadcast client enables computers running Windows 98 to be client systems for many types of broadcast networks. The broadcast client is a standard computer enhanced with hardware and software components that enable it to process video, audio, and data from a variety of sources.

Some networks that broadcast clients can support are

- Broadcast TV and cable networks that broadcast digital data to viewers in the VBI of the television signal

- High-speed broadcast networks, such as direct broadcast satellite (DBS) networks

- The Internet's multicast backbone (MBONE) and the networks and telephone lines that support it — integrated services digital network (ISDN), Ethernet-compliant networks, Asymmetric Digital Subscriber Line (ADSL), and others

- Corporate networks that support multicasting

Of course, for any given network, the receiving device must have appropriate hardware and software drivers (software that controls the hardware and allows it to communicate with the operating system). Receiving data over the VBI, for example, requires analog television tuning hardware. Receiving data via satellite requires satellite receiver hardware.

The Broadcast Architecture is designed primarily for receiving data over broadcast networks. However, it can also be used over any traditional two-way network (such as a corporate network) that supports IP Multicast.

Broadcast networks, like traditional television, send data in only one direction. Therefore, these networks are ideal for sending the same information to large numbers of users, just the way television has always done. When users want to transmit information back (for example, when performing a transaction, making a purchase, or participating in a chat or poll) they must use a different, two-way network to do so. A user's existing Internet connection normally acts as the back channel.

In the future, clients receiving data on a broadcast network might be able to request data that they are interested in, much as some viewers today can request particular movies through pay-per-view.

Data Loss

Because the sender and receiver aren't connected, data loss is the most important issue to consider when transmitting or receiving data over a broadcast network:

- In a broadcast environment, servers can periodically resend data. The receiver can replace the entire piece of content or can simply fill in pieces of data that were lost. The frequency of retransmission depends on the amount of bandwidth available and the value of the data, among other factors. In the future, it is conceivable that clients could connect to special servers to download specific packets of information that were lost.

- In addition, servers can use special encoding methods to transmit redundant data that allow receivers both to detect errors and to reconstruct missing data quickly. Forward error correction (FEC) algorithms at both the network transport level and the application level can protect against data loss. For data transmitted over the VBI, for example, a low-level FEC algorithm is used, allowing the client to recover data even before it looks at the individual IP packets contained in the stream. At a higher level, the libraries used for sending and receiving files include additional methods for encoding redundant data.

An important implication of data loss is that a client might receive only some portion of the data it was expecting. If the client doesn't properly handle the display of such data, the user might have a poor viewing experience. For example, when some — but not all — interactive content is received, an underlying HTML page might be displayed but the content elements it references, such as static images, might be missing. To avoid such problems, it is possible to bundle groups of content together, such as a page and all of its dependences, so that the user gets an all-or-nothing experience. It's up to the content producer to make the right decision about how much content is required to give the viewer a good experience. WebTV for Windows supports the use of cabinet (CAB) files for bundling files together; the ATVEF specification supports a standard called multipart MIME (Multipurpose Internet Mail Extensions).

Data Navigation

In his landmark essay at the end of World War II, Vannevar Bush, the director of the Office of Scientific Research and Development, wrote, "Our ineptitude in getting at the record is largely caused by the artificiality of systems of indexing."

Over 50 years later, increasing amounts of content—such as digital moving and static images and television programming—make the finding and cataloging of data even more challenging. When it comes to the ever-expanding number of cable, broadcast, and satellite television channels, Electronic Program Guides might be the solution.

Electronic Program Guides combine information from multiple broadcast sources, each of which has its own channel numbering scheme. On the receiving device, guide data is stored in a local database. Figure 12.1 shows how guide data providers might use different transports (from data transmitted in the VBI to data transmitted through Internet downloads) for distributing the data to the end user.

There are three critical issues to consider in handling guide data from multiple sources:

- How to deal with overlapping channels (for example, channels from a satellite provider and a local cable provider)

- How to move data into the guide database

- How to store data that is provided in different formats but allow the

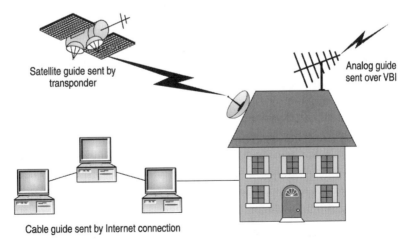

Figure 12.1   Various ways in which guide data can be transmitted to a broadcast client.

Electronic Program Guide to display the data from any of those providers in a uniform manner

Beyond the Set-Top Box: Harnessing Computer Power

As implemented for WebTV for Windows, the Broadcast Architecture uses the versatility and power of personal computers to enhance the viewing experience beyond what is possible with a set-top box. The computer promotes flexibility in planning television viewing, and it displays program guide information conveniently and clearly. Other advantages include

- *Processing power.* Use of processor-intensive technologies, such as Liquid Motion, which provide complex two-dimensional animation capabilities

- *Flexibility.* The ability to use complete Win32 applications and associated technologies such as ActiveX controls

- *Personalization.*

- *Open platform.* Use of third-party technologies such as Shockwave Flash, which lend incredible flexibility to multimedia presentations and enhancements

- *Storage capabilities.* Larger local storage capabilities for cached content and large, digitally encoded video and audio streams

- *Expansion.* Features such as the Universal Serial Bus (USB) that make it easy for consumers to add functionality to their computers

Today's computers support high-end graphics display, networked game playing, and other multimedia capabilities, in addition to television reception. New power-saving instant response technology, such as OnNow, keeps the system available at all times. The Internet is fully accessible by modem, and some Internet content is already loosely coordinated with television, as demonstrated by the MSNBC network.

Personal computers, acting as broadcast clients, offer an incremental, flexible, and affordable migration path to higher resolution television. Instead of buying a new digital television when broadcast technologies shift to a new standard, users will be able to upgrade by simply plugging a new hardware card into their computers or by attaching additional hardware using standard USB or 1394 interfaces.

Finally, broadcast clients display different types of program guide information in a single form. In this combined program guide, shows can easily be previewed,

WebTV for Windows Minimum Hardware Recommendations (Broadcast Client)

- Intel Pentium 150 megahertz processor.

- PCI bus with at least four slots available.

- Computer case of the consumer electronics type, with low-noise fan or noiseless cooling system. A user should not hear broadcast client noise from a distance of 6 feet in a quiet living room environment.

- Coordination with initiatives such as OnNow, Drive Bay, 1394, and the USB to provide a more consumer friendly appearance to the user.

- 16 megabytes (MB) random-access memory (RAM) or more.

- Hard disk of 2 gigabytes (GB) or larger with a fast data transfer rate.

- 3.5-inch 1.44 MB disk.

- 6X-speed CD-ROM drive or digital video disk (DVD).

- 31-inch monitor capable of 800 ¥ 600 resolution with a noninterlaced refresh rate of 60 hertz.

- Internal fax modem with a speed of 28,800 baud or higher that is compatible with the AT command set. Modem functionality can be incorporated on expansion cards for the broadcast client, so the modem does not need to be a separate peripheral.

- Wireless keyboard that responds to radio or infrared frequencies, is battery operated, and has a built-in pointing device.

- Wireless, television-style remote control.

- Combination remote control and wireless mouse with power and sleep button, TV buttons (channel up and down, volume up and down, and mute). This remote control-mouse should be battery operated.

- Sound-system expansion card with the following features:

  - Digital audio, specifically pulse code modulated (PCM) digital input.

  - MIDI port.

  - MIDI-controlled wave-table synthesizer.

  - Multiple analog and digital audio inputs.

Continues

**WebTV for Windows Minimum Hardware Recommendations
(Broadcast Client)** (Continued)

- Audio mixer and preamplifier that is software controllable and low noise.

- Multiple audio outputs.

- Sound-card functionality can be incorporated on the motherboard or on expansion cards for the broadcast client so that the sound card does not need to be a separate peripheral.

- Built-in microphone or a front-mounted microphone jack suitable for teleconferencing, education, karaoke, and other applications requiring sound input.

- Audio compression using the AC-3 algorithm for DVD compatibility.

- Infrared remote control capable of controlling consumer electronic devices.

scheduled, and, if necessary, purchased. Broadcast clients offer the convenience and ease of finding, selecting, and scheduling entertainment and information in one place, using one familiar interface.

Conclusion

By building on common, existing standards, WebTV for Windows and the Broadcast Architecture provide an evolutionary way for personal computers, set-top boxes, and other devices to support broadcast functionality. In the future, a common content standard, such as that proposed by the ATVEF, will make it easier for content producers — from local stations to production houses — to add value to their television programming. Although consumers will ultimately decide which interactive television devices they prefer and what types of enhanced content they are interested in, a flexible and robust architecture will allow new devices and improved content to find a consumer market.

Interactive Programming and the ATVEF

Data delivered over broadcast networks today — whether in the form of TV Crossover Links, interactive content, or stand-alone data feeds — will pave the way for the more advanced, informative, and entertaining content of tomorrow. A solid understanding of the issues involved — from embedding video in a Web page to synchronizing content with television programming — will serve you well as you enter the digital age of television.

N O T E

In this chapter, the words *client* and *receiver* are used interchangeably to refer to a device capable of displaying an Electronic Program Guide and of receiving and displaying television programming with interactive content.

Interactive Content Streams

An *interactive content stream* is a set of data files and triggers tied to video, transmitted using IP Multicast. Interactive content can take many forms:

- Simple text
- Images
- Recurring combinations of text and images, such as rotating advertisements
- Animated images
- Sound
- Links to Web content
- More elaborate content, such as interactive chat controls that enable viewers to discuss a show with other viewers

Any type of content that can be delivered over the Web can be used in an enhancement. An enhancement can incorporate functionality such as rotating content, hyperlinks, Java applets, and ActiveX controls.

An enhancement stream is composed of the following enhancement events:

- Announcements, which describe the IP address and port on which triggers will be sent for a particular enhancement.

- Triggers, which tell the client to perform particular actions.

- Data files, including the base page, which are either packages containing interactive content files or the interactive content files themselves. The data files are transferred using a file transfer protocol specially designed for unidirectional file transfer. Data files are stored to the interactive cache on the client. Triggers use the *bpc://* uniform resource locator (URL) syntax to refer to content stored in the interactive cache.

- Announcements, triggers, and data files are all sent on separate IP addresses and ports.

Receiving and Displaying Interactive Content and Video

To receive and display interactive content and video, three components are required:

- The enhancement filter. The announcement listener, a system service, loads the enhancement filter to receive and process enhancement announcements.

- An enhancement trigger control (referred to as the enhancement control), also hosted in a Web page, which receives interactive content (data files) and triggers. The enhancement control is instantiated through the following HTML OBJECT tag:

```
<OBJECT ID="EnhCtrl" CLASSID="clsid:3A263EF8-D768-11D0-911C-
00A0C91F37E3" WIDTH=0 HEIGHT=0></OBJECT>
```

- A video control, which is an ActiveX control hosted in a Web page that tunes a particular channel, displays it on the screen, and plays the accompanying audio. A Web page instantiates the control through an HTML OBJECT tag, as follows:

```
<OBJECT ID="Vid" WIDTH=100% HEIGHT=100% classid="clsid:a74e7f00-
c3d2-11cf-8578-00805fe4809b"></OBJECT>
```

Although the enhancement control is embedded in the page, it is invisible to the user.

Figure 13.1 shows the process flow for enhancements.

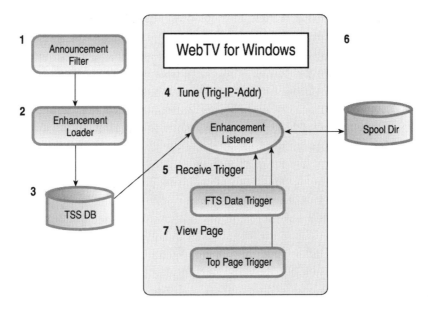

Figure 13.1 The process flow for enhancements.

First, the announcement filter receives the announcement. It passes relevant information to the enhancement loader, which then stores that information in the Electronic Program Guide database, TSS.MDB.

Enhancement Announcements

Enhancement announcements inform a broadcast client that a television show is interactive and provide details about the enhancements.

Announcements are based on the Internet standard Session Description Protocol (SDP). An announcement is made up of lines of text, with identifiers on the left of an equal sign and associated text on the right. An announcement can be stored as a text file until it is ready for broadcast. Table 13.1 describes a sample announcement.

On the client, the announcement listener, a system service, runs the enhancement announcement filter to receive and process enhancement announcements. Enhancement information is then stored in the Electronic Program Guide database. The presence of enhancement data in a show listing in the database indicates that the show is interactive. When a user tunes WebTV for Windows to a new channel, WebTV for Windows checks the database to see if the new show is interactive. If it is, and if the user has enhancements enabled, WebTV for Windows displays a special icon indicating that the show is interactive.

Table 13.1 A Sample Announcement

Example	Description
v=0	SDP version number, must be 0.
o=enhID 2 1 IN IP4 155.55.55.55	EnhID specifies a user identifier. 2 is the session identifier. 1 is the version identifier. 155.55.55.55 is replaced with the IP address of the server transmitting or encoding the content. As a whole, this field serves as an identifier for an enhancement.
s=Title	Contains the title for the enhancement.
c=IN IP4 233.17.43.44/3	Indicates the IP address on which triggers will be sent.
t=2208988801 2208990601	Start and finish time for an enhancement.
a=EnhID:{9E2E8B20-083E-11d1-898F-00C04FBBDEBC}	Identifies the announcement as an enhancement announcement (as opposed to some other type of announcement).[a]
m=data 17832 udp 0	Specifies the port used for sending triggers.

a. The value specified after EnhID is known as a UUID (universally unique identifier). For more information, see *http://www.ietf.org/internet-drafts/draft-leach-uuids-guids-01.txt.*

NOTE

The information passed to the enhancement filter through announcements specifies only parameters for the enhancements to come. This data does not contain actual content, such as enhancement HTML files. Enhancement files are broadcast to a user's computer separately from announcements.

There are four types of enhancement announcements:

- *Current announcements* refer to a show that is currently on.
- *Channel announcements* refer to a given channel.
- *Timeslice announcements* refer to a range of episodes.
- *Future announcements* refer to an episode that is on in the future.

The two most common announcements are current announcements and channel announcements because they are the most practical and easiest to use. They are described here.

Current Announcements

A current announcement specifies that the triggers broadcast on the specified IP address apply to whatever show (episode) the viewer is currently tuned to. The enhancement will be loaded in association with the current episode. If the episode ends at a certain time (for example, the show begins at 8 P.M. and ends at 9 P.M.), the enhancement will expire at the end of the time period and the viewer will no longer see it. To ensure that the viewer receives the content associated with a current announcement, you should transmit a current announcement at regular intervals during a broadcast. A current announcement is shown in Figure 13.2.

If a viewer tuned to this show in the middle of its broadcast, the viewer's computer might not have received the initial enhancement trigger at the beginning of the show. Current announcements provide a method for you to start an enhancement during a show.

Current announcements can also be used when a show's broadcast time is not known. For example, television programming and its enhancement stream, including enhancement announcements, might be recorded for later broadcast. Using current announcements ensures that the announcements work no matter when the show is broadcast.

A current announcement expires immediately; in other words, its expiration date is the same as its transmission date. This functionality ensures that the announcement listener receives again each broadcast of a current enhancement announcement. Otherwise, the default behavior of the Announcement Listener is to ignore duplicate announcements.

Current enhancement announcements use relative times to specify when the enhancement expires, rather than fixed times. When the enhancement filter receives a current announcement, some further computation and data gathering must be performed. The enhancement filter calculates the episode's end time and

Figure 13.2 A current announcement.

```
v=0
o=EnhAnn 1 1 IN IP4 155.55.55.55
s=EnhancementAnnouncements
c=IN IP4 233.17.62.1/3
t=2208988800 2208998800
a=EnhID:{9E2E8B20-083E-11d1-898F-00C04FBBDEBC}
m=data 18700 udp 0
```

passes the connection information to the internal Broadcast Architecture object that loads the episode into the guide database.

If a current announcement does not specify either a show reference for the enhanced episode or the PreloadURL that specifies the enhancement's base page, an internal Broadcast Architecture object gets this information from the enhancement control. When the enhancement information is complete, an internal object loads the enhancement data into the guide database.

Channel Announcements

A channel announcement contains information about an enhancement for the current channel. A channel enhancement enhances a particular channel. For example, MSNBC might create a channel enhancement that displays MSNBC-related content, such as which shows air next, news items, or sports scores. In this example, the channel enhancement is displayed whenever a viewer tunes to MSNBC. If an interactive show is broadcast over a channel that is enhanced, the viewer can choose to watch either the show enhancements or the channel enhancement.

Like current announcements, channel announcements expire immediately and can gather some enhancement information from the client they are sent to. A channel enhancement does not specify a start time. Typically, channel enhancements are displayed continuously whenever the channel they enhance is displayed.

A current channel enhancement assumes that the channel enhancement is associated with whatever channel the viewer is tuned to. A current channel enhancement announcement is the easiest announcement to use and the most likely to succeed because it does not require guide data on the client.

A sample channel announcement is shown in Figure 13.3.

Figure 13.3   A channel announcement.

```
v=0
o=davefe 2 1 IN IP4 155.55.55.55
s=MSNBC Ticker
c=IN IP4 233.43.17.32/3
t=2208988800 2208999900
a=EnhID:{9E2E8B20-083E-11d1-898F-00C04FBBDEBC}
a=EnhTime:Current Channel
m=data 17832 udp 0
```

Triggers

Triggers are notifications that are sent to broadcast clients at specific times during an interactive show. Triggers cause an action to occur on a client. The enhancement control receives the triggers, handles some of them directly, and passes others to the control's container, which is normally a Web page itself loaded by WebTV for Windows.

Each type of trigger sent to an enhancement control has a different format. However, all triggers are formatted as strings containing three parts: a *key* or *numerical identifier*, the *trigger data*, and a *checksum value*. The key is separated from the data by white space, typically a space or tab character.

The format of a trigger is as follows:

```
"Key TriggerData[Checksum]"
```

where *Key* is the numerical identifier, *TriggerData* is the trigger data, and *Checksum* is the checksum value.

For example, the following string might be transmitted to the client for a Nav trigger, which causes the browser to navigate to the specified page, which is stored locally in the interactive cache:

```
"2 bpc://MSNBC/default.htm[BA7E]"
```

This trigger causes the enhancement control to navigate to the MSNBC base page, *default.htm*. The *bpc://* URL syntax specifies that the content is located in the interactive cache (much as *http://* specifies that content is located on a remote Web browser).

The trigger topics listed in Tables 13.2 and 13.3 follow the trigger format used to specify a trigger in an enhancement stream—in other words, the trigger format using relative paths instead of Broadcast Architecture URLs and without the checksum value.

A number of basic types of triggers are shown in Table 13.2.

Table 13.3 provides further details on some of the individual triggers.

An FTS data trigger indicates the subdirectory in which to store an enhancement and the IP address and port on which files will be transferred. Here is a sample FTS data trigger, followed by a sample URL:

```
"1 <FTS> 233.43.17.17:17817&MyEnhancement"
```

The trigger indicates that all files received on the specified IP address and port should be stored in the *MyEnhancement* subdirectory.

Table 13.2   Basic Triggers

Key	Name	Description
0	Error	No action is taken.
1	Data	Receives data using the specified transfer protocol.
2 or 3	Nav	Displays a page. If a target is specified by, for example, using a FRAME or DIV tag set, the page is displayed in that target. (2 and 3 have the same functionality and have both been maintained for compatibility with earlier versions.)
4	Script	Runs the specified script.
6–999	Reserved	Reserved for future use.
1000 and up	UserTrigger	Sends a user-defined trigger event.

Data Files

Interactive content files are stored in the *interactive cache*, a local directory on the user's machine. The base page is the HTML page that resides at the top level or base of the enhancement pages loaded into the Web browser or into WebTV for Win-

Table 13.3   Individual Triggers, Their Uses, and Examples

Trigger Type	Description	Format
Navigation		
Top Page Navigation	"Home page" for enhancements	"2 <bpc://MyEnhancement/toppage.htm>"
Target Navigation	To navigate to a named target	"2 <itv.htm>[targ:LOGO_FRAME]"
Script	Execute ECMAScript (JScript) in the top page	"4 alert('Hi!');" "4 Navigate('VIEW_FRAME', 'http://www.microsoft.com');"
Data		
FTS	Starts listening for FTS data	"1 <FTS> 233.17.43.44:2000&MyEnhancement"
CAB	Unpacks CAB files	"1 <CAB> bpc://MyEnhancement/toppage.cab"

dows. Before WebTV for Windows can display an enhanced show, it must first navigate to a base page. The recommended way to display the base page is by using a trigger; however, the base page can also be specified as part of an announcement using a special tag called the *PreloadURL*.

Dependencies

Enhancement pages, like Web pages, are typically composed of several files. Some of these files must be downloaded for the enhancement page to display properly. Such required files are the enhancement file's *dependencies*. You must ensure that an enhancement's dependencies are stored on a broadcast client before that enhancement is displayed on the client. Otherwise, the user might end up viewing an incomplete enhancement and might perceive that the content is broken.

There are several strategies for handling dependencies:

- Transmit the dependencies and the base page together in a CAB file.

- Allocate broadcast bandwidth to download the dependencies repeatedly.

- Have the user explicitly download or install the dependency files, either from a Web site or from a portable medium such as a CD-ROM.

Contents of the Interactive Cache

When enhancement files are received on the client, they are stored in either the *spool folder* or the *base page folder*, both of which reside in the interactive cache.

The Spool Folder

The spool folder stores all enhancement files received during a broadcast. WebTV for Windows creates the spool folder during installation. The location of this folder is stored on a broadcast client in the following registry key:

```
HKLM\Software\Microsoft\TV Services\Interactive Cache
```

For each interactive show episode for which data is received, the enhancement control that receives the data creates a subfolder, called an *episode folder*, within the spool folder. The control gives the episode folder a unique name, for example "MyEnhShow.5." The control then saves the enhancement files for that show episode in the episode folder.

The Base Page Folder

The base page folder contains the HTML page that resides at the top level (base) of the enhancement pages loaded in the user's Web browser. The location of each enhancement's base page is stored in the guide database. When WebTV for Windows tunes to an interactive show, it retrieves this information and passes it to the show's enhancement control.

An enhancement control extracts path information from the base page. It then uses that path for the base page folder. If a base page is broadcast along with other enhancements for a show episode, then the base page folder is the same as the episode folder. However, the base page can also reside in some other folder on the broadcast client.

Navigating to an Enhancement

When an enhancement control receives a trigger to navigate to a file, the following process occurs:

- The control looks for that file in the episode folder (or in a subfolder of the episode folder if one is specified).

- If the file is not found there, the control looks in the base page folder. An episode can use enhancement files from the episode folder, the base page folder, or both.

- If the file is not found there, the enhancement control displays an error message if the control appears in Internet Explorer. The control does nothing if it appears in WebTV for Windows.

On a broadcast client, all data, including enhancements, is processed as a stream of digital data. Analog television signals are digitized before display. From this incoming stream, the video and audio data is extracted and sent to a video control. At the same time video is received by its control, enhancements and triggers are received by an enhancement control. An enhancement control is an ActiveX control that responds to enhancement stream events. Like a video control, the enhancement control is hosted in an enhancement page displayed by WebTV for Windows or by a Web browser.

Comparison of Windows 98 Interactive Television Implementation and the ATVEF Specification

This section describes the goals of the ATVEF specification and some of the differences between the WebTV for Windows implementation (as shipped in Windows 98) and the implementation proposed by the ATVEF. Many companies collaborated on a framework for supporting interactive television content based largely on existing Internet standards. In this way, the ATVEF specification is quite similar to the Windows 98 implementation of interactive television. As mentioned earlier, a second edition of Windows 98, still to be named at press time, is expected to provide full ATVEF support.

A goal of the creators of interactive television has been the development of a platform that can be supported across all television broadcast environments, including analog, digital, cable, satellite, or terrestrial formats. The preferred platform would utilize the huge base of tools, media, and knowledge that has developed for the Web. Although often called an "HTML-based" solution, this framework in fact builds on both HTML and several other components:

- The Internet Protocol (IP) is the primary transport for all data, with IP Multicast used over unidirectional links.

- The Session Announcement Protocol and Session Description Protocol (SAP/SDP) announces streams of interactive content.

- HTML and related data formats are the mechanisms for describing the presentation of graphics, text, video, and other multimedia features.

- Uniform resource identifiers (URIs) are the mechanism for referencing all multimedia elements, including television broadcasts and other content delivered over unidirectional links.

- ECMAScript and the Document Object Model (that is, JScript) for dynamic control of HTML content and the synchronization of HTML content to broadcast video.

- Multipurpose Internet Mail Extensions/hypertext transport protocol-style (MIME/HTTP-style) headers as the representation for content meta-data.

These six elements provide nearly all the services necessary to design and deliver compelling interactive television content. Only a handful of new elements are additionally required:

- A protocol for transporting content and related meta-data over unidirectional links using IP Multicast (in other words, an IP Multicast–based unidirectional HTTP).

- A specific URI scheme for describing television broadcasts.

- A specific URI scheme for describing content delivered over a unidirectional link (and therefore not available on demand).

- A mechanism for sending fragments of ECMAScript over a unidirectional link to specific pages on a client in order to trigger actions that synchronize those pages with the television broadcast.

Thus, the standard proposed by the ATVEF uses existing Internet standards where possible but innovates where necessary. It is based on technologies found in WebTV and WebTV for Windows, so both platforms remain good development and target platforms while an implementation of the ATVEF specification is developed.

The following are important elements of WebTV for Windows:

- Data is delivered via IP Multicast, which offers a standard transport mechanism on which to build higher level data delivery and synchronization functionality. IP Multicast can be delivered over all television broadcast formats, including analog, digital, cable, satellite, or terrestrial.

- Enhancements are simply HTML pages. HTML provides a framework, both on the Web and in WebTV for Window, to describe the presentation of multimedia content.

- SDP is used to announce enhancements. The announcements are transmitted on a well-known IP address and port.

- A forward error correction (FEC) algorithm facilitates recovery from lost or damaged data.

- Triggers are used to synchronize interactive content with television programming.

- HTML and other content is delivered by a unidirectional file transfer protocol.

- The mechanism for referencing delivered content is based on URLs.

- A trigger object is embedded in an HTML page expecting to receive triggers.

Here are the differences in the ATVEF implementation, as compared with WebTV for Windows:

- The syntax for embedding television in a Web page is slightly different, but, as with WebTV for Windows, an object tag is used to embed a video object.[1]

---

1. In the ATVEF specification, TV is embedded using syntax similar to the following: `<object data="tv:" width="60%" height="60%">` or `<img src="tv:" width=320 height=240>`.

- SDP announcements indicate the address and port for both triggers and data streams (rather than just for triggers). SDP syntax is expanded to address additional requirements (such as identifying the announcement as an enhancement announcement and tying the announcement to a particular television program).

- Triggers are based primarily on TV Crossover Links, which are specified in the Electronic Industries Association (EIA) standard EIA-746A. The only triggers supported are script triggers (which were the primary ones used in WebTV for Windows). All other triggers are handled by scripting. Also, the trigger object is specified slightly differently than the WebTV for Windows trigger object.

- Rather than sending a file transfer service (FTS) data trigger to initiate data reception, the data address and port are specified in the announcement. Although this reduces flexibility, it offers a simpler process for initiating reception of interactive content.

- Rather than grouping files together using cabinet (CAB) files, a multipart format known as multipart MIME is used instead. The multipart format, like CAB files, supports "all-or-none" delivery.

- The Unidirectional File Transfer Protocol (UFTP), based on the WebTV for Windows Broadcast File Transfer Protocol (BFTP), is used to deliver HTML and other content. The error detection and correction mechanisms remain the same, but the format of the headers is different (with BFTP, each transmission is preceded by a number of headers; with UFTP, each packet has header information preprended).

- A slightly different FEC algorithm, along with retransmission, is used to increase the reliability of data transfer.

- The naming scheme for referencing interactive content is based in general on the WebTV for Windows "bpc:" protocol but instead uses the protocol "uhttp:" (for unidirectional hypertext transfer protocol).

All of the features of the ATVEF specification are expected to appear in the next version of WebTV for Windows included with the next Windows 98 release and in WebTV set-top boxes around the same time.

CHAPTER 14

Server Overview

The case studies in Part 3 provide details of how particular networks created and delivered content to WebTV for Windows. This chapter provides a foundation for understanding those case studies: It offers an introduction to some of the software that will allow you to create and deliver interactive content and data broadcasts. Although such software is in its infancy, a familiarity with it now will help you determine what kind of functionality you'll need from software in the years ahead.

Broadcast Server

The components of the Microsoft Broadcast Server (the Broadcast Server is available with Microsoft NetShow Theater) enable you to deliver interactive content and broadcast data feeds. The Broadcast Server is designed to work with existing TV production and broadcasting facilities, thereby protecting and extending existing network investments. Initially, you can use the Broadcast Server with analog delivery networks by encoding data into the Vertical Blanking Interval (VBI) of analog TV signals.

- Because the Broadcast Server is designed specifically to deliver data to clients built on the Broadcast Architecture, you can easily leverage your existing investment in hardware and content production and authoring tools in the future. In particular, the Broadcast Server components use the Internet Protocol (IP) to encode and deliver data over networks that support IP Multicast.

- No major changes are required to start producing and delivering interactive content for digital television. By simply adding new software modules, it's possible to support a wide variety of encoding formats and broadcast networks. The Broadcast Router, in particular, makes this possible.

- During the transitional period — when many broadcasters will simulcast using analog and digital signals — the same content can be routed at regulated rates to the right transmission hardware. For example, the same interactive television programming can be simultaneously routed and broadcast to both VBI encoders (for analog broadcasts) and digital multiplexers used for satellite or digital TV broadcasts (for digital broadcasts).

Components of the Broadcast Server

The Broadcast Server consists of three components:

- **Broadcast Router.** The Broadcast Router forwards multicast or tunneled data to broadcast head-end hardware or to peer Broadcast Routers. The Broadcast Router supports address and bandwidth reservation via the built-in Address Reservation Service (ARS) and Bandwidth Reservation Service (BRS). Several types of broadcast hardware are supported by default, and additional hardware can easily be supported via pluggable virtual interfaces (VIFs).

- **Internet Channel Server (ICS).** The ICS service enables transmission of Web content specified by industry standard channels over broadcast and other multicast-enabled networks. ICS also enables delivery of files that are located on a network share or stored locally. Administrators configure ICS via a Microsoft Management Console (MMC) plug-in and specify Web content to broadcast using a database interface.

- **Interactive Television Authoring Tools.** The ITV tools are sample applications that make it possible to author and play HTML-based interactive television content. Interactive television content is typically displayed in association with the television signal. The enhancement tools enable authoring and transmission of both synchronized and nonsynchronized content. They include the *Enhancement Player*, a simple player for transmitting enhancements; the *Enhancement Author*, a sample postproduction editing tool; and the *Live Broadcast Editor*, which incorporates interactive content into a live broadcast such as a newscast or sports event. The enhancement tools also include reusable components, in the form of component object model (COM) objects, that allow third-party tool vendors to implement authoring and transmission capabilities in their own applications.

Figure 14.1 shows how the Broadcast Server components operate together:

- The Broadcast Router acts as the gateway between a variety of content server applications and head-end hardware. In this example, the Broadcast Router sends data to the VBI virtual interface, which then sends data

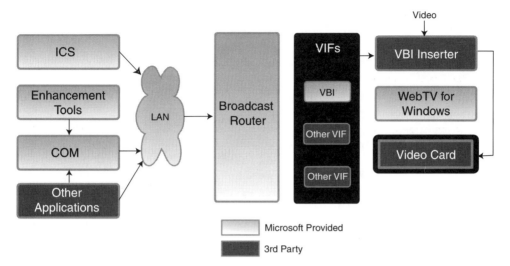

Figure 14.1   Diagram of the Broadcast Server components.

to a Norpak VBI Inserter. The Broadcast Router receives data over a local area network (LAN).

- The enhancement tools use COM objects, which are reusable software components, to gather interactive content, package it, and send it to the Broadcast Router.

- ICS collects intranet or Internet Web content over a network connection or from a local drive and then transmits that content to the Broadcast Router.

- Other content server applications, such as tickers or third-party content authoring tools, can use the COM objects or can independently send data via tunnels or IP Multicast to the Broadcast Router.

- You might use the ARS and BRS (which are part of the Broadcast Router) to allocate IP addresses and bandwidth for use by the various content server applications.

Broadcast Router System Requirements

- Windows NT 4 Server with Service Pack 3 (or later) installed
- Internet Explorer 4.01
- Windows NT 4 Option Pack 4
- A server with at least 50 megabytes (MB) of available hard disk space.

The Windows NT Service Advantage

The Broadcast Router and ICS run as Windows NT services. This offers three advantages, among a variety of others:

- They can be set up and managed through the Microsoft Management Console (MMC), a common console framework for management applications.

- They can be administered remotely, which means that a service running on one machine can be configured from any other machine running the right software and connected to the primary machine via a network.

- They can be configured to restart automatically when Windows NT starts, which means that no user intervention is required in the case of a power reset or machine restart.

In addition, the Broadcast Router requires a supported interface, such as the following:

- Intranets and Internet: A network card supported by Windows NT 4 using TCP/IP

- Analog video broadcast: A serial communications port connected to a supported VBI Inserter

The ARS (a separate Windows NT service accompanying the Broadcast Router) must be set up with one or more unique IP address blocks. These address blocks are leased for broadcasting content and cannot overlap address blocks used on other ARSs or multicast routers.

ICS Requirements

- Windows NT 4 Server with Service Pack 3 (or later) installed
- Internet Explorer 4.01
- Windows NT 4 Option Pack 4
- A server with at least 1 gigabyte of available hard disk space for content storage and at least 64 MB of memory

In addition, ICS requires Microsoft Access 97 and a connection to either a LAN or a multicast router connected via a network. A connection to the Internet is required in order to gather content from Internet sites.

Interactive Television Authoring Tools Requirements

The interactive television (ITV) authoring tools can run as shown in Table 14.1.

For all components, the following minimum computer configuration is recommended:

- 166-megahertz (MHz) Pentium processor
- 32-MB random-access memory (RAM)
- 1-gigabyte (GB) hard disk

Broadcast Router

Because the Broadcast Router, shown in Figure 14.2, is such a critical piece of software, several key issues are detailed here. Today, a number of TV networks, digital satellite networks, and TV production houses are already using the Broadcast Router. Using the Broadcast Router as the interface between a server network and a broadcast network has three key advantages:

- Content server applications, such as interactive television tools and ticker applications, can be written independently of a particular head-end hardware configuration or network type. This means that you can use the Broadcast Router now to transmit data over an analog television network and you can continue to use it with new digital TV head-end hardware in the future.

- The ARS and the BRS make it easy to allocate IP addresses and reserve bandwidth for a broadcast network.

- The Broadcast Router accepts data either through standard IP Multicast transmissions or through TCP/IP tunnel connections, which enables it to

Table 14.1 Platforms for Interactive Television Authoring Tools

Tool	Windows 98	Windows NT
Enhancement Author	X	
Live Broadcast Editor	X	
Enhancement Player	X	X

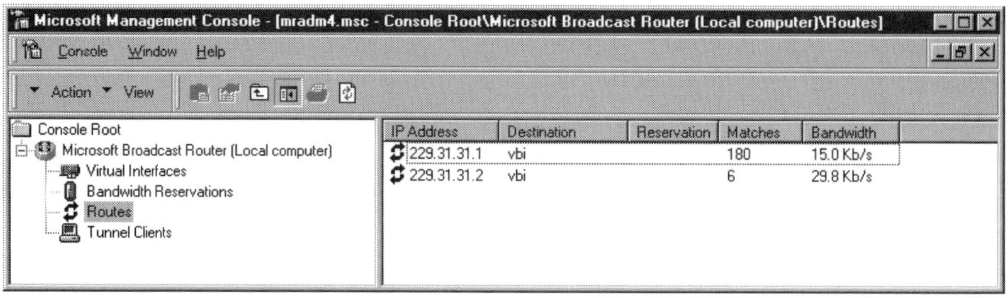

Figure 14.2 shows the Microsoft Management Console interface window with the following details:

```
Microsoft Management Console - [mradm4.msc - Console Root\Microsoft Broadcast Router (Local computer)\Routes]
Console   Window   Help

Action   View

Console Root
  Microsoft Broadcast Router (Local computer)
      Virtual Interfaces
      Bandwidth Reservations
      Routes
      Tunnel Clients
```

IP Address	Destination	Reservation	Matches	Bandwidth
229.31.31.1	vbi		180	15.0 Kb/s
229.31.31.2	vbi		6	29.8 Kb/s

Figure 14.2   The interface for configuring the Broadcast Router.

throttle content server applications so that they don't exceed the amount of bandwidth available.

Administrators can configure the Broadcast Router, the ARS, and the BRS via an MMC plug-in; applications can programmatically control the router through COM or remote procedure call (RPC) interfaces.

Multicasting and Tunneling

A content server application can send data to the Broadcast Router in two ways: by *multicasting* or by *tunneling*.

- With multicasting, content servers use IP Multicast interfaces to send data on a given IP address. The Broadcast Router passes these packets directly to the VIF for transmission. The content server is responsible for sending data at times and speeds that are acceptable to the transmission medium. For example, if the VIF is designed to send data to a device that inserts data in the VBI, the content server application must send the data at a rate slow enough for the VBI data inserter to keep up. In addition, if another content server application is using the same VIF, both content server applications must be designed so that they do not send too much data.

- With tunneling, applications use TCP/IP tunnels to transmit data to a Broadcast Router. A TCP/IP tunnel connects two applications and sends data packets within other data packets. Tunneling allows packets encoded with one protocol to be transferred using another protocol. In the case of the Broadcast Router, this data consists of IP Multicast packets destined for the VIF. The advantage of using a TCP/IP tunnel is that it gives the Broadcast Router an opportunity to send messages back to the content server application. These messages tell the content server application when it is sending too much data or sending data at the wrong time. In other words, the Broadcast Router can throttle the application sending data, depending on the amount of bandwidth available.

The advantage of multicasting is that applications do not have to be modified to use the Broadcast Router. The disadvantage is that if an application sends data too fast and not enough bandwidth is available, data will be lost. With tunneling, content server applications gain the benefits of flow control. However, the applications must use simple, but special, Broadcast Router application programming interfaces (APIs) to transmit data.

Internet Channel Server

Internet Channel Server (ICS) allows you to transmit industry standard channels over broadcast and other multicast networks. Initially, you might simply want to transmit links from your own Web site; later, you can expand to transmitting other content from the Internet as well. Although all content is received on the client Windows 98 machine, WebTV for Windows stores the content associated with only those channels to which the user has subscribed. The content is stored in the Internet Explorer cache and can be browsed off line.

Interactive Television Authoring Tools

Microsoft provides a number of sample tools that you can use to prepare the enhancements for an interactive TV show. The tools have two goals:

- Provide basic authoring functionality for the most common types of interactive content, to producers, broadcasters, and other content creators.

- Provide examples for third-party companies developing more refined and full-featured tools.

A detailed explanation of the use of these tools is beyond the scope of this book. However, here is a brief description of the tools:

- **Enhancement Author** creates a stream script — a file that synchronizes enhancement files with the main video broadcast of an interactive show.

- **Enhancement Player** is a lightweight tool for playing finished stream scripts. The Enhancement Player is shown in Figure 14.3.

- **Live Broadcast Editor** broadcasts enhancement files with the main video broadcast of a live interactive show.

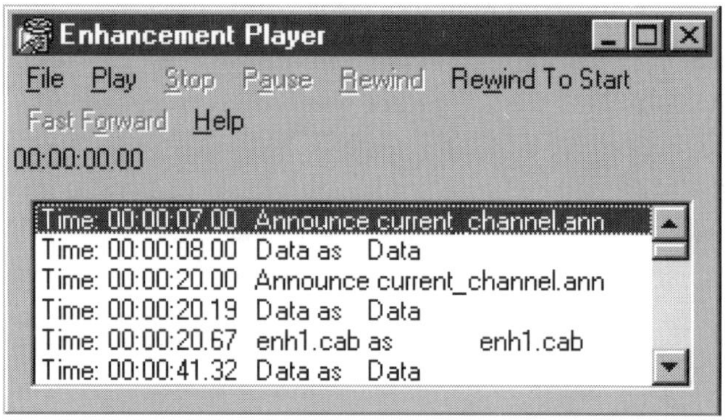

Figure 14.3 The Enhancement Player.

Choosing Tools

With the right server tools and network architecture, it's possible for producers and content creators to create exciting content and for broadcasters and networks to deliver that content. Keep in mind that many existing products, from Web servers (such as Internet Information Server, IIS) to hypertext markup language (HTML) authoring tools (such as Microsoft FrontPage), will also help you in creating and delivering interactive content. The tools you choose will vary depending on a number of factors:

- Where you are in the chain. Are you a creator of content (a television producer), a content deliverer (a network), or both?

- The type of service you want to offer. Do you want to offer a high-speed data broadcast service that delivers technical manuals or software, or do you want to deliver interactive television programming?

- The level of complexity involved in your service or content. Do you want viewers to chat on line and participate in polls while viewing your content, or is it sufficient to link them to a Web site? Are there commercial transactions involved that require underlying security and encryption mechanisms?

- The source of your content or data. Is your content coming from one location (a particular machine, for example) or from many locations (on a global corporate network, for instance)?

- The necessary frequency of your content delivery. How often is your content updated? Does your content rely on proprietary data feeds, databases, or protocols that could require the development of some custom software?

COM Objects

The ITV Authoring Tools are built on top of a set of reusable software components called *COM objects*, which are described here briefly for reference:

- **IPSend** sends file-based announcements, enhancement triggers, and FTS files to specified IP Multicast addresses.

- **WalkDocument** retrieves dependencies, targets, and script functions from a specified HTML file.

- **CAB object** creates and extracts cabinet (CAB) files.

- **File Transfer Service** (FTS) provides file transmission capabilities.

- **Announcement Generation Object** generates enhancement announcements.

Interactive Programming Suite

The Interactive Programming Suite (IPS) is a database-driven, template-based authoring system for creating basic interactive broadcasts. Microsoft makes IPS available on its Web site. The primary purpose of IPS is to offer an easy way for broadcasters and networks to produce and deliver simple, template-based enhancements. Producers can choose from a number of templates or add their own. Like the other authoring tools that Microsoft offers, IPS will not meet everyone's needs, but it will get you started in broadcasting interactive content.

IPS is based on three core components: the Live Content Wizard, the Live Content Manager, and the Live Content Stream Server.

Live Content Wizard

- Allows producers to design custom live pages for interactive broadcasts.
- Simple question-and-answer process.
- Users add backgrounds, station logos, advertisements, or other graphics.
- Users set up buttons that viewers will click to see the types of interactive content viewers want (such as news, sports, and TV listings).

Live Content Manager

- Main component of the IPS, the Live Content Manager is an easy-to-use, Web-based tool that allows a user to create, edit, and schedule interactive content.

- Provides for dynamic changes.

Live Content Stream Server

- Checks the Live Content Manager for live page content — new or updates.
- Collects the content.
- Packages the files into a CAB file.
- Transmits the CAB file as encapsulated IP Multicast data — also known as IP packets — to the Broadcast Server.
- Transmits the CAB file using IP Multicast.

Figure 14.4 shows one of the IPS templates.

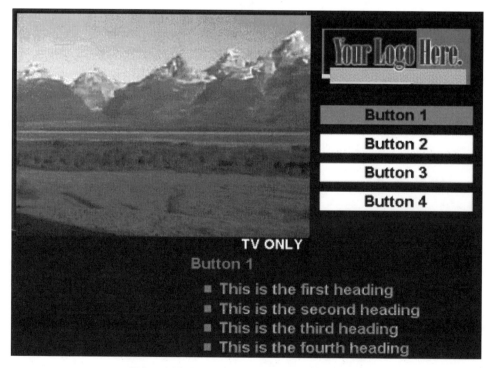

Figure 14.4   Screen shot of an IPS template.

Here are some details about the templates:

- TV image (upper left): Viewers can easily toggle to full-screen video or interactive view by clicking **TV Only**. The wizard templates give you a choice of upper left or upper right placements. The aspect ratio of the video image is always 4:3. The size of the video image will vary depending on the template used in the wizard and on the screen resolution chosen by the viewers.

- Advertiser logos (not shown): IPS allows you to import advertiser or promotional logos and schedule when they will be updated. These ads or promotions can also double as links to Web sites. They adhere to current Internet Advertising Bureau (IAB) standards. Wizard templates give you a choice of two sizes for advertiser logos: 125 ¥ 125 pixels and 234 ¥ 60 pixels.

- Station logos (upper right): You can make your station logo a part of a live page. The wizard templates accommodate station logos between 240 ¥ 118 pixels and 300 ¥ 70 pixels.

- Buttons (middle right): These display text or Web links (or both) when viewers click them. The wizard allows you to customize these buttons.

Templates

The fastest way to get on the air with interactive content is to use simple templates—whether you're enhancing a particular television show or a channel. Templates can include areas for branding and promotions and provide content that might be associated with any given show. Interactive content can be delivered in the form of separate enhancements—for example, where users can choose from separate enhancements provided by a show's producer, a network, or a broadcaster. Alternatively, different members of the food chain could work together to deliver more integrated content. Show producers can deliver content relevant to a particular show, while stations could deliver nonassociated content, such as weather radar images, traffic information, and news headlines. Networks could provide information about upcoming programs. With the right tools, all of these types of content can easily supplement the existing audio–video broadcast and turn it into a multimedia viewing experience.

If you're trying to decide whose tools to use, a quick look at the IPS feature set will give you an idea of what to look for in Microsoft and third-party tools. If you're designing your own content authoring tools, a brief look at the IPS feature set will help you determine what functionality is important to include in your own tool set.

- Content area (lower right): This is the information viewers see when they click one of the buttons. Using the Live Content Manager, you can enter headings, subheadings, and links to Web sites.

- Background: With IPS, you can import custom background images that reflect your station's look and feel. You can also choose a solid color for your background or one of dozens of textured backgrounds included in IPS.

The flow of data in the IPS is shown in Figure 14.5.

Testing

Initially, you will probably want to test broadcast services and interactive content over a LAN before sending data over an actual broadcast network. Your network must be capable of transmitting IP Multicast packets. If you don't already have a corporate network, or if you want to set up a basic network to be used only for test-

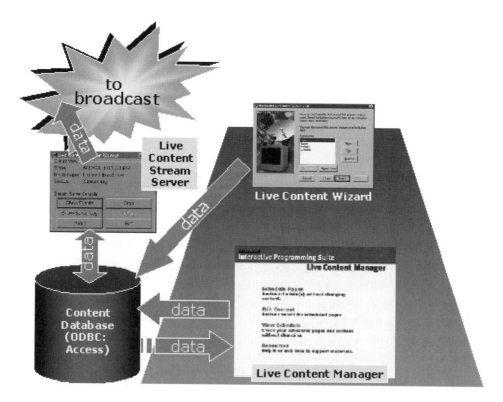

Figure 14.5 IPS components diagram.

ing of broadcast services, simply use an Ethernet hub and Ethernet cables to connect a server machine and a client WebTV for Windows machine together. (Don't connect the machines directly to each other — provide a hub in between the two machines. Alternatively, you can use a network crossover cable if you are using only two machines.)

Figure 14.6 shows a sample test configuration.

To confirm that multicasting is working and that your network is properly configured, you can use some simple multicast utilities included with the Broadcast Server. These utilities allow you to send and receive test data.

Your First Enhancement

In the future, tools such as the Interactive Programming Suite and Digital Renaissance's T.A.G. authoring tool (discussed in Chapter 10) will make it easier to create and broadcast interactive content. The following information is provided for reference but will give you an idea of the components of an enhancement.

Controls

An enhancement uses two controls:

- Enhancement video control, which displays the video in WebTV for Windows

- Enhancement listener control, which receives enhancements

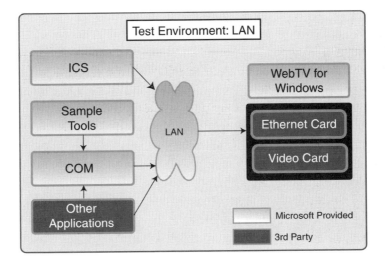

Figure 14.6 Test LAN configuration.

The code for the two controls is shown in Figure 14.7.

To receive triggers, you will need a small amount of script that listens for the enhancement control trigger event. In Visual Basic Script, the command utilizes the following code:

```
Sub BPCOC_Trigger( ID, TriggerString, CkSum )
```

The same command in JavaScript uses this code:

```
SCRIPT LANGUAGE="JavaScript" FOR="BPCOC" EVENT="Trigger(ID, TriggerString,
CkSum)"
```

After you have created your enhancement pages, you will want to transmit the pages and triggers to display them. The Enhancement Player provides a basic way to broadcast preauthored interactive content. The Enhancement Player makes use of a simple file called a *stream file* to determine what announcements, files, and triggers to transmit.

Stream File

The stream file performs the following tasks:

- Transmits an announcement
- Tells the client to initiate a file transfer reception
- Sends down a CAB file containing an enhancement
- Sends a trigger to unpack the CAB file
- Displays an HTML page from the CAB

Figure 14.7   The HTML for controls used to display video and receive interactive content.

```
<DIV ID="id_vid" STYLE="position:absolute; top:0; left:0;">
    <OBJECT ID="vid" classid="clsid:a74e7f00-c3d2-11cf-8578-
00805fe4809b"
    BORDER=0 VSPACE=0 HSPACE=0 ALIGN=TOP HEIGHT=100% WIDTH=100%
STYLE="position:absolute; top:0; left:0; width:100%; height:100%">
    </OBJECT>
</DIV>

<OBJECT ID="EnhCtrl" CLASSID="clsid:3A263EF8-D768-11D0-911C-00A
C91F37E3" WIDTH=0 HEIGHT=0>
</OBJECT>
```

Figure 14.8 shows a sample stream file.

Figure 14.8   A sample stream file.

```
Bandwidth = 9600 ;
ShowLength = 00:04:00.00 ;

// Sends the current channel announcement:
00:00:07.00  announce ( "current_channel.ann" ) ;

// This data trigger informs the client of the address & port
// that will be used for transmission of files.
// It is repeated once every 2 seconds until 18 seconds into the show
// to ensure that the receiving computer gets the message about where
to
// place the files it receives.
00:00:08.00  Data (" 0.0.0.0:0&EnhSample" "FTS") repeat 00:00:02.00
until 00:00:18.00 ;

// Another instance of an announcement and an FTS trigger.
// The announcement tells the computer tuning in late what IP
addresses
// to listen to for receiving assets, and the FTS trigger tells it
what
// folder to deposit the assets in. It's best to couple these two
events
// just prior to a download event.
00:00:20.00  announce ( "current_channel.ann" ) ;
00:00:20.19  Data (" 0.0.0.0:0&EnhSample" "FTS") ;

// Downloads the first CAB file, whose contents will appear in the
// target region of the screen defined in default.htm as enhframe1.
00:00:20.67  "enh1.cab" ;

// Unpacks the CAB file enh1.cab so that it is ready to be triggered
after
// default.htm is triggered.
00:00:41.32  Data (" enh1.cab" "CAB") ;

// Displays the file enh1.htm (and its one dependency) in the
// target region of the screen defined in default.htm as enhframe1.
00:01:30.00  Nav ("enh1.htm" "enhframe1") only onefile ;
Here is the announcement referenced in the stream file:
v=0
o=UserID 1 1 IN IP4 144.44.44.44
```

Continues

Figure 14.8   A sample stream file. (Continued)

```
s=Current Channel Enhancement Sample
c=IN IP4 0.0.0.0/3
t=220890001 2208912001
a=EnhID:{9E2E8B20-083E-11d1-898F-00C04FBBDEBC}
a=EnhTime:Current Channel
m=data 0 udp 0
```

In the future, better tools of production-grade quality will make it much easier for you to broadcast interactive content in the future. Once you have tested your enhancement over a LAN, you are ready to encode the content in the VBI, using the Broadcast Router and a supported VBI inserter.

Recording to Tape

After you have fully authored a show, you will probably want to record the enhancements and video to a Betacam tape. Regular VHS tapes do not store the enhancement data or other data contained in the VBI (except for closed captioning). Therefore, you must use a Betacam for enhancements to be stored. Storing enhancements on tape provides the following advantages:

- You don't have to worry about synchronizing the content to the video later.

- The data does not have to be maintained separately from the video.

- No server equipment is required (other than the tape player) to send video with enhancements.

You always want your master tape to provide high-quality video. To maintain video quality, therefore, you will normally want your source video to be a Betacam tape (as opposed to a regular VHS tape) as well. Connect the audio straight from the source tape player to the one you are recording to. Connect the video from the output of the source player to the VBI inserter, then from the output of the VBI inserter to the input of the recorder.

On the recorder, make sure you configure the options (normally under the Advanced menu) such that the VBI lines you are recording on are set to "through." This means that VBI will be recorded on these lines. If you are simply making a copy from one tape to another, make sure the player is also set to "through" so that it will transmit the data stored on the tape.

TV Crossover Links

Although Microsoft provides some rudimentary tools for encoding TV Crossover Links, it is preferable to contract with a company that already does closed caption encoding to encode the links.

Hardware

This section details some of the common hardware components useful in creating and delivering interactive content:

- **VBI inserter.** A VBI inserter is used for encoding digital data into an analog television signal. The Broadcast Router currently supports Norpak TES3 and TES5 VBI inserters. TES3 inserters are used in analog head ends, while TES5 inserters are used in digital head ends. The Broadcast Router communicates with the VBI inserter via a serial cable. In the future, the TES4, which has an Ethernet interface, might be supported as well, along with other VBI inserters. Many TV stations already have VBI inserters installed — for use with the Nielsen ratings system, for example. Some VBI inserters also support TV Crossover Link insertion.

- **Betacam deck.** A Betacam deck is required for encoding VBI data to tape, Ethernet hub, or crossover link cable. To connect a server and a client machine together, use either an Ethernet hub in between them or a network crossover cable. Both are commonly available.

- **Video feed source.** When initially testing with a VBI inserter, you need to provide a video feed. (For a TV station, this is the station's actual video feed.) For a test configuration, you can use a VCR, laser disk, or some other constant video source. Alternatively, you can use a demodulated TV channel, but you run the risk that the channel already contains some data, so a reliable, data-free video feed is preferable.

- **Modulator.** In a test configuration, you have two options. Take the output of the VBI inserter and hook it directly to a WebTV for Windows computer, or modulate the video onto a channel using a commonly available modulator.

Service Guidelines

Producing and delivering interactive content or data services is much like running an actual television broadcast or maintaining a Web site. Service, as used here, refers to the delivery of interactive content or broadcast data, whether on a full-time basis or with a particular show. We have developed the following service guidelines, based both on experience with our own internal test network and on our work with broadcasters, networks, and other content producers. You should follow these service guidelines to ensure the quality of your own service or content:

- Institute a clear set of policies for your service.

- Have a clear chain of command that identifies key personnel in the event that the service goes down or interferes with the video feed. Keep pager and cell phone contact information readily available.

- Secure access to your content server and bridge machines. Even though you might be "testing" VBI data or content services, you don't want unfamiliar users modifying the machine or the services running on it.

- Maintain a log that includes the date, the time, and a description of action taken and the name of the person who acted. If the service stops running or if you receive support calls, you can refer to the log to see what was changed and by whom. All changes (including machine reboots, restarts of services, and so on) should be noted in the log.

- Keep close to the machine a clear set of instructions on how to restart the service components. The instructions should be available in printed form near any servers as well as in electronic form.

- Clearly label all machines with machine name, IP address, brief description of purpose, and contact information.

- Label all connections going in and out of the server machines.

- Maintain a wiring diagram that shows how to reconnect cables in case they are disconnected or servers need to be moved.

- Check your server at least twice a day. If you can't provide a full-time employee to run the service, implement a round-robin service policy. Certain individuals are responsible for checking the service on specific days or at specific times. For example, one individual can check the service in the morning when arriving at work; another individual can check in the afternoon before going home.

- Set up a client machine next to or near the content server so that you can see the experience that the user is having and make sure that content is being received properly.

- When changing content, upgrading software, or modifying the service, test the changes over a LAN or over a nonlive VBI inserter before implementing the changes on the production server.

- Before making changes, notify potential users and administrators of the changes that will take place ahead of time. Don't surprise your administrators or your end users. If you need to take any of your servers down for maintenance and do not have backup equipment in place, set a specific time for when service will be resumed. Note the predicted time and the actual service restart time in the log.

Looking ahead, many changes will be necessary before authoring and delivery tools are fully functional and robust. But remember — we're in the very early stages of developing interactive content and the tools to create it. Among Microsoft products, certain tools — ICS, the ITV Authoring Tools, TV Crossover Link tools, and IPS — clearly need to be better integrated with each other. Alternatively, and ideally, third-party toolmakers will use the tools Microsoft has created as learning instruments and then build production-grade tools in the future.

CHAPTER 15

Using Television in Your Web Site

This chapter briefly describes how to use television as part of a Web site. You can

- *Determine whether WebTV for Windows is installed.*

- *Allow users to launch WebTV for Windows tuned to a particular channel.*

- *Integrate video functionality directly into a Web page, using the WebTV for Windows video control.*

You can also add these capabilities to Windows 98 applications — you could even build your own television viewing application.

Determining Whether WebTV for Windows Is Installed

Before integrating TV viewing capabilities into your Web site, you must determine whether WebTV for Windows is installed on the user's system. To do so, check for the existence of an ActiveX control installed by WebTV for Windows. For example, the code in Figure 15.1 checks for the video control (which loads only if video can be properly displayed — that is, if the viewer has the hardware and software necessary to display television).

The code performs the following steps:

- Determines whether Windows 98 is installed on the client by checking the value of *navigator.userAgent.indexOf("Windows 98")* to see if it is greater than –1.

- Uses the *isReady* function to determine whether the video control is loaded or not. If the *readyState* property of the video control equals 4 (a reserved Internet Explorer value), then video can be properly displayed on the user's system. Visual Basic Script is used to provide adequate error handling if the control is not available.

The video control is referenced using the ID idVidOcx1, but you could use any ID. The CLASSID attribute is the globally unique identifier (GUID) of the video control.

Figure 15.1 Determining whether the WebTV for Windows video control is installed.

```
<HTML>
<BODY STYLE="background-color:black; color:white;">
<DIV STYLE="position:absolute; width:240; height: 180;
     top:15; left:15; border:1px solid white">
     <OBJECT ID="idVidOcx1" WIDTH="100%" HEIGHT="100%"
          CLASSID="clsid:31263ec0-2957-11cf-a1e5-00aa9ec79700">
          Microsoft Windows® 98 with WebTV for Windows Required
</OBJECT>
</DIV>
</BODY>
</HTML>

<SCRIPT LANGUAGE="VBScript" TYPE="text/vbscript">
Function isReady(myObj)
     isReady=False
     On Error Resume Next

     If myObj.readyState <> 4 Then
          isReady=False
     Else
          isReady="True"
     End If
End Function
</SCRIPT>

<SCRIPT LANGUAGE="Javascript" TYPE="text/javascript">
     var iCurrentChannel = 7;
     var bIs98 = navigator.userAgent.indexOf("Windows 98") > -1;

     if (bIs98)
          if(IsReady(idVidOcx1))
               document.idVidOcx1.Tune(3,iCurrentChannel,-1,-1);
</SCRIPT>
```

The video control's GUID is 31263ec0-2957-11cf-a1e5-00aa9ec79700. This attribute enables the Web browser to obtain the location of the video control from the registry.

Launching WebTV for Windows from Your Web Site

The TV URL syntax (TV://) lets you launch WebTV for Windows from your Web site.[1] Table 15.1 shows how the value that follows the syntax causes WebTV for Windows to tune to a particular channel.

---

1. In the future, the TV:// syntax will cause video to be embedded in the Web page, according to the standard proposed by the Advanced Television Enhancement Forum (ATVEF).

Table 15.1 Use of the TV Syntax[a]

Statement	Example	Description
TV://channel_number	Tv://32	Tunes to channel 32
TV://network_call_letters	Tv://NBC	Tunes to the local NBC affiliate
TV://station_call_letters	Tv://KOMO	Tunes to channel number associated with KOMO

a. Two different syntax styles (TV: and TV://) are equally valid. The syntax is not case sensitive — TV:, tv:, and other variations will all work, as will TV:MSFT, TV:msft, and mixed upper- and lowercase usages.

Here is an example in hypertext markup language (HTML):

```
<a href="tv://NBC">Watch NBC</a>
```

When the user clicks the specified text, WebTV for Windows is launched:

- If WebTV for Windows is already running, it will tune to the specified channel in full-screen mode.

- If network or station call letters are specified, WebTV for Windows looks up the channel number corresponding to the call letters. This allows WebTV for Windows to tune to the channel in the local program guide database. If the user doesn't have any programming information, or if no call letters are found that match those specified, WebTV will simply launch to the last selected channel.

NOTE

The TV:// URL syntax is supported through the combination of a special registry setting installed by WebTV for Windows and command line parameters of the TVX.EXE program. If WebTV for Windows is not installed, clicking the link might result in an error dialog in your browser. Therefore, when including a TV: link in your Web site, you should either determine that WebTV for Windows is installed or indicate that the link is available only to WebTV for Windows users.

Alternatively, end users can type *tv:* plus the desired channel number directly into the edit box of the Run command (for example, *tv:7*). They can also create shortcuts on the desktop, as shown in Figure 15.2.

Figure 15.2   A WebTV for Windows shortcut on the Windows 98 desktop.

Embedding Television Video in Your Web Page

You can embed television video directly in your Web pages. Two controls are available:

- The **video control** (vid.ocx) should be used in stand-alone Web pages that are loaded in a Web browser and not loaded in WebTV for Windows or in Windows 98 applications. The video control supports properties for setting input devices and channels. The video control is referenced using the CLSID *31263ec0-2957-11cf-a1e5-00aa9ec79700*.

- The **enhancement video control** (msepg.ocx) should be used in pages that will be loaded in WebTV for Windows. WebTV for Windows sets the channel and input devices for this video control. The enhancement video control is referenced using CLSID *a74e7f00-c3d2-11cf-8578-00805fe4809b*.

The following statement embeds the control itself in the page:

```
<OBJECT ID = "idV1" STYLE = "width:100%; height:100%;"
  CLASSID = "clsid:31263ec0-2957-11cf-a1e5-00aa9ec79700">
</OBJECT>
```

By placing the control inside a <DIV> tag, as demonstrated in the following statement, you can gain greater control over the size and position of the control:

```
<DIV STYLE="position:absolute; width:40; height:30;
  top:15; left:15; border:1px solid white">
  <OBJECT ID = "idV1" STYLE = "width:100%; height:100%;"
    CLASSID = "clsid:31263ec0-2957-11cf-a1e5-00aa9ec79700">
    Microsoft Windows® 98 with Web TV for Windows Required
  </OBJECT>
</DIV>
```

Tuning the Video Control

Next, you will want to tune the video control to a particular channel and resize the video, as shown in Figure 15.3.

- The variable *iCurrentChannel* contains the channel to tune to, and *iTuningSpace* contains the tuning space.[2] The variable *bIs98* uses the *userAgent* string to determine whether the page is running on a Windows 98 machine.

- The script then tests whether the page is running in Windows 98 and whether the video control is properly instantiated. If the video control is properly instantiated, the script sets a global event handler for the *window.onresize* and *window.onload* events so that the script can later adjust the video to a size corresponding to that of the window.

Figure 15.3   Tuning the video control.

```
<SCRIPT LANGUAGE="Javascript" TYPE="text/javascript">
var iCurrentChannel = 7;
var iTuningSpace = 3;
var bIs98 = navigator.userAgent.indexOf("Windows 98") > -1;

if (bIs98 && isReady(idV1)) {
  window.onresize = sizeVideo;
  window.onload = sizeVideo;
  document.idV1.Tune(iTuningSpace,iCurrentChannel,-1,-1);
}

function sizeVideo() {
  var iHt = document.body.offsetHeight-41;
  var iWi = document.body.offsetWidth-51;
  if (iHt < 0) iHt = 0;
  if (iWi < 0) iWi = 0;
  if ((iHt * (4 / 3)) > iWi) {
    idV1.style.height = iWi / (4 / 3);
    idV1.style.width = iWi;
  }
  else {
    idV1.style.width = iHt * (4 / 3);
    idV1.style.height = iHt;
  }
}
</SCRIPT>
```

2. A tuning space is a set of nonoverlapping channels that are all available through the same type of physical channel tuner, such as an analog television tuner. A broadcast client with multiple tuning devices can provide channels from multiple tuning spaces.

- Finally, the script tunes the television channel. When the browser loads the page, the *onload* event is immediately fired, causing the *sizeVideo* function to be called. This function maintains the 4:3 aspect ratio of the video, which is the normal ratio viewers are used to seeing on television sets. The additional reduction in width and height (–41 and –51) accommodates the screen real estate used by the status bar in the browser window and between the video control and the edge of the browser window.

Looking Ahead

This chapter has provided a brief look at how to add television functionality to your Web site. Here are some other ideas to pursue in the future:

- **Displaying video on the desktop.** Windows 98, with Active Desktop, allows HTML pages to be displayed on the desktop. You can easily set up Active Desktop to display a Web page containing the video control embedded in it. Broadcasters, networks, or shows could offer desktop themes that include video.

- **Designing your own TV viewing application.** With the components of the Broadcast Architecture, it's easy to design your own personalized TV viewing application or environment. You can use Web pages or design a full-fledged application using Visual Basic or another development tool.

- **Setting reminders from a Web page.** WebTV for Windows can remind viewers about particular programs. An obvious way to capitalize on this functionality is to allow users to set reminders from the Web site of a particular network, station, or show.

CHAPTER 16

Everything Else You Need to Know about Enhancements

The information in this chapter is specific to the first version of WebTV for Windows. You will find it of value after you decide to create, produce, and broadcast interactive content. (If you're not yet at that point, you might want to return to this chapter at a later date.) The utilities and controls described in this chapter are available in one or more of the following places:

- *Broadcast Architecture Software Development Kit (SDK)*
- *Broadcast Server (a part of NetShow Theater)*
- *Microsoft's Web site (*www.microsoft.com*)*

Testing the End-to-End Setup

Before using enhancements or other data services, you should test the delivery and receipt of data with some simple test utilities. Use the utilities *wsend* and *wlisten*, end to end, to confirm that you have the underlying network set up properly before trying enhancements. Using wsend, first create a tunnel to the Broadcast Router. Choose a packet size under 1400 bytes. You might also want to use wsend on the addresses you choose for enhancements to confirm that the addresses are being properly forwarded by the Broadcast Router before sending enhancements.

Beacon

To ensure that you are reliably sending and receiving data, you should leave a "beacon" transmitting on a fixed Internet Protocol (IP) address using the wsend utility. A good address to use is 224.1.1.1 port 1000 at a low bit rate and a packet size of 400 bytes. (Remember to set the router up to forward this address.) With this configuration, you can always run wlisten on the client and know whether data is making it through the system successfully. (An interesting and useful application for the future would be one that scans all channels for the beacon and reports which channels are transmitting data.)

Replication

If you need to supply the same data to two separate video feeds, you can transmit data from a single router machine to two Vertical Blanking Interval (VBI) inserters. For example, you have a primary and a backup video feed and want to send data to both without having to change any software configurations, cabling, or machines. In this case, set up the router service to have two virtual interfaces (VIFs) with identical bandwidths (and identical bandwidths specified in the VBI inserters). Then configure the Broadcast Router to transmit data on IP addresses over both VIFs.

Redundancy

If your greatest concern is a possible failure of the router machine, set up the highest degree of redundancy with two completely separate routers, both configured to forward the same routes to their respective inserters. In this configuration, either set up your content server applications to tunnel to both routers or use multicast only.

IP Multicast Addresses

Some common addresses for enhancements are as follows (the beginning numbers are the IP address; the numbers after the colon are the port):

- Announcement IP: 227.37.32.6:22706

- Trigger IP: 233.43.17.32:17832

- FTS IP: 233.43.17.33:17833

Whether sending enhancements over a local area network (LAN), over the VBI, or over some other transport, it is important to use unique addresses for each set of enhancements. In general, it is a good idea to have applications transmit data on separate addresses. Moreover, when transmitting multiple enhancements simultaneously over one VBI feed, you must use a separate set of addresses for file and trigger transmission for each enhancement.

Configuring Client Announcement Addresses

You can add additional IP address–port combinations for Announcement Manager to listen on. For example, if you want to do testing but don't want to have everyone on your network matching announcements you send, add in your own announcement address–port and then use that address and port in the Enhancement Player or authoring tool.

To determine whether you are receiving announcements in Windows 98, you can use the built-in Announcement Manager UI component, located in *C:\Program Files\TV Viewer\annui.exe*. If you are receiving announcements, the # *Matched* count for the Enhancement Filter will increment.

For testing purposes, whether over a LAN or over a VBI inserter, it is best to use your own announcement address. As noted earlier, the Announcement Listener listens for announcements on a set of addresses specified in the registry. If you use an announcement address other than the default addresses specified in the registry, only your system will see the announcements. To view, change, or add announcement addresses, use the registry editor (regedit), and browse to *HKLM\Software\Microsoft\TV Services\Announcements*. For example, you might add the key Webcast7, with address 227.37.32.7:22707. After adding or changing addresses in the registry, you will need to restart Announcement Listener for the changes to be reflected. You can do this by launching annui.exe, selecting Exit and Halt service, and then restarting, or simply by rebooting.

N O T E

Make sure to specify the new announcement address in your authoring tool or in the announcement if you choose an announcement other than the defaults in the registry.

If you are testing over the VBI, the data (announcements, triggers, and files) is received only when you are tuned to the channel on which the data is being broadcast. When testing over a LAN, the data will be associated with the channel the viewer is currently tuned to, as it is not arriving over a particular channel but rather over a separate network. Thus, if you are tuned to a channel other than the channel you want to enhance, the enhancements will still appear on that channel.

Before You Start Testing Enhancements

In order to provide program guide data and enhancement information, WebTV for Windows uses data stored in the local program guide database. Before doing any enhancement testing, it is a good idea to make a backup copy of the program guide database (C:\Program Files\TV Viewer\tss.mdb). If you have successfully received an enhancement, the enhancement title will appear in the "I" drop-down menu available from the WebTV for Windows banner, which can be displayed by pressing F10.

Enhancement Cache and File Transmission

To support Internet security zones, the client implements a pluggable protocol called *bpc://*. Similar to the http:// protocol used for Web addresses, it allows the installed bpc:// protocol to provide files stored locally to Internet Explorer (IE) rather than have those files come from the IE cache.

All files to be transmitted as enhancements must be stored locally on the server — they can't be referenced from a network drive or referenced as a uniform resource locator or URL (http://) on the Web. The current enhancement engine does not allow files to be received into the IE cache. Files are received into the bpc:// enhancement cache, which is located at C:\Program Files\TV Viewer\interactive cache. The bpc:// cache allows the enhancement engine to utilize the IE security features while making sure that files are not prematurely deleted from the cache by IE garbage collection. To determine whether the client is properly receiving enhancements, you might want to browse to this directory and watch the files being received in Windows Explorer. In addition, during enhancement testing, you can manually delete subdirectories and files from this directory when you want to restart a test.

Replacing Files and Timeout Values

In the current version of the client, you can't replace files that have already been received.

Enhancements support two timeout options, after which the enhancement expires:

- **Announcement Expiration.** The announcement contains the title of the enhancement and the time for which the enhancement is valid. After the specified time, the enhancement item will be removed from the list of enhancements available for the channel or show being watched and the user will no longer be able to gain access to it. This expiration time does not remove any of the content (files) associated with the enhancement from the user's hard disk.

- **FTS Trigger Timeout.** Trigger (1 "<FTS> Address:Port&Subdirectory[& timeout]"). This timeout value, explained in detail later, specifies the time after which the files will be removed from the user's hard disk.

If you are transmitting a channel enhancement, it is possible to work around the limitation of not being able to delete previously received files. You should cycle through a list of directory or file names over the course of a certain time period (say several days) and then restart the cycle, because garbage collection will have gathered the files by the time you reuse the names.

Alternatively, it is possible to write a lightweight control that would allow you to replace or rename files through scripting. Check Microsoft's Web site to see if such a control has been made available.

NOTE

Garbage collection on the client occurs only when a tune occurs — that is, when

- An episode boundary is crossed (if guide data is present and one show ends and another begins).
- The user changes channels.
- WebTV for Windows is restarted.

If the user does not have guide data and does not change channels, garbage collection will not occur.

Commonly Asked Questions

Q. How do I replace files I have already transmitted to the client?

A. It is not possible to delete files already received by the client in the first version of WebTV for Windows. A future version may fix this problem.

Q. How do I receive triggers more reliably?

A. Triggers, unlike data transmitted using the file transfer service (FTS), have no built-in redundancy other than the underlying error correction implemented by the North American Basic Teletext Standard (NABTS)–VBI transport layer. Therefore, you should transmit each trigger twice to ensure that the client receives it.

Q. How do I determine whether a file has been received so that I can reference it from my hypertext markup language (HTML) pages?

A. A simple control allows you to make this determination; you will need to transmit the control as part of your enhancement.

Q. When should I use CAB files and how do I create them?

A. Use cabinet (CAB) files as much as possible to save on file transfer overhead, to utilize compression, and to keep your files and their dependencies together.

Q. My server application is sending data and the client is receiving data on some addresses but not others. What should I do?

A. A common mistake is to start transmitting data using a given application without setting up the corresponding route in the Multicast Router.

Known Issues and Bugs

NOTE

Some of the bugs noted here have workarounds or are fixed in Windows 98 service packs. This section documents the known issues and bugs that exist in WebTV for Windows as shipped in the original release of Windows 98.

- The second octet in the multicast IP address used over the VBI must be less than 128. For example, 224.127.x.x works but 224.128.x.x fails.
- Files cannot be replaced in the bpc:// enhancement cache.
- Enhancement garbage collection occurs only on a tune and it is possible that, if the user does not change channels and does not have guide data, a tune will never occur.
- Ideally, all enhancement server applications should automatically create routes so that addresses don't have to be entered both in the server application and in the router.

Useful Utilities

The following section describes a number of useful utilities. They are categorized by type:

- IP Multicast–Router utilities
- VBI-related utilities
- Enhancement utilities

IP Multicast–Router Utilities

The following utilities are useful for testing IP data transmission.

wlisten

The utility wlisten is a simple IP Multicast listener. It lets you save specific multicast groups that you are interested in. When you join a multicast group, a green icon appears if the operation was successful. The display is refreshed every second and displays the packets that have been received. Optionally, you can view the contents of the packets or collect stats (these work only with the stream that wsend.exe sends out) for packets lost, errors, and so on. The "Errors" column is valid only if you are collecting stats. For more details on stats, see wsend.exe.

wsend

This utility sends known data either via IP Multicast or via a tunnel. If you wish to examine and confirm the transmission of these packets, use wlisten.exe to do so.

MCTunnel

This simple utility receives IP Multicast packets and forwards them via a tunnel to a Multicast Router host. Note that a static queue can be configured to fit the needs of the multicasting host. For example, if the sender transmits multicast packets in bursts that exceed the bandwidth reservation on the Multicast Router or exceed the maximum bandwidth of the VIF, MCTunnel will queue these packets internally and transmit them to the Multicast Router. The read buffer size and the number of packets in the queue are configurable but are not preserved from session to session. MCTunnel works on Windows NT and Windows 98.

ipstat

Ipstat is a console utility that prints out the IP addresses and ports on which multi-cast data was recently received over the VBI. Ipstat will work on Windows 98 only with the WebTV for Windows component installed. Ipstat will also list the time at which data was last received on each address or port.

> **N O T E**
>
> Because of reception errors, ipstat will occasionally report erroneous addresses. Look at the times listed — if data has not been received for a long time on a particular address, that address is more likely than others to be an erroneous address (although it is also possible that data transmission simply stopped on that address).

VBI-Related Utilities

The following utilities resolve issues related to NABTS–FEC and closed-caption data reception.

Scope

The scope utility is similar to a standard video scope and allows the user to view graphically the waveforms of individual VBI lines. This allows the user to verify that the capture filter is functioning and helps identify which lines carry data in the video signal.

When VBI data is present, the scope presents a graphical view of any line from 10 through 21. The scope supports two waveform windows to allow viewing of two lines simultaneously.

The scope application provides a simple user interface for monitoring the video, changing channels, and switching video sources. Some basic channel-changing controls are present, and two buttons expose the property sheets of the TV Tuner and the ATI Crossbar.

> **N O T E**
>
> The scope application builds a filter graph similar to the graph that WebTV for Windows would build. However, it adds the scope filter along with the other standard codecs to the consumers of captured VBI information.

VBIScan

VBIScan is a utility that presents status information from the VBI core components. There are three categories of status information: NABTS–FEC groups detected, VBI lines with NABTS waveforms detected, and VBI lines with closed-caption waveforms detected.

To obtain a list of current NABTS/FEC Group IDs detected, click the NABTS–FEC Reader button. The Group IDs and respective Bytes and FEC Buffers read will be presented in the list box directly above the NABTS-FEC Reader button. The list is cumulative and can be reset at any time by clicking the Clear button below the list box.

Enhancement Utilities

The following utilities provide functionality that can be useful when delivering and displaying interactive content. You might want to deliver these controls over the VBI as part of your enhancement. The best way to do this is to put the control itself in a signed CAB file (if it is not already in such a form) and then include the signed CAB file as part of your enhancement CAB file. On the receiver side, viewers will receive the CAB file and be shown the standard IE security dialog asking whether they would like to install the control. Note that if IE already trusts the signature on the CAB file containing the control (Microsoft, for example), the control will simply be installed with no prompting. Moreover, once the control is installed, the user will not be prompted again.

CacheCtrl

CacheCtrl supports three functions that did not make it into the initial WebTV for Windows release. The following functions act on the bpc:// cache:

- RenameURL(strSourceURL as String, strTargetURL as String) — renames the source file to the target file. If the target exists, it is replaced.

- ExistURL(strURL as String, bRetVal as Boolean) — determines whether the specified file exists.

- GarbageCollect() — causes enhancement cache garbage collection to occur.

Figure 16.1 shows the HTML for using the CacheCtrl control.

InTVView

InTVView allows you to determine from script in a Web page whether your content is being displayed inside WebTV for Windows (rather than inside stand-alone IE).

Figure 16.1   An HTML page that uses the CacheCtrl control.

```
<HTML>
<HEAD>
<TITLE>Enhancement Test Case</TITLE>

<SCRIPT language="VBScript">
Sub Test0_OnClick()
     CacheCtrl.RenameURL "BPC://test/page1.htm",
"BPC://test/page2.htm"
End Sub

Sub Test1_OnClick()
     CacheCtrl.ExistURL "BPC://test/page2.htm", bRet
     MsgBox bRet
End Sub

Sub Test2_OnClick()
     CacheCtrl.GarbageCollect
End Sub
</SCRIPT>
</HEAD>
<BODY>
     <INPUT TYPE="Button" VALUE="RENAME" ID="Test0">
     <INPUT TYPE="Button" VALUE="EXIST" ID="Test1">
     <INPUT TYPE="Button" VALUE="GC" ID="Test2">
     <OBJECT id="CacheCtrl"
         classid="clsid:69FCE094-E9C2-11D1-AE95-00C04FBBDEBC"
     >
     </OBJECT>
</BODY>
</HTML>
```

This can be useful for determining which video control you use, for example, or for showing different content based on the context in which you are running. Figure 16.2 provides a sample page that shows how to use the control.

stpushch

This control provides a lookup function for station call letters when provided with a channel number. To do this, it automatically uses the locally stored guide database (tss.mdb). You must have guide data in the database for the control to work.

Here is the HTML that instantiates the control:

Figure 16.2 Using the InTVView control.

```
<html>
<head>
<title>Untitled Normal Page</title>
<meta name="GENERATOR" content="Microsoft FrontPage 1.1">
</head>

<SCRIPT LANGUAGE="JavaScript">
<!-- hide away...
function hello()
{
     foo1 = myObj.IsControlContainedByTvViewer;
     alert('Are we inside TV Viewer ? = ' + foo1 );
}
// End of hide away.. -->
</SCRIPT>

<BODY leftmargin=0 topmargin=0 onLoad="hello()"; onClick="hello()";>
     <OBJECT
          ID="myObj"
          CLASSID="CLSID:730D3051-AD2E-11D1-B334-00A0C96F72A7"
     >
     </OBJECT>
</BODY>

</html>
```

```
<OBJECT ID = "idP1" STYLE = "display:none; width:0; height:0;"
  CLASSID = "clsid:C501A64E-44A4-11D1-9156-000000000000"
  CODEBASE =
  "http://webtv.microsoft.com/activex/stpushch.cab#version = 1,0,0,1">
</OBJECT>
```

Notice the inclusion of an inline style to help define the control's appearance. The control has no visible interface. It provides several subroutines and functions, including the following:

Subroutines

SetManualUpdate(ManualUpdate As Boolean) —Sets the manual update state.

SetPushChannel(CallLetters As String, ChannelNumber As Long, TuningSpace As Long) — Sets the default data channel (the channel that WebTV for Windows tunes to when you are not watching TV but want to receive data).

- Functions

GetCallLetters() As String — Gets the call letters for the current push channel.

GetChannelNumber() As Long — Gets the current channel number.

GetManualUpdate() As Boolean — Determines whether channel content is updated manually or automatically.

GetTuningSpace() As Long — Determines the current tuning space.

IsBPCEnabled() As Boolean — Determines whether the client has the WebTV for Windows components installed.

ResolveCallLettersFromChannel(TuningSpace As Long, ChannelNumber As Long) As String — Returns a string containing call letters based on a channel number and tuning space.

ResolveChannelFromCallLetters(CallLetters As String, TuningSpace As Long) As Long — Returns a channel number given call letters and a tuning space.

ResolveChannelFromNetwork(Network As String, TuningSpace As Long) As Long — Given a network name and a tuning space, returns the associated channel number.

The subroutines have no return value, whereas the functions do. Figure 16.3 shows a sample page that uses the control.

Figure 16.3   An HTML page that uses the stpushch control.

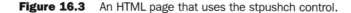

```
<HTML>
<HEAD>
<STYLE TYPE="text/css">
  BODY, TD {background-color:black; color:white; font:8pt verdana}
</STYLE>
</HEAD>

<BODY>

<OBJECT ID = "idP1" STYLE = "display:none; width:0; height:0;"
```

Figure 16.3 (Continued)

```
  CLASSID = "clsid:C501A64E-44A4-11D1-9156-000000000000"
  CODEBASE = "http://webtv.microsoft.com/activex/stpushch.cab#version
= 1,0,0,1">
</OBJECT>
<TABLE ID="myTable" RULES=ROWS>
  <CAPTION><B>Results of stpushch</B></CAPTION>
  <TR><TD>Testing...</TD></TR>
</TABLE>
</BODY>
</HTML>
<SCRIPT LANGUAGE="VBScript" TYPE="text/vbscript">
Function isReady(myObj)
  isReady=False
  On Error Resume Next
  If myObj.readyState <> 4 Then
    isReady=False
  Else
    isReady=True
  End If
End Function
</SCRIPT>
<SCRIPT LANGUAGE="Javascript" TYPE="text/javascript">
var iCurrentChannel = 7;
var iCallLetters = "KIRO";
var iTuningSpace = 3;
var bIs98 = navigator.userAgent.indexOf("Windows 98") > -1;
var x = window.setTimeout("start()", 1000);
function start() {
  var sTemp = "";
  if (bIs98 && isReady(idP1)) {
    sTemp = sTemp + "Setting push Channel to '" + iCallLetters +
        "', Channel " + iCurrentChannel + "..." + "<BR>";
    idP1.SetPushChannel("KIRO", iCurrentChannel, iTuningSpace);
    sTemp = sTemp + "Setting the update to MANUAL..." + "<HR>";
    idP1.SetManualUpdate(true);
    sTemp = sTemp + "Current Push Channel (Call Letters): "
      + idP1.GetCallLetters() + "<BR>";
    sTemp = sTemp + "Current Push Channel (Channel Number): "
      + idP1.GetChannelNumber() + "<BR>";
    sTemp = sTemp + "Manual Update is set to "
      + idP1.GetManualUpdate() + "<BR>";
    sTemp = sTemp + "The Tuning Space ID is "
      + idP1.GetTuningSpace() + "<BR>";
```

Continues

Figure 16.3   An HTML page that uses the stpushch control. (Continued)

```
    sTemp = sTemp + "IsBPCEnabled returns "
        + idP1.IsBPCEnabled() + "<BR>";
    sTemp = sTemp + iCurrentChannel + " has the call letters "
        + idP1.ResolveCallLettersFromChannel(iTuningSpace, iCurrentChan-
nel) + "<BR>";
    sTemp = sTemp + iCallLetters + " is on channel "
        + idP1.ResolveChannelFromCallLetters("KIRO", iTuningSpace) +
"<BR>";
    sTemp = sTemp + "PBS is on channel "
        + idP1.ResolveChannelFromNetwork("PBS", iTuningSpace) + "<BR>";
    }
    else {
      sTemp = "Microsoft Windows® 98 with Web TV for Windows Required"
    }
    myTable.rows(0).cells(0).innerHTML = sTemp;
  }
</SCRIPT>
```

A sample of the output for the preceding page is shown in Figure 16.4.

VBI Inserter Overview

This section describes the details of a Norpak VBI inserter, which the Broadcast Server supports by default. Other inserters are available from other companies. However, many stations and networks already have Norpak inserters installed. For analog networks (most cases), order a TES3; for digital head ends order a TES5. Both of these use a serial interface to transmit data from the computer to the inserter. In the future, Microsoft plans to support the TES4, which has a LAN inter-

Figure 16.4   Sample output from the page that uses the stpushch control.

```
Settings push Channel to 'KZZZ', Channel 7...
Setting the update to MANUAL...
Current Push Channel (Call Letters): KZZZ
Current Push Channel (Channel Number): 7
Manual Update is set to true
The Tuning Space ID is 3
IsBPCEnabled returns true
7 has the call letters KZZZ
KZZZ is on channel 7
PBS is on channel 9
```

face. If ordering a TES3 or TES5, order the inserter with at least one NABTS module and with closed captioning enabled.

If you do not have an inserter, you can test enhancements over a LAN.

Setting Up a Norpak Inserter

Settes is a DOS-based program provided with the inserter that allows you to configure the inserter. To use settes, depress the Load button on the front of the inserter using a paper clip or pen for 5–10 seconds while powering on the inserter. After the lights stop flashing, run settes. If you get a "carrier not detected error, repeat the process, but hold the load switch in longer and make sure the cable is securely connected between the computer and the inserter. Using settes, turn hardware handshaking on. Turn BERT lines off. Broadcasters typically allocate two to five lines for data transmission. If you are setting up a test environment, you might want to mimic a typical broadcast environment by using lines 14–17, both fields. To determine which NABTS address to use, look at Table 16.1; if you are unsure which address to use, use 0x8F0. For baud rate, use a baud rate that will at least match the number of lines you are using (average baud rate is 9600 baud per line). Therefore, for two lines, use 19,200; for three lines, uses 28,800; for four lines, use 38,400; and so on.

NOTE

If you install the Broadcast Router software and then want to reconfigure the inserter, you must first stop the router software to free up the component object model (COM) port. See the section on Multicast Router for more information on how to reconfigure the inserter.

NOTE

The baud rate in the inserter VIF for the Multicast Router and the baud rate configured in the inserter must match. If they do not, you might notice a flickering red–green status light on the front of the inserter, which indicates an error.

Setting Up a Modulator–Video Feed

You must provide a video feed into the inserter. For a television station, this is your actual video feed. For a test setup, use a VCR, laser disk, or some other constant video source. You can use a tv channel, but this is risky (that channel could already

Table 16.1 Recommended NABTS Addresses

Group ID	Description
0x800	Data content created by individuals and placed within the footage of original shows
0x810	Data content created by individuals and placed in the advertisement portion of the footage of original show.
0x820	Data content created by production companies and placed in previously finished shows
0x830	Data content created by production companies and placed in the advertisement portion of previously finished shows
0x840	Data content created by broadcast syndicates and placed in syndicated shows
0x850	Data content created by broadcast syndicates and placed in the advertisement portion of syndicated shows
0x860	Data content created by television networks and placed in shows that the networks broadcast
0x870	Data content created by television networks and placed in the advertisement portion of shows that the networks broadcast
0x880	Data content created by individual television stations and placed in shows that those stations broadcast
0x890	Data content created by individual television stations and placed in the advertisement portion of shows that those stations broadcast
0x8A0	Data content created by local cable companies and placed in shows broadcast from those companies' cable head ends
0x8B0	Data content created by local cable companies and placed in the advertisement portion of shows broadcast from those companies' head ends
0x8C0–0x8EF	Unused
0x8F0–0x8FF	Unused

be inserting data), and so a known empty video feed is best. Take the video out of the inserter and run it through a modulator. You can get inexpensive modulators from Home Automation Systems or a professional quality modulator from General Instruments (M6II is recommended). You can also run the video directly from the inserter to the composite input of the video card in the computer.

NOTE

If you have a scope available, you might want to look at the output of the inserter to confirm that data is being inserted and that the data is not interfering in any way with the video signal.

Conclusion

This chapter has provided a look at some of the details you need to be familiar with to start producing your own enhancements. The chapters in the third part of the book let you see how several companies have put this information to use in enabling their own interactive broadcasts.

Technical Case Studies

The four case studies in this section show how various companies are putting interactive television to use today. Previous chapters have talked about high-level business and architecture goals. These chapters describe what's really involved in creating and delivering interactive content. Here you'll read about everything from user interface and content design issues to network configurations and HTML coding.

I picked NBC, MSNBC, Tribune, and Home & Garden in part because I've worked closely with the members of their technical staffs and because they offer a wide variety of experiences. These companies have also been some of the most aggressive in delivering interactive content and are all broadcasting today.

- NBC has been producing interactive content for more than 2 years, focusing primarily on show-related enhancements. As a content producer (news, sports, and entertainment shows such as *Saturday Night Live*), NBC also acts as a content production house.

- Tribune Broadcasting owns stations in major cities throughout the United States. Tribune brings a wide variety of media assets to the table — from newspapers to Web sites to television stations — that they were able to leverage in producing their interactive feeds. The case study provides an excellent example of how stations can add significant value to their programming.

- The MSNBC case study offers a unique look at creating and deploying channel enhancements for an all-news station. A relatively new network, MSNBC was able to leverage its strong Web presence, technical resources, and media assets to build its interactive service. The case study focuses on MSNBC's channel enhancement — an enhancement that isn't tied to specific shows but rather provides an interactive viewing environment to users throughout the day.

- The Home & Garden/TV Food Network/Do-It-Yourself chapter examines several up-and-coming cable networks whose "how to" focus made them ideal interactive programming candidates.

NBC Case Study

Jonathan Boltax, Manager and Producer,
NBC Enhanced Broadcast Group,
with David Feinleib, Microsoft

w w w . n b c . c o m / e t v

Chapter 4 described the genesis and philosophies of NBC's Enhanced Broadcast Group (EBG). This chapter demonstrates the implementation of enhancements during interactive broadcasts. Although the 1998 U.S Open golf tournament is used as the prime example, this chapter also describes enhanced broadcasts of Saturday Night Live, NBA on NBC, NFL on NBC, *and* Homicide: Life on the Street.

This chapter evolved from interviews with Jonathan Boltax in New York in June, 1998. All of the experiences, ideas, and information that made this chapter possible came from Jonathan and his group. Hence, throughout the chapter, where "we" is used, it refers to Jonathan and his staff at the NBC Enhanced Broadcast Group.

The Interactive Content Evolution

Initially, in 1996 we created content for nose-to-screen environments. This suggests that viewers are watching the enhanced broadcast at a desk and sitting directly in front of the screen. In early 1997, we changed our content initiatives to create content visible in a couch-to-screen environment, which meant the text and graphics had to be visible from 10 feet away. This stems in part from the proliferation of set-top and cable boxes that enable enhanced TV.

In considering how to design your content, keep three things in mind:

- Are you creating for a TV-device or a PC-device? How will the device be used in the home?

- With the formation of the ATVEF (Advanced Television Enhancement Forum), cross-platform content is becoming a reality. Content developers now need to be cognizant of creating content that will be displayed on television screens as well with technologies such as WebTV Plus and advanced analog and digital cable boxes.

- The viewing experience is more enjoyable if the content is larger, easier on the eyes, and simple to use.

Making Statistics Graphical

For sports such as basketball or football, our plan was to create an enhanced experience that would make viewers feel as if they were at the game. We wanted viewers to have a scoreboard and all the ancillary information that is available to any fan at an arena. Depending on the sport, we provided real-time game statistics, the updated game score, as well as other game-related statistics. However, this focus on data cluttered our screen with numbers. Again, it is important to note that the viewer could turn off the enhancements at any time.

In later broadcasts of football and basketball, we began to display statistics and numbers graphically (Figure 17.1). We wanted to change the experience from viewing content at your desktop to viewing content from your couch. A graphical display became the method for showing data in a form that was more accessible than raw numbers. However, we ultimately settled on a compromise: We allowed users to access numbers in raw as well as graphical form.

Enhancements have evolved significantly, from a slide show–like presentation seen in early broadcasts such as the 1996 Summer Olympics and the 1996 NFL season to a highly interactive presentation with choice and user feedback as the key. It became a better user experience if we provided three to five clear and intuitive broadcast-related enhancements. If the users interacted with only one of those, we felt that was a successful enhancement. In our latest iteration of the 1997–1998 NBA enhancements, we provided a cornucopia of elements, including a graphical display of statistics, a statistics feed, and targeted Web links.

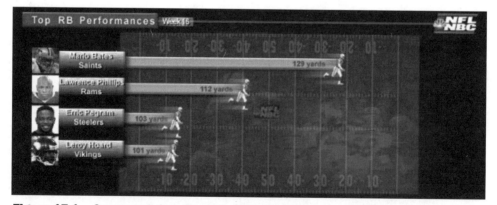

Figure 17.1   Screen grab from *The NFL on NBC* (1996) interactive broadcast using Intercast 1.6 technology. Credit: Keith Wichowski.

1998 U.S. Open Golf

The enhanced broadcast of the 1998 U.S. Open golf tournament was designed so that the viewer would not experience a data barrage. Golf as a sport has some unique qualities. Most people who watch football on television will not play football the next day. On the other hand, adults often play golf. Therefore, we wanted the interactivity to be a player's companion. One of the most compelling types of content was the Hole-by-Hole information (Figure 17.2). The enhancement presented the viewer with a combination of value-added information and animation in a concise and useful way.

The enhanced portion of the golf broadcast had six content areas and two or three different templates per area. (Although polling and chat areas are normally standard features in our broadcasts, they were not part of this particular one.) The six content areas were

- **Hole-by-Hole:** Fly-throughs of each hole, expert analysis, and hole statistics
- **Bios:** Golfer's biographies, statistics, tour victories, earnings, and position among all other golfers for the year

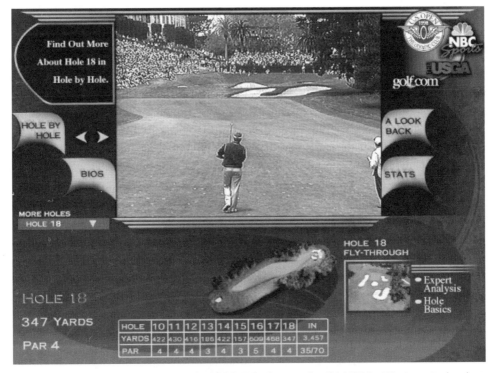

Figure 17.2   Screen grab from the 1998 U.S. Open using WebTV for Windows technology. Credit: Jennifer McCoy.

- **A Look Back:** Brief stories about last year's U.S. Open and previous winners

- **Stats:** Charts and graphs about players' performances

- **Chip Shots:** Facts and figures about the golf course, tournament, and the event

- **Ticker:** Scrolling news stories and a leader board that is updated throughout the tournament.

Information in the six content areas was downloaded and displayed at the appropriate time within the broadcast. For example, when Payne Stewart prepared his shot from the first tee, the viewer received Hole-by-Hole information about hole one, along with Stewart's biography. A spinning golf ball in the upper-left corner of the interface, followed by a text alert and a flashing graphic, indicated that content was available. These images were a nonintrusive way to alert the viewer to the presence of interactive content. This nonintrusive graphic (Figure 17.3) became the ubiquitous symbol for new content throughout the broadcast. The accompanying text prompt for the U.S. Open enhancement is shown in Figure 17.4.

Preparation

- To outline and plan their work, team members watched previous U.S. Open broadcasts from the NBC tape library and learned more about the broadcast flow. Understanding the broadcast flow is critical to planning the enhancements.

- The team then met with the television graphic artists to coordinate our enhancement design with the look and feel of the television show. All templates were a seamless extension of the television output.

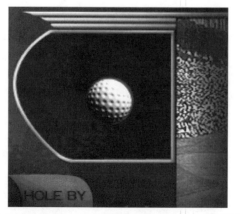

Figure 17.3   Spinning golf ball from the 1998 U.S. Open using WebTV for Windows technology. Credit: Jennifer McCoy.

Figure 17.4 Text prompt from the 1998 U.S. Open using WebTV for Windows technology. Credit: Jennifer McCoy.

- The final step in preparation was to break down a broadcast golf tournament into six content areas that we wanted to target, areas that we felt would be important to the individual viewers. These six content areas are listed earlier.

At this point, we were in our second week of production and we followed the template cycle described in Chapter 4.

Bringing New Meaning to the Term "Armchair Quarterback": The Digital Playbook

The Digital Playbook has evolved significantly as a content element. It was first used under the heading "How Do They Do That?" in the Olympics broadcast. As gymnasts flipped and divers dived, we took images of the athletes. We edited the sequence and an expert analyzed the event. This became an always accessible enhanced version of an instant replay with commentary.

By the time the NFL season arrived, we had refined the process and renamed it "The Digital Playbook." The Digital Playbook featured a frame-by-frame analysis of offensive plays and their execution by each team, with commentary by an NBC analyst. Variations from the Digital Playbook are shown in Figure 17.5 and Figure 17.6.

In the latest NBA iteration, using dynamic HTML (DHTML), the Digital Playbook evolved again. We provided viewers with a digital console that enabled them to

Figure 17.5   Example of Digital Playbook variation from the 1996–1997 *The NFL on NBC* interactive broadcasts using Intercast 1.6 technology. Credit: Keith Wichowski and Jennifer McCoy.

choose plays that each team used. The viewers used buttons such as play, rewind, and fast forward to see how these plays were executed.

Mixing Content Delivered through the VBI and Content Requested over the Web

Our philosophy to date has been to provide 80% of the interactive experience through content delivered over the Vertical Blanking Interval (VBI). The remaining 20% of the content comes to the viewer through the Web and a back channel. You will often use the same information that is on the Web but will need to repackage it

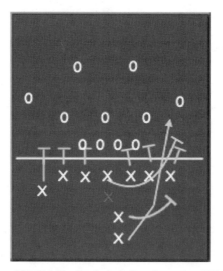

Figure 17.6   Example of Digital Playbook variation from the 1997–1998 *The NFL on NBC* interactive broadcasts using Intercast 1.6 technology. Credit: Keith Wichowski and Jennifer McCoy.

in a way that does justice to the medium of interactive television. However, you should not ignore existing Web properties. They can be leveraged in areas that provide two-way capabilities such as chat and commerce. Moreover, you can use links to the Web to create what we call a "customized browsing experience." This experience features links that give the users targeted, enhanced content rather than directing them to the home page of a given site or some other general home page that isn't really associated with the television content itself

We are also moving toward a model that designates two distinct areas in the interface (although they might take up more than one physical space on the screen): one dedicated to Web links and the other to enhanced content delivered over the VBI. In Figure 17.7, the stage lights to the left and right of the television image are dedicated to enhanced content, and the navigation bar at the bottom provides links to the *Saturday Night Live* Web site.

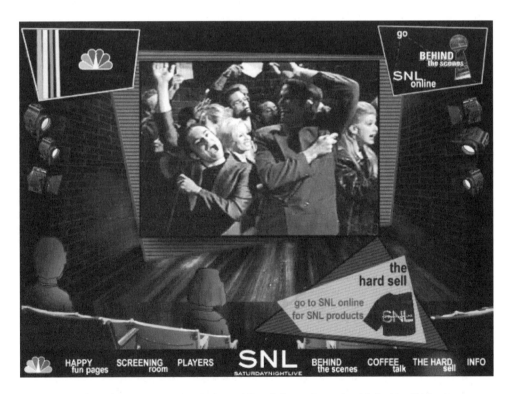

Figure 17.7   Bottom navigation bar providing links to *Saturday Night Live* Web site: screen grab from *Saturday Night Live* using WebTV for Windows Technology. Credit: Jennifer McCoy.

Technical Side Note

The innovations that have advanced Web technology have had an equally significant impact on interactive television in an analog ITV environment. Since we
began in 1996 several key technologies have advanced the presentation of interactive television content: GIF animations,[1] which have put movement in the
medium; DHTML and the enhanced interface, which has created a look and feel
similar to those of a CD-ROM, data binding, which allows us to display statistics
easily, and Cascading Style Sheets and JavaScript.

DHTML and data binding were both introduced in Internet Explorer 4. Figure
17.8 provides an example of how data binding was used for the Chicago Bulls'
roster. This shows how we manage a large amount of text data in an easy-to-
update format. The accompanying text file is shown in Figure 17.9.

Figure 17.8   HTML code.

```
<OBJECT ID="home" WIDTH=100 HEIGHT=51
    CLASSID="CLSID:333C7BC4-460F-11D0-BC04-0080C7055A83">
    <PARAM NAME="FieldDelim" VALUE=",">
    <PARAM NAME="DataURL" VALUE="home.txt">
    <PARAM NAME="UseHeader" VALUE=True>
</OBJECT>

<TABLE id="hdataform"
style="position:absolute;visibility:visible;top:0;left:-200;
                          height:25;width:100"
                       WIDTH=100%>
<TR>
<TD> <INPUT id="hnum" TYPE="TEXT" DATASRC="#home" DATAFLD="NUM"> </TD>
</TR>
<TR>
<TD> <INPUT id="hplayer" TYPE="TEXT" DATASRC="#home" DATAFLD="PLAYER">
</TD>
</TR>
<TR>
<TD> <INPUT id="hpos" TYPE="TEXT" DATASRC="#home" DATAFLD="POS"> </TD>
</TR>
<TR>
<TD> <INPUT id="hht" TYPE="TEXT" DATASRC="#home" DATAFLD="HT"> </TD>
</TR>
<TR>
```

1. GIF animations refer to image files that contain multiple images, resulting in an animated image assembled out of a
number of static images.

Figure 17.8 (Continued)

```
<TD> <INPUT id="hwt" TYPE="TEXT" DATASRC="#home" DATAFLD="WT"> </TD>
</TR>
<TR>
<TD> <INPUT id="hdob" TYPE="TEXT" DATASRC="#home" DATAFLD="DOB"> </TD>
</TR>
<TR>
<TD> <INPUT id="hfrom" TYPE="TEXT" DATASRC="#home" DATAFLD="FROM">
</TD>
</TR>
<TR>
<TD> <INPUT id="hyrs" TYPE="TEXT" DATASRC="#home" DATAFLD="YRS"> </TD>
</TR>
</TABLE>
```

Successful Content Elements

In addition to the successful Digital Playbook and the golf fly-throughs, we created a number of other value-added enhanced broadcast content elements:

- **Live statistics.** We've provided live statistics for NBA and WNBA games, often converting the statistics into graphs and charts to make the raw data more interesting.

Figure 17.9 Data binding from *The NBA on NBC* interactive broadcasts, using WebTV for Windows technology. Credit: Ethan Holda.

```
NUM,PLAYER,POS,HT,WT,DOB,FROM,YRS
23,Michael Jordan,Guard,6-6,216,2/17/63,North Carolina '84,12
9,Ron Harper,Guard,6-6,216,1/20/64,Miami (Ohio) '86,11
33,Scottie Pippen,Forward,6-7,228,9/25/65,Central Arkansas '87,10
91,Dennis Rodman,Forward,6-6,220,5/13/61,Southeastern Oklahoma State
'86,11
7,Toni Kukoc,Forward,6-11,232,9/18/68,Croatia '93,4
25,Steve Kerr,Guard,6-3,181,9/27/65,Arizona '88,9
1,Randy Brown,Guard,6-2,191,5/22/68,New Mexico State '91,6
30,Jud Buechler,Guard,6-6,228,6/19/68,Arizona '90,7
53,Joe Kleine,Center,7-0,271,1/4/62,Arkansas '85,12
22,Keith Booth,Forward,6-6,226,10/9/74,Maryland '97,R
24,Scott Burrell,Forward,6-7,218,1/12/71,Connecticut '93,4
35,Jason Caffey,Forward,6-8,256,6/12/73,Alabama '95,2
5,Rusty LaRue,Guard,6-2,185,12/10/73,Wake Forest '96,R
13,Luc Longley,Center,7-2,292,1/19/69,New Mexico '91,6
34,Bill Wennington,Center,7-0 277,4/26/63,St. John's (NY.) '85,10
C,Phil Jackson,Coach,6-8,-,9/17/45,N. Dakota,11
```

- **Sense of community.** A sense of community is created through viewer participation in chats, polls, and bulletin boards. This was apparent during the *Homicide: Life on the Street* enhanced broadcasts. Each week we posed a question to the viewers about the current story line. From the responses we received, we then selected one question. During the production week, we would seek the answer from the appropriate actors, in or out of character, on the set. The next week, viewers saw the answer to the question from the actors and the name of the person who asked the question. Our goal was to create a strong sense of participation and make the viewer say, "I was just on an enhanced broadcast!"

- **Polling simplicity.** The use of simple and concise polling has generated the most activity. A good example is Scott Wolf's appearance as guest host of *Saturday Night Live*. He joked in his monologue about his resemblance to the actor Tom Cruise. We then asked the question, "Does Scott Wolf look like Tom Cruise?" By asking a simple question, we enabled the viewers to interact with the show and see what other viewers were thinking, without having them lose the main focus — Scott's monologue.

- **Coupons.** Our Clip and Save feature on *Saturday Night Live* demonstrated how coupons can enhance advertising (Figure 17.10). Although used for humorous effect on *Saturday Night Live*, the coupons showed a

Figure 17.10 Coupon: Screen grab from *Saturday Night Live* using WebTV for Windows Technology. Credit: Jennifer McCoy.

clear way to add value to the existing advertising model, provided the user with additional ties to the show, and developed viewer loyalty. The goal of the Clip and Save feature was to provide the user with a physical item from the broadcast. By collecting items throughout the season, viewers have something tangible to remind them how much they enjoyed the program.

- **The story behind the story.** One example of how we deployed this concept was seen in the *Homicide: Life on the Street* enhanced broadcast. Mike Kellerman, a character on the show, was reading a newspaper story about an arson in Baltimore. The user could click on the article to see exactly what Mike was reading (Figure 17.11).

- **Purchasing.** Through a partnership with MyLaunch (*www.nbc.mylaunch .com*) we provided the opportunity to purchase music. As a band performs on *Saturday Night Live*, we provide biographies, a discography, and a Purchase Here button. A click takes viewers to the appropriate order form on the NBC.LAUNCH Web site, which can lead to impulse purchases of the music.

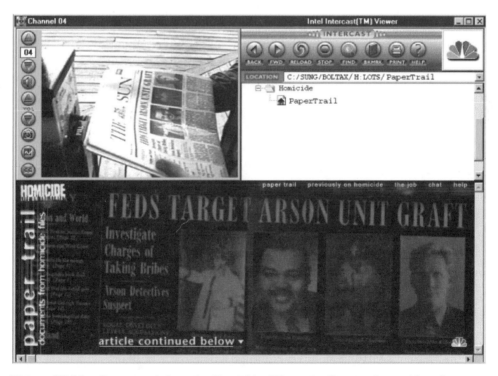

Figure 17.11 Screen grab from the *Homicide: Life on the Street* enhanced broadcast using Intercast 1.6. technology. Credit: Sung Chang.

Audio, however, is one area that requires significant development. There are currently severe conflicts between audio provided as part of an enhancement and audio provided by a television. We could not achieve smooth transitions between the two types of audio, and as a result, to date we have offered limited additional audio as part of the enhanced experience.

The Road Ahead

The content evolution continues with each enhanced broadcast. Groups such as ATVEF are defining a common content specification to make the creation of content easier for producers. Focus group research and user responses we collect continue to improve our viewers' experience. If enhanced television is created with sensitivity, there should be no difference in a viewer's mind between watching interactive and watching "traditional" television. For this to happen, viewers must be able to get to "traditional television" easily and the interface must not conflict with the television picture. Interactivity should be just as easy to use as a channel click on a remote. If these models are followed, interactive television will begin to seep into homes. Television viewers will begin to vote in polls, purchase products, and access statistics and related information with just as much enjoyment as they apply to watching television today. HDTV also opens up a new and exciting world to ITV. As bandwidth becomes larger, the content becomes more dynamic and exciting. What we do in the analog world is only a precursor to what can be done with the added bandwidth of digital. With easy interactivity, a wide variety of choices, and rich experiences, television viewing will soar to the next level.

CHAPTER 18

Case Study: Interactive Television and Tribune Company

Gary Wong, Senior Developer
Matt Thompson, Internet Producer
Tribune Company
w w w . t r i b u n e . c o m

Tribune Company is a media company involved in publishing (print and online), broadcasting, and education. Their varied media offer a unique ability to leverage their assets across a variety of media. For this project, they sought to leverage their news and online content for use in enhancing their television broadcasts.

As an early adopter of the interactive television technology available in WebTV for Windows, Tribune provides you with insight into the possibilities available with this new medium. The terms interactive and enhanced are used interchangeably throughout the chapter.

Our History with Interactive Television

Tribune became involved with Microsoft's interactive TV project in 1997. By March 1998, we had created broadcast enhancements for a live event in multiple markets (including Chicago, New York, and Los Angeles). Our first event was the pre-Oscar show, the red-carpet event prior to the Academy Awards presentation. During the show, hosts Sam Rubin and Leanza Cornett interviewed celebrities as they entered the awards hall. Our challenge was to enhance the broadcast with interactive content and to synchronize the enhancements with the fast-changing, unscripted show.

For example, when Robert Duvall stopped to talk with our hosts, we quickly broadcast an enhancement with a Robert Duvall filmography, including a photo and another enhancement that listed the "degrees of separation" between Duvall and fellow actor Kevin Bacon. (Degrees of separation in film appearances from Kevin Bacon, a popular pastime, was a running game during the broadcast. For more information about "Degrees from Kevin Bacon," see the Web site *www.cs. virginia.edu/~bct7m/bacon.html.*) In Figure 18.1, the area on the left is the enhanced content, displayed translucently over the video.

Network Infrastructure

The infrastructure behind our broadcast was complex. Our content was created and "played" live from our Chicago station WGN. The enhancements were then relayed (via IP tunneling over our intranet) to the Broadcast Router — a service running on Windows NT in our Los Angeles station KTLA — which inserts the enhancements into the Vertical Blanking Interval (VBI) of the live video feed. This master feed was then uplinked to a satellite carrier and downlinked by multiple stations across the country for terrestrial broadcast (WLVI Boston, WHPL Philadelphia, KTZZ Seattle, and others). The uplink came from KTLA because the show "Live from the Academy Awards" was filmed in Los Angeles (Figure 18.2).

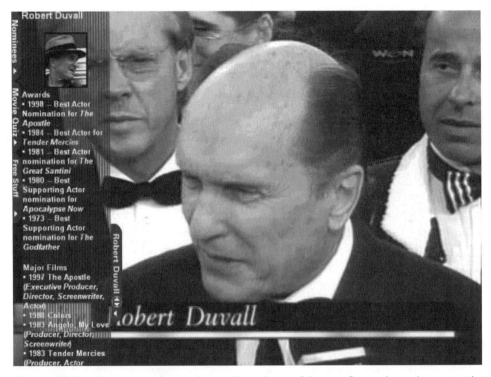

Figure 18.1   Screen shot from enhanced broadcast of the pre-Oscar show, demonstrating content displayed translucently over the video.

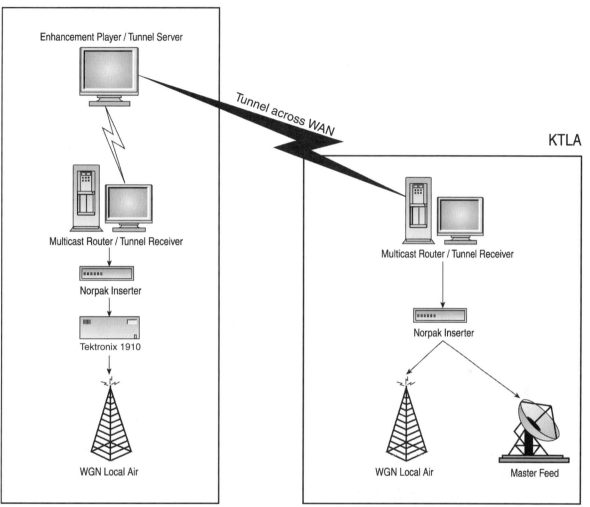

Figure 18.2   Network infrastructure diagram showing the WGNTV-to-KTLA enhanced TV transmission path.

Database-Driven and Automated Content Delivery

When Windows 98 was launched in May 1998, we had in place a system for delivering around-the-clock updated enhancements for WGN in Chicago. Viewers in the Chicago area[1] can tune into WGN and receive constantly updated news, weather,

---

1. Some cable companies strip the VBI. Consequently, only terrestrial broadcasts (noncable) are guaranteed to contain our enhancements.

and sports enhancements. The news enhancement contains national headlines that, when clicked, yield the text of the full story. The sports enhancement displays sports scores updated every 15 minutes. The weather enhancement graphically displays the 7-day forecast, a satellite image of the Chicago area, as well as current still photos from multiple vantage points in the city (including one from the 96th floor of the John Hancock Tower and one from Tribune Tower on Michigan Avenue). Figure 18.3 shows weather information and a live shot from Michigan Avenue.

Content

When designing WGN-TV's WebTV for Windows experience, we had several goals in mind: a consistent look for all media (WGN-TV on-air, the WGN Web site, and WebTV); a simple and familiar user interface; a short wait time before receiving enhancements; and a fun, interactive experience.

Figure 18.3 Weather information and a live shot from Michigan Avenue displayed in an enhanced broadcast.

Consistent Look

When viewing WGN-TV content through WebTV for Windows (Figure 18.3), the Web (Figure 18.4), or traditional television (Figure 18.5), there is a consistent look and feel. This shared design supports the brand equity of WGN across all media. When new users visit our Web site, the site seems familiar because they recognize elements from television. When creating enhancements for WGN-TV, we used many of the same elements.

Colors

We use the same red and yellow colors both in enhanced TV broadcasts and on our Web site. These colors are also the same shades as those used in the on-air graphics for WGN. If the WebTV enhancements are on screen at the same time as a WGN on-air graphic, the graphics will be integrated. Because the on-screen and on-air features can be viewed simultaneously, the need for a consistent look and feel becomes even more important.

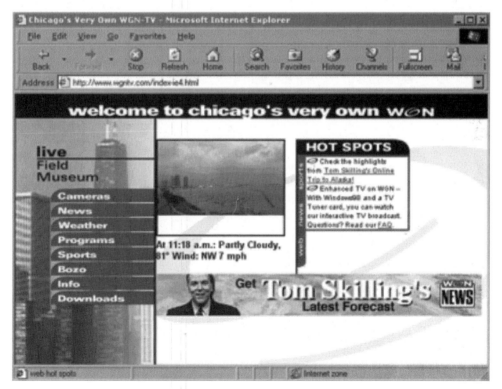

Figure 18.4   The WGN-TV Web site.

Figure 18.5   Screen shot from a WGN-TV television broadcast.

Menu Bar

To navigate through the WGN-TV enhancements, users click buttons on a bar at the bottom of the TV viewer window. This bar (Figure 18.6) contains a series of text buttons that can be clicked to display another page in the frame above it. The bar closely resembles the tool bar next to the Start menu in Windows 95 and Windows 98. The text buttons stretch or shrink as the user resizes the TV Viewer window. As more enhanced content is sent through the VBI, additional text buttons appear on the bar. Enhanced content is always visible without degrading the television experience. Users have complete control over the display of content.

The menu bar works just like the Windows Start button. When a user clicks a text button, the button becomes activated. The user can click another button to display different content or click the same button to remove the content.

Pop-Ups

When the user clicks a button on the menu bar, a new page appears in the space above the bar in the TV viewer window. Unlike most WebTV designs, the size of the

CHICAGO'S VERY OWN
ENHANCED TELEVISION **News**   **Sports**   **Weather**   **Recipe**   **Bubble**

Figure 18.6   The WGN-TV enhancement menu bar.

TV image does not change. Instead, the content appears on top of the TV images but in such a way as to minimize impact on the TV picture itself.

The enhanced content of WGN-TV appears as floating windows, or pop-ups. Pop-ups allow users to watch television and view interactive content at the same time. Pop-ups can be moved with a drag-and-drop operation anywhere inside the TV Viewer window. The background of the pop-up is translucent, allowing the TV image to remain visible. Figure 18.7 demonstrates how to create a translucent background.

Pop-up navigation should be familiar to users. They can scroll text using up and down arrows. Users can minimize pop-ups by clicking on the "X" icon. By dragging the tab with the name of the pop-up on it, users can move the pop-up across the screen. Users can also click on hyperlinks within the text of the pop-ups to display more information.

The pop-up window (Figure 18.8) is only 150 pixels wide. To accommodate larger images, thumbnail images appear on the pop-up. When a thumbnail image is clicked, a new window is created containing the image at full resolution.

Fun

Live television combined with the Web opens up all sorts of new interactive entertainment possibilities. With a little dynamic HTML and JavaScript, you can have a lot of fun. For our pre–Academy Awards interactive broadcast, we allowed users to throw virtual tomatoes at the TV screen, as shown in Figure 18.9.

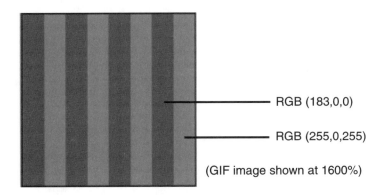

RGB (183,0,0)

RGB (255,0,255)

(GIF image shown at 1600%)

Figure 18.7   This illustration shows how to create a translucent background by alternating bands of color with the TV transparency color of magenta.

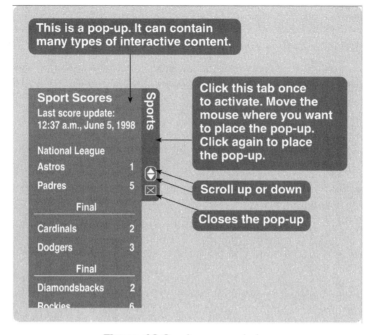

Figure 18.8   A pop-up window.

Figure 18.9   Screen shot showing, for sample purposes, virtual tomatoes on top of the TV picture.

The Technology of Tomato Toss

In this example, there are six layers. The bottom layer, named "bot," has a magenta background, so the TV image is visible. When the user clicks anywhere on the layer, it calls the "toss()" JavaScript function. This function records location of the mouse click and then moves a tomato layer across the screen to that location. When the layer arrives, it changes the tomato GIF image from a whole tomato to a splattered tomato. The code is shown next and can be adapted as needed.

```
<head>
<script>
tomnum=0; //tomnum is the number of the current tomato layer
divs = document.all.tags("div");
imgs  = document.all.tags("img");
function toss(){
    /* This function runs any time the user clicks on
    the screen. It turns on the correct tomato layer
    and then moves the layer to wherever the user
    clicked.*/
    tomnum++;
    if (tomnum>5){tomnum=1;}
    imgs[((tomnum)-1)].src="art/tomato.gif";
    xhere = x2= window.event.x; //captures the mouse position
    yhere = y2 = window.event.y; //captures the mouse position
    divs[tomnum].style.visibility="visible";
    mox=0; // The starting X position
    moy=700; // The starting Y position
    move2(tomnum,x2,y2);
    }
function move2(num,xer,yer){
    /* the move2 function moves a layer to the
    two coordinates specified. */
    num2=num;
    go=0;
    xme=xer;
    yme=yer;
    if (mox<xer){
        mox = mox + 30;
        divs[num2].style.left = mox;
        go = 1;
        }
    if (moy>yer){
        moy = moy -30;
        divs[num2].style.top = moy;
        go =1;
        }
```

Continues

The Technology of Tomato Toss (Continued)

```
    if (go==0){
        /* When go=0, the layer has moved to the
        correct place. Until that happens,
        the function continues to cycle.*/
        imgs[((num2)-1)].src="art/splat.gif"
        }
    if (go == 1){
        setTimeout("move2(num2,xme,yme)",5);
        }
    }
</script>
</head>
<body bgcolor="magenta">
<div id="bot"
style="top:0;left:0;width:800;height:600;position:absolute;"
onclick="toss();">
</div>
<div id="tom1"
style="width:30;height:30;position:absolute;visibility:hidden;">
<img src="art/tomato.gif"></div>
<div id="tom2"
style="width:30;height:30;position:absolute;visibility:hidden;">
<img src="art/tomato.gif"></div>
<div id="tom3"
style="width:30;height:30;position:absolute;visibility:hidden;">
<img src="art/tomato.gif"></div>
<div id="tom4"
style="width:30;height:30;position:absolute;visibility:hidden;">
<img src="art/tomato.gif"></div>
<div id="tom5"
style="width:30;height:30;position:absolute;visibility:hidden;">
<img src="art/tomato.gif"></div>
</body>
```

Streams

The look and feel of the WebTV for Windows experience of WGN-TV are also integrated into the design of our *stream files*. Stream files are text files that contain time codes that indicate when to transmit triggers and files. Instead of one long stream file that plays for the duration of the broadcast, we play a series of small stream files that can easily be swapped in and out. This allows us significant flexibility in what we can broadcast.

The base framework of our design is sent through a base stream file. Playing this stream sends out a page referencing the WebTV video and enhancement controls, the navigational images used throughout the content, and the HTML page containing the IFRAME tags that set the framework of the pages. The menu bar described earlier is also contained in these HTML files.

The rest of the enhanced content is sent through other stream files, depending on the topic. We have a *news.str*, *weather.str*, *sports.str*, and so on. Each stream file sends an HTML page and a custom trigger that adds that subject to the menu bar.

Users cannot view anything until after the base stream is played. The base stream is played as often as possible, allowing as many users as possible to view the enhanced content. We typically play the base stream first, followed by two additional streams. The base stream is played again, followed by two more streams, and then the base stream plays again. Each stream is about 30 to 60 seconds in duration. A user will never have to wait more than 2 minutes to view the enhancements. A sample *news.str* file is shown in Figure 18.10.

Tribune's Enhanced TV Scheduler

Our system, collectively called the *ETV Scheduler*, delivers these enhancements with no manual intervention. The system consists of a database of content, a scheduling system, and Microsoft's Enhancement Broadcast Server components, as shown in Figure 18.11. The content database is derived from Tribune Interactive, Inc.

These database-driven feeds are formatted for various online customers (primarily Web sites). In our case, we requested news, sports, and weather content formatted in HTML templates we had developed for enhanced TV. In addition, Tribune Media Services (TMS) automatically creates stream files based on the file names and lengths of the content files. The content files (HTML and image files) and stream files are then transferred (via File Transfer Protocol or FTP) to our scheduling system.

The scheduling system determines which streams to play for any given half-hour time period during the day. The scheduling system checks the database every half-

Figure 18.10   Sample news.str.

```
bandwidth=38400;

00:00:00.00     announce ( "wgn.ann" ) ;

// Download base page
00:00:02.00     trigger ( 1 "233.43.17.33:17833" "WGN" "30") only ;
00:00:05.00     "news.htm"; // Send the news html file
00:00:20.00     trigger (2000 "News+news4") only;
```

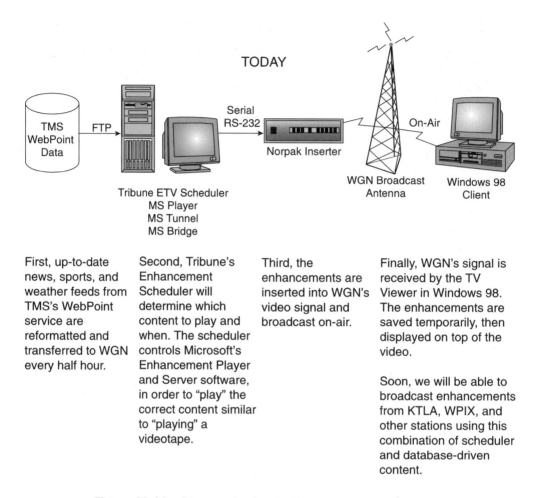

Figure 18.11   Diagram showing the Tribune Enhanced TV Network.

First, up-to-date news, sports, and weather feeds from TMS's WebPoint service are reformatted and transferred to WGN every half hour.

Second, Tribune's Enhancement Scheduler will determine which content to play and when. The scheduler controls Microsoft's Enhancement Player and Server software, in order to "play" the correct content similar to "playing" a videotape.

Third, the enhancements are inserted into WGN's video signal and broadcast on-air.

Finally, WGN's signal is received by the TV Viewer in Windows 98. The enhancements are saved temporarily, then displayed on top of the video.

Soon, we will be able to broadcast enhancements from KTLA, WPIX, and other stations using this combination of scheduler and database-driven content.

hour to determine which streams to play. If the scheduler finds streams listed for a given time period, it will play those streams sequentially and repetitively for the entire half-hour segment. If the scheduler finds no streams listed for a given half-hour, it will play a set of default streams. Thus, the content producer needs to schedule only streams that vary from the default set of streams. Content producers program the scheduler by entering schedule information via a convenient Web page form from anywhere on the corporate intranet. Figure 18.12 shows the Web page form that allows a content producer to schedule streams for later playback.

During normal hours, we normally want to play the local news, sports, and weather streams sequentially all day. These streams become our defaults and will play con-

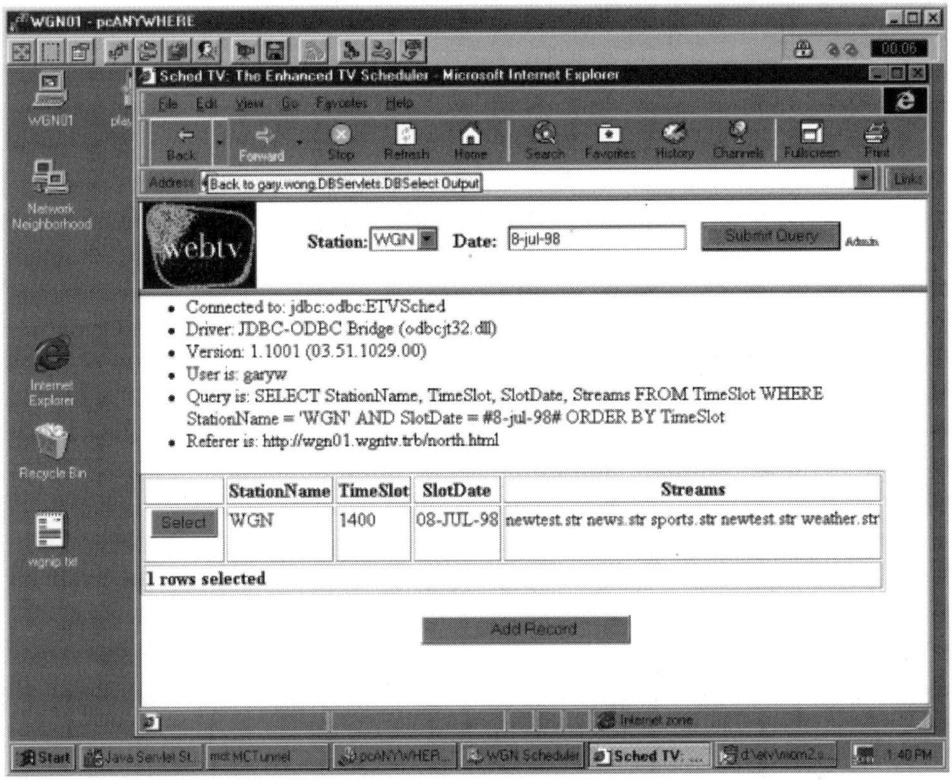

Figure 18.12   The Web page form for scheduling stream playback.

tinuously. (Note: the stream file names won't change but the content in them is updated every half-hour.) On special occasions, for example, during the program *Earth: Final Conflict*,[2] we will want to break away from the regular streams and play special "Earth" streams for the course of the 1-hour show.

Unfortunately, a scheduling system as described earlier was not available from Microsoft in our time frame. Thus we "rolled our own." Although Microsoft plans to deliver a generic scheduler by the time this book is published, we will probably continue to use our scheduler because it provides the flexibility and key functions that we need.

Our task was to write a scheduler that delivered the desired functionality and then have it built and tested in a very short time. We used Java because it is the standard development language at Tribune. However, because the Enhancement Player, MCTunnel, and Broadcast Router all require Windows NT or Windows 98, you could

2. *Earth: Final Conflict.* Copyright „ Tribune Entertainment.

develop a similar scheduler in Visual Basic or Visual C++ as well. Figure 18.13 shows the scheduler at work.

Our scheduler consists of two primary parts. The first part allows content producers to update the scheduling database, while the second part queries the database and controls the Enhancement Player. We used Microsoft Access as the database, but you can easily switch to any other Object Database Connectivity Protocol (ODBC) compliant database, or you can replace the Java Database Connectivity to ODBC (JDBC-ODBC) bridge to use any other database.

When we had to update the scheduling database, we developed a set of Java servlets that provided convenient Web access to the database. The servlets use a JDBC driver (in this case, Intersolv's JDBC-ODBC bridge, downloadable from *java.sun.com/products/jdbc*) to connect to the scheduling database. For more information about servlets, see *java.sun.com/products/servlet*.

Figure 18.13 The scheduler at work.

Our scheduling database consists of two simple tables, Station and TimeSlot. The Station table contains information about each station such as the IP address of the station's Broadcast Router, name and phone number for the station's technical contact, and a list of the station's default streams. StationName is the primary key for the Station table. The TimeSlot table contains information for each half-hour segment for each station. The fields are StationName, SlotDate, SlotTime (in 24-hour military time), and the list of streams to be played during this time period. StationName, SlotDate, and SlotTime are the primary key for the TimeSlot table.

The second part of the scheduler queries the database every half-hour to determine which streams to play. It then plays the streams in sequence and repeats the sequence until the end of the half-hour time period. The class etvScheduler handles the database querying and stores the default streams and multicast addresses for a given station. The etvScheduler class is started with the name of a station. For example, to start the scheduler for our Chicago station, WGN, the command line would be, "java etvScheduler WGN."

When necessary, etvScheduler creates an instance of the class smartPlayer, which is initialized with the proper IP addresses and list of streams for the given station and time period. The smartPlayer class then launches the Microsoft Enhancement Player as a process. To launch the player, we rely on the command-line options of the Enhancement Player. Figure 18.14 lists the command-line options for the current version of the player:

In starting EnhPlay.exe, smartPlayer uses the "EnhPlay.exe –g –x –n# -a#:# -t#:# -f#:# streamfile" options, where # is replaced by the appropriate IP addresses for the given station. When a given stream is finished, the player exits and the next stream

Figure 18.14   The command line options for the player.

```
EnhPlay.exe Usage:
enhplay [-switches] [filename]
-g Go immediately
-x exit when done
-m minimize
-0 continuous
-# play #times
-r reload file on each iteration
-n# set netcard
-a#:# set Announcement IP
-t#:# set Trigger IP
-f#:# set FTS IP
```

is started. When the time period is over, smartPlayer ends the EnhPlay.exe process and waits for the next half-hour time period.

Centralized Control of Multiple Stations

As a large station group, we have multiple broadcast stations that we want to transmit enhancements from. However, information systems staff at most stations are already very busy and are unlikely to embrace more demands on their time. Also, we expect that revenue from enhanced shows in these early days of interactive television is likely to be low. Thus, from a business standpoint, variable costs for producing enhancements must be similarly low.

To minimize costs and maintenance, we wanted to serve multiple stations from one machine. Centrally located, this master server would store content for each station and play the content to each station over the network. Each station would need only a Windows NT computer running the Broadcast Router software and a Norpak inserter. Figure 18.15 shows our future Enhanced TV network for broadcasting interactive content.

As this book goes to press, we are in the testing phase of such a scenario. We've found that by using different multicast IP address groups (sets of Announcement addresses, file transfers or FTS addresses, and trigger addresses) for each station, we can have multiple instances of the player tunneling to multiple stations. As for addresses, note that valid multicast addresses range from 224.0.0.0 to 239.255.255.255. Announcement addresses in the Windows 98 registry, in the format of "IP address (colon) port number," are 227.37.32.1:22701 through 227.37.32.6:22706. Thus, you must use one of the six valid Announcement addresses and any valid, unique multicast addresses for your FTS and triggers. The scheduler database allows you to store different multicast address groups for each station.

Looking Ahead

Much of what we've discussed here applies only to the over-the-air broadcasts of enhanced television. Unfortunately, the possibility of hitting weak links in cable broadcasts of enhanced television is high. For example, some cable companies and satellite services strip the VBI of incoming feeds. You might be forced to track the VBI signal path of your station to determine whether your cable viewers will receive enhancements. You need to know if your enhancements will be carried by the cable company; this will affect how you promote your enhancements to the public.

TOMORROW

TMS WebPoint Data

FTP

Tribune ETV Scheduler
MS Player (one for each station)
MS Tunnel

IP Tunnel IP Tunnel IP Tunnel

WGN
MS Tunnel
MS Bridge

Serial RS-232

KTLA
MS Tunnel
MS Bridge

Serial RS-232

WPIX
MS Tunnel
MS Bridge

Serial RS-232

Norpak Inserter Norpak Inserter Norpak Inserter

WGN Broadcast Antenna

KTLA Broadcast Antenna

WPIX Broadcast Antenna

On-Air On-Air On-Air

Windows 98 Clients Windows 98 Clients Windows 98 Clients

First, up-to-date localized news, sports, and weather feeds from TMS's WebPoint service are reformatted and transferred to the central ETV player every half hour.

Second, Tribune's Enhancement Scheduler will determine which content to play and when. The scheduler controls Microsoft's Enhancement Player and Server software, in order to "play" the correct content similar to "playing" a videotape.

Third, the enhancements are inserted into each station's video signal and broadcast on-air.

Finally, WGN's signal is received by the TV Viewer in Windows 98. The enhancements are saved temporarily, then displayed on top of the video.

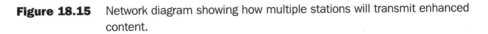

Figure 18.15 Network diagram showing how multiple stations will transmit enhanced content.

The Enhancement Player today inherently uses multicasting. However, multicasting can consume unnecessary resources on the network or even be filtered out by certain router configurations. Thus, we recommend the use of IP tunneling for directing enhancements from the Enhancement Player to the Bridge Router. With IP tunneling, your data packets will be received only by the intended machine.

As we look ahead, we see enhanced television as a way to give our stations a competitive advantage in their local markets. Moreover, it prepares us as a broadcaster to enhance programs, a skill that will become critical during the transition to digital television. Digital television promises to deliver many megabits per second of bandwidth for the transmission of data (as opposed to kilobits per second available through the VBI), opening a myriad of new and compelling content possibilities. Committees such as the Advanced Television Enhancement Forum (ATVEF) are proposing standards for enhancement syntax that will be similar to the enhancement syntax we have been using here.

Credits

Tribune: Jeff Scherb, Ira Goldstone, Marc Drazin, Mike Silver, Dennis Fitzsimons, Jim Dowdle, Sharon Mandell, Jeff Sciackitano, Rich Kittelstved, Clark Bender, Nedra Plonski, Joel Summy, Brian Durand, Ricardo Cheriel, Pooneh Rassekh, Ardell Banas.

Microsoft: David Feinleib, Chuck Mount, Steve Wilkes, Noel Gamboa, Isaac Sheldon, Matthijs Gates, Andamo Deming, Gernot Ross.

Case Study: MSNBC and Interactive Television

www.msnbc.com

On June 15, 1998, MSNBC launched the first version of its Vertical Blanking Interval–based (VBI-based) interactive service for Windows 98. This chapter documents several aspects of the service and describes how MSNBC plans to use the technology in the future.

Prior to the specification and rollout of the production grade version one (V1) service, the Windows 98 team worked with MSNBC to design and build a prototype VBI-based MSNBC service for use by WebTV for Windows beta testers. The prototype served as a catalyst to get the proper hardware, policies, and personnel in place for the real service.

The prototype service included three phases:

1. Redmond test. Test data was inserted, delivered, and received over the internal Microsoft cable television network.

2. Secaucus test. Test data was inserted in a national video feed for MSNBC and received on computers running beta copies of Windows 98 in Redmond.

3. National test. Delivery to Windows 98 beta testers. The prototype included an ActiveX ticker control for displaying news, weather, and sports information with links back to the MSNBC Web site.

Target Platforms

MSNBC originally targeted both Windows 98 computers and WebTV Plus set-top boxes. However, due to a delay in enabling VBI reception for WebTV set-top boxes, MSNBC ultimately launched the service targeted only at computers running WebTV for Windows.

Table 19.1 shows the initial client requirements, network topology, and types of content that MSNBC planned to deliver:

Table 19.1   Requirements and Content Type

Client	Network Topology	VBI-Delivered Content Type
Windows 98 computer	5 Lines VBI — 48 Kbps	Single page
TV tuner card	No back channel for initial rendering	Headline ticker
Modem	Assume 28.8 Kbps connectivity for back-channel actions	Client-filtered local information? Weather?
800 ¥ 600 screen		
WebTV Plus v2.x	5 Lines VBII — 48 Kbps	Single page
New VBI-enabled WebTV will not ship until end of year	No back channel for initial rendering	Headline ticker
	Assume 56 Kbps connectivity for back-channel actions	Client-filtered local information? Weather?

V1 Specification

MSNBC created a priorities and feature list as shown in Table 19.2.

Feature priorities are shown in Table 19.3, and expanded explanations of the priority 1 features are provided.

Headline Ticker

Goal: Cycle through the top three headlines of each top tier MSNBC section (News, Commerce, Sports, Tech, Living, On Air, Opinions) and provide an interface for users to skip to headlines of a particular section. Cycle period would be continuous but tied to the headlines present upon display of the page.

Table 19.2   Priorities and Their Definitions

Priority	Definition
1	Must have: cannot ship without this feature
2	Should have
3	Nice to have
4	Not doing

Table 19.3 Features and Their Priorities

Feature	Priority
Headline ticker	1
Show scheduling	1
Links to personalization	1
Standing links	1
Advertising space	1
Interactive advertising mechanism	2
Personalization	3
Client-side filtering of personalized data	4

Development task: Determine the mechanism for delivering MSNBC headlines:

- Understand the feasibility of using the existing ActiveX ticker client and the resulting user experience. (Although an ActiveX ticker control had been used in the prototype service, MSNBC wanted to investigate the feasibility of providing a "lightweight" interface that did not require the control.)

- Review the server-side parser system to determine MSNBC production compatibility.

- Compile a time estimate for development of lighter client delivery, using dynamic HTML (DHTML), for example.

- Investigate the feasibility of modifying one or many index files to include editorial selection of included headlines.

Editorial–Development task: Ensure that all sections have the means and a system to update the ticker information.

Show Scheduling

Goal: Include scheduling information for all MSNBC and NBC news shows.

MSNBC and NBC scheduling information is already entered into a database used by the "On Air Scheduler" page (as shown at *www.msnbc.com/oasched.asp*).

Development task: Determine system for including information from the Scheduler Database in a VBI-delivered page.

Editorial task: Ensure means and system for updating of Scheduler Database.

Links to Personalization

Goal: Have a prominent and standing link to the MSNBC Personal Front Page (PFP), Local Traffic, News, and Weather.

Development task: Determine the feasibility of creating PFP sign-up page.

Standing Links

Have standing links, with editable headlines and target URLs, to two out of four of the following items each day:

- Question of the day

- Featured interactive page

- Featured bulletin board system (BBS) thread

- Play for MSNBC.com story packages

Advertising Space

Goal: Have an advertising and sponsorship ad space using a GIF image.

Design task: Provide advertising team members with space dimensions.

Advertising task: Provide design team members with ad mockup that meets design dimensions.

Other Requirements and Opportunities

MSNBC determined that the ITV service would not require any back-channel connectivity to render the page, although a back channel would be required to see links provided by the page. In addition, the interactive team determined that

- The page had to be deliverable in 30 seconds given the amount of VBI bandwidth available.

- A headline ticker might be possible using DHTML.

- Its overall development task was to assess the feasibility of creating tools to facilitate editorial tasks necessary in building the page on a daily basis.

Interactive Team

MSNBC put together a development team that included a number of members. Only core members worked on the service on a day-to-day basis; however, the support of each of the following members was critical:

- Project Lead — director-level responsibility for the project, approval of funding, and so forth

- Project Manager — day-to-day management and responsibility for project

- On-Air Coordinator — coordinator for MSNBC broadcast (in Secaucus, New Jersey)

- Design Lead — user interface designer

- Development Lead — specification of requirements, features, and priorities

- Development — implementation of supporting tools, HTML, and JavaScript

- Usability — handling of focus groups and user feedback

- Operations — maintenance of VBI insertion, network infrastructure, and equipment

- Test Lead — testing of the underlying tools and the implemented service

- Promotion — marketing of the service on the Web and internally at Microsoft

- Advertising — coordination with advertisers such as Barnes & Noble

Schedule

After the prototype service had been running for approximately 2 months, MSNBC began designing and implementing the production service. A significant portion of the work actually occurred in the final 2 to 3 weeks.

The schedule in Table 19.4 shows the planned rollout timetable for MSNBC.

Table 19.5 shows the revised, actual rollout schedule with task owners:

MSNBC Interactive Service Overview and Goals

In building the first version of its interactive service, MSNBC had the following key design goals:

- Integration with the existing MSNBC television and Web look and feel.

- Scalability. For example, when the user resizes a window, the enhancement must degrade gracefully at different resolutions.

- Delivery of basic content service by the launch of Windows 98 with a "first layer" of information — timely news headlines and links back to the MSNBC Web site.

Table 19.4   Planned Rollout Timetable for MSNBC

Milestone	Planned	Description
Complete specification	3/28/98	Finalize requirements, specifications
Complete task schedules	4/03/98	All team leads compile schedule for main spec
Prioritization of features	4/15/98	Reports by various team leads and prioritization of functionality, based on available resources
Design complete	4/24/98	Page and all page elements are complete
Design and usability review	4/27/98	Core team reviews design
Development begins	4/01/98	
Development complete	5/15/98	
Testing and usability review	5/16/98	
Final review and rollout	6/01/98	Core team approves

- Asynchronous content — in other words, content not tied to a particular show but generic to the channel.

- Stability. The service had to run on a continuous basis.

The limitations of the V1 design were due to time constraints and the fact that the team wanted to become familiar with the technology and understand what was possible. The team traded off vision and depth of content for stability and schedule. Because interactive TV was uncharted territory, the team didn't want the enhancements to be overly complex. The team members decided against an ambitious content specification for the first version, which allowed them to focus on getting the process down and making the service stable.

Table 19.5   Actual MSNBC Rollout Schedule

Section I Date	Task	Owner
4/29/98	First draft functional spec for MSNBC ITV V1	Beth
5/09/98	Usability prototype done	Brian
6/03/98	Beta for all elements: ITV Ticker Feed; ITV Ticker Editor; ITV Page	Peter, Curtis, Brenden, Brian
6/03–6/14	Test and fixes	

Elements of the Service

The MSNBC-ITV service has three elements: ticker data feed, MSNBC enhancement page, and ITV ticker editor.

- The **ticker data feed** creates a data file by combining existing MSNBC headline content with TV/cable schedule information from an existing Scheduler Database along with manually inserted headlines and Web links (URLs). It also generates a stream file, which is compatible with the Broadcast Server enhancement player.

- The **MSNBC enhancement page** is a DHTML page transmitted via the VBI to Windows 98 users with WebTV for Windows and compatible TV tuner hardware. Data from the ticker data feed is used to populate the DHTML ticker. The enhancement page also displays some standing links to the MSNBC home page, weather, and so on.

- The **ITV ticker editor** is a wizard that allows the ITV associate producer (AP) to enter headlines and URLs manually into the ticker data feed. Users of the ITV ticker editor do not need knowledge of HTML.

System Description

- The MSNBC ITV V1 service requires the user to be running a Windows 98 machine with a compatible TV tuner card installed.

- Content Server ("Webcast") Machine runs

    Enhancement player 1 (runs *triggers.str* to send out the headline triggers).

    Enhancement player 2 (runs *msnbc.str* to send out the enhancement page).

    MCTunnel (takes the packets and tunnels them to the Broadcast Router PC).

Network Topology

This section describes the underlying network topology for MSNBC, which has an especially complex setup. Content is created and served up in Redmond, Washington but is transmitted from the MSNBC head end in Secaucus, New Jersey.

Data Flow from Feed to Broadcast

Figure 19.1 illustrates the flow of video and data on the MSNBC network. Content is served from the Content Server (Webcast PC) at MSNBC Interactive in Redmond, Washington. It is tunneled over the MSNBC wide area network (WAN) — using a simple multicast tunneling utility provided with the Broadcast Server software — to the Broadcast Router server at the MSNBC head end in Secaucus, New Jersey. A special serial connector allows the data to be sent over a lengthy serial interface to the Norpak TES5 VBI inserter located in the MSNBC all-digital head end. There the data is combined with the video.

Data Flow from Data Sources to Feed

Figure 19.2 illustrates the data flow between the various data sources that make up the MSNBC ITV service and the Broadcast Router, which transmits the data to the VBI inserter. Of note is that the Broadcast Router PC sends out the same data over two serial ports to two separate Norpak VBI inserters: a primary and a backup. This

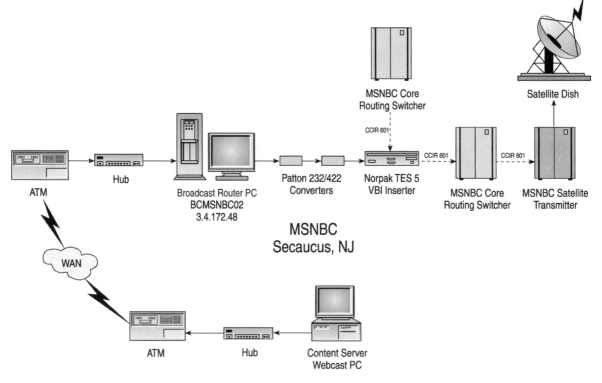

Figure 19.1 The flow of video and data on the MSNBC network.

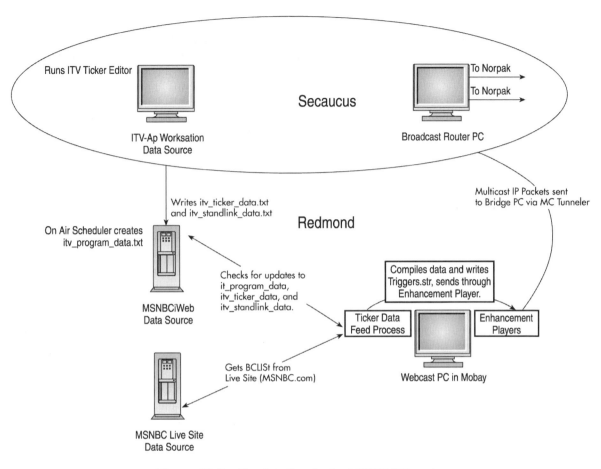

Figure 19.2 The data flow for the MSNBC ITV service.

allows MSNBC to switch between two video paths for maintenance or in case of failure. In the future, MSNBC will use two separate Broadcast Router machines that will eliminate a single point of failure.

MSNBC Enhancement Page

The MSNBC enhancement page is an HTML page with JavaScript, DHTML, and other types of code packaged into a cabinet (CAB) file and broadcast to the user. The ticker on the page is coded to cycle through a set of text triggers containing the headlines to be displayed, along with a link to an associated part of the MSNBC Web site. When clicked, the links launch the back channel and a child browser window.

There are several advantages to using a CAB file. CAB files offer the capability to compress the contained files. Moreover, because CAB files can contain multiple files, CAB files enable you to keep files and their dependencies (for example, an HTML page and the graphics it references) together so that the user either sees the entire enhancement in its complete form or sees no enhancement at all.

Figure 19.3 shows the MSNBC-ITV V1 enhancement interface.

End users activate the enhancement page when they view MSNBC through their Windows 98 computer with WebTV for Windows installed. To turn the enhancement

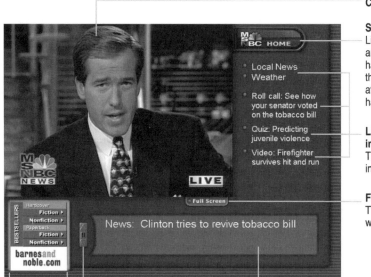

MSNBC Cable TV

Static Links: Link to Home page, weather, and Local News. If the user has chosen a local affiliate, they will be redirected to their affiliate front page. Links are hardcoded into the ITV Page.

Links to daily interactives: This data is editied/managed in the ITV Ticker Editor.

FullScreen: TV takes over full screen when button is clicked.

Up/Down Arrows: Clicking on the up and down arrows cycles through the headlines. Up arrow exposes previous headline and down arrow exposes next headlines.

DHTML Ticker: Section Name, Headlines, URLs, scheduleinfo, etc. brought in from Ticker Data Feed. Headlines transition by fading to bgcolor.

DHTML Ads: This ad features flydown menus with content that changes on a weekly basis. Need to support dynamic ads.

Figure 19.3 The MSNBC-ITV enhancement interface.

on or off, the user clicks the "Interactive *I*" in the upper right corner of the screen or the MSNBC logo that appears in the lower right corner of the screen.

Advertising in Version 1 is coded directly into the enhancement page. It is maintained by the AP, in coordination with members of the advertising team.

Enhancement Page Details

The MSNBC page demonstrates a number of key enhancement-scripting functions:

- Receiving headlines as triggers and accumulating them in the ticker

- Fading in and fading out of the ticker (using DHTML)

- Using a *Full Screen* button to return to full-screen mode

The MSNBC enhancement page operates as follows:

1. The enhancement page itself is received and displayed in WebTV for Windows.

2. The enhancement page receives triggers containing the headlines for the ticker and stores them as elements in an array. The enhancement page also receives triggers for the standing headlines and links entered by the AP.

3. The page operates on a timer to cycle through all of the triggers, fading from one headline to the next.

4. Each headline has an associated Web link (URL). If the user clicks a headline, a child browser window is created in which the referenced page is displayed.

The ticker data is stored in three arrays defined as shown in Figure 19.4.

The array *MSNBC_Category* stores the headline category; *MSNBC_URL* stores the link associated with the headline; and *MSNBC_Headline* stores the actual headline

Figure 19.4 Arrays for storing ticker data.

```
// MSNBC Headlines
MSNBC_Category = new MakeArray(40);
MSNBC_URL = new MakeArray(40);
MSNBC_Headline = new MakeArray(40);
```

Figure 19.5 Adding lines to the ticker.

```
function ChangeHeadline(tnum,tcat,turl,thl)
{
tnum—;
if(tnum >= 0 && tnum < 40)
  {
  MSNBC_Category[tnum] = tcat;
  MSNBC_URL[tnum] = turl;
  MSNBC_Headline[tnum] = thl;
  }
}
```

text that is displayed in the ticker. Each array can store up to 40 elements corresponding to ticker headlines. The array is initially filled with empty strings. As the ticker cycles through the arrays, it ignores any element that is an empty string. To fill out the arrays and thereby add headlines to the ticker data, the content server transmits a trigger that calls the JavaScript routine *ChangeHeadline*, as shown in Figure 19.5.

The *ChangeHeadline* function inserts the headline *thl* at the array index *tnum*. The value specified in *tnum* allows the content producer to order the headlines in a particular fashion. The ticker cycles through the arrays in numeric order, skipping empty array elements.

Figure 19.6 shows some examples of triggers that call *ChangeHeadline*. Trigger type 4 causes the trigger listener control on the enhancement page to execute the script specified in the trigger.

Figure 19.6 Examples of triggers that add headlines.

```
00:00:05.00  trigger 4 (
"top.main.ChangeHeadline(1,'Brian','http://msw','Test 1 Headline');" )
only;
00:00:10.00  trigger 4 (
"top.main.ChangeHeadline(10,'Seattle','http://msw','Test 10 Headline
Test 2 Headline Test 2 Headline Test 2 Headline Test 2 Headline Test 2
Headline Test 2 Headline Test 2 Headline Test 2 Headline');" ) only;
00:00:15.00  trigger 4 (
"top.main.ChangeHeadline(11,'Seattle','http://msw','Test 11 Headline
Test 2 Headline Test 2 Headline Test 2 Headline Test 2 Headline Test 2
Headline Test 2 Headline Test 2 Headline Test 2 Headline');" ) only;
```

Figure 19.7   Removing headlines.

```
00:00:15.00  trigger 4 ( "top.main.ChangeHeadline(11,'','','');" )
only;
```

The trigger in Figure 19.7 will remove the headline from the array at index 11.

An excerpt from an actual stream file as generated by the MSNBC tools is shown in Figure 19.8.

The standing links for the MSNBC page, as shown in Figure 19.9, are located in an HTML list with the same DHTML ID, which makes it possible to access the elements as a collection.

To update the standing links, the content server transmits a trigger that calls the *ChangeStanding* subroutine to update the standing links as shown in Figure 19.10. If the specified text string is empty, the standing link, *hl*, at index *tnum* is hidden. ChangeStanding also updates the URL, *turl*, for the headline. (The function *openLink* causes the specified URL to be opened in a child window at a preconfigured size.)

Figure 19.8   Excerpt from a stream file.

```
bandwidth=38400;
00:00:01.00     trigger 4 ( "top.main.ChangeStanding(0, 'http://www.
msnbc.com/news/itv_redir.asp?http://www.msnbc.com/modules/starr/
default.asp', 'Starr&#39;s growing web of investigations');" ) only;
00:00:02.00     trigger 4 ( "top.main.ChangeStanding(1,
'http://www.msnbc.com/news/itv_redir.asp?http://www.msnbc.com/news/180
095.asp', 'Sabotage may have killed U.S. envoy');" ) only;
00:00:03.00     trigger 4 ( "top.main.ChangeStanding(2,
'http://www.msnbc.com/news/itv_redir.asp?http://www.msnbc.com/
modules/clinics/default.asp', 'Clinic violence, state-by-state');" )
only;
00:00:04.00     trigger 4 ( "top.main.ChangeHeadline(1, '',
'http://www.msnbc.com/news/itv_redir.asp?', '');" ) only;
00:00:05.00     trigger 4 ( "top.main.ChangeHeadline(2,
'Time &amp; Again',
'http://www.msnbc.com/news/itv_redir.asp?/news/TIMEAGAIN_front.asp',
'JFK&#39;s presidential nomination. Wednesday, July 15 12:00AM');" )
only;
```

Figure 19.9   Standing links.

```
<SPAN style="DISPLAY: list-item">
    <UL style="MARGIN-RIGHT: 0px; MARGIN-TOP: 0px; list-style:
url(./graphics/dot.jpg) inside">
    <LI ID="Standing" STYLE="TEXT-INDENT: -30px;visibility:hidden"><A
ID=hl HREF="" style="cursor:hand" onmouseout=colorText(this,0)
onmouseover=colorText(this,1)></A></LI>
    <BR style="LINE-HEIGHT: 10px">
    <BR style="LINE-HEIGHT: 10px">
    <LI ID="Standing" STYLE="TEXT-INDENT: -30px;visibility:hidden"><A
ID=hl HREF="" style="cursor:hand"  onmouseout=colorText(this,0)
onmouseover=colorText(this,1)></A></LI>
    <BR style="LINE-HEIGHT: 10px">
    <BR style="LINE-HEIGHT: 10px">
    <LI ID="Standing" STYLE="TEXT-INDENT: -30px;visibility:hidden"><A
ID=hl HREF="" style="cursor:hand"  onmouseout=colorText(this,0)
onmouseover=colorText(this,1)></A></LI>
    </UL>
    </SPAN>
```

The enhancement page toggles between two states: full screen and interactive. In full-screen mode, the user can click on an overlaid translucent logo to go to interactive mode. The *GoToInteractive* function sets the visibility style of a number of elements to *visible* in order to display them, as shown in Figure 19.11.

The ticker itself is defined as a Span, with the Dynamic HTML filter *revealTrans* that allows the headlines to fade in and out as shown in Figure 19.12.

The page uses a timeout to cycle through the headlines, calling the function *Run-Transition* after each timeout. The function *RunTransition* calls *apply* on the

Figure 19.10   Updating the standing links.

```
function ChangeStanding(tnum,turl,ttext)
{
if(ttext != "")
  Standing[tnum].style.visibility = "visible";
else
  Standing[tnum].style.visibility = "hidden";

hl[tnum].href = "javascript:openLink('"+turl+"');";
hl[tnum].innerHTML = ttext;
}
```

Figure 19.11   Making the elements visible.

```
function GoToInteractive()
{
    overlay.style.visibility = "hidden";

    bot.style.visibility = "visible";
    right.style.visibility = "visible";
    adborderdiv.style.visibility = "visible";

    shadow_right.style.visibility = "visible";
    shadow_bot.style.visibility = "visible";

    exit.style.visibility = "visible";
    logo.style.visibility = "visible";

    view = "Interactive";
}
```

ticker filter to freeze the current text. Then it executes the play function to make the fading transition to the next headline. Note that if play were called without first calling apply, the new text would appear before the fade occurred rather than making a transition into the fade. A portion of the *RunTransition* function is shown in Figure 19.13.

RunTransition calls the function *SetHeadline*, which builds a table that allows the sports scores and headlines to be properly aligned. *SetHeadline* builds the table to display the category and headline on the fly using *tempCategory* and *tempHeadline*. This is shown in Figure 19.14.

To return to full-screen mode, the user clicks the Full Screen button, which calls the function *GoToFullScreen*, as shown in Figure 19.15.

Figure 19.12   Fading the headlines in and out.

```
<TD WIDTH=* HEIGHT=* ALIGN=middle VALIGN=center bgcolor=#4240b4>
    <SPAN ID=ticker STYLE="BACKGROUND-COLOR: #4240b4;
FILTER: revealTrans(Transition=12, Duration=1);
HEIGHT: 100%; LEFT: 0px; POSITION: relative; TOP: 0px;
VERTICAL-ALIGN: middle; WIDTH: 100%">
    </SPAN>
</TD>
```

Figure 19.13 The *RunTransition* function.

```
function RunTransition()
{
…

hindex = GetNextHeadlineIndex();
ticker.filters[0].apply();

ticker.innerHTML = SetHeadline(MSNBC_Category[hindex],
MSNBC_Headline[hindex],
        MSNBC_URL[hindex]);

ticker.filters[0].play();
…
}
```

A set of tiled graphics, used to fill the background, provided a polished look and feel for the MSNBC interactive interface, while also conserving bandwidth, as shown in Figure 19.16. The code fragment causes the viewer to tile the image repeatedly across the table cell. The image is also specified in an IMG tag so that the cell maintains its proper height.

Conclusion

Reviewing the implementation and deployment of its first interactive TV service, the MSNBC team was extremely happy with the results. Although the initial content

Figure 19.14 The function *SetHeadline*.

```
function SetHeadline(tempCategory,tempHeadline,tempURL)
{
tempCategory = stripSpaces(tempCategory);
return("<TABLE WIDTH=100% HEIGHT=100% BORDER=0 CELLPADDING=0
CELLSPACING=0><TR><TD WIDTH=50 ALIGN=LEFT VALIGN=TOP><SPAN
style='color:#4240b4;cursor:default'>1 </SPAN><A CLASS='tick'
HREF='javascript:openLink(&quot;"+tempURL+"&quot;)'>"+ tempCategory +
":  </A></TD><TD ALIGN=LEFT VALIGN=TOP><A CLASS='tick'
HREF='javascript:openLink(&quot;"+tempURL+"&quot;)'
style='color:white' onmouseout='this.style.color = &quot;white&quot;'
onmouseover='this.style.color = &quot;lightblue&quot;'>
"+tempHeadline+"</A></TD><TD> </TD></TR></TABLE>");
}
```

Figure 19.15 The function *GoToFullScreen*.

```
function GoToFullScreen()
{
    vid.style.width = document.body.offsetWidth;
    vid.style.height = document.body.offsetHeight;

    bot.style.visibility = "hidden";
    right.style.visibility = "hidden";

    adborderdiv.style.visibility = "hidden";

    shadow_right.style.visibility = "hidden";
    shadow_bot.style.visibility = "hidden";

    exit.style.visibility = "hidden";
    logo.style.visibility = "hidden";

    overlay.style.visibility = "visible";

    view = "FullScreen";
}
```

specification was not overly ambitious, the team was able to deliver a highly useful, stable service that appeals to viewers. The ITV effort was also the team's first experience with a completely new platform.

When viewing both MSNBC interactive TV and the Web site, users chose two types of interactive content most often:

- "Top teases," the most prominently displayed links that are part of the top layer of content.

- Links that are mentioned on air as part of the broadcast.

Use of this information on viewer behavior will play an important role in driving site traffic in the future.

Figure 19.16 Tiling the background image.

```
<TD WIDTH=* HEIGHT=35 VALIGN=bottom ALIGN=middle
BACKGROUND=graphics/bottom_middle.jpg>
    <IMG SRC="graphics/bottom_middle.jpg" BORDER=0>
    </TD>
```

MSNBC currently utilizes an extremely complex system that allows cable companies to opt in and out of the various overlays that are provided as part of the video signal, including the MSNBC "bug" (logo) and the weather, among others. The current system relies on a series of tones generated by specialized equipment to enable local cable headends to turn particular overlays on or off. For now, therefore, the MSNBC team is acting conservatively when it comes to overlaying interactive content on top of the video, because it doesn't want the content to conflict with existing video-based overlays.

In the future, the MSNBC interactive team would like to see

- Scheduling capabilities available through a seamless content management and producer interface. Such capabilities would make it easy to associate a group of assets with a scheduled time.

- Improved integration with existing tools and data sources.

The objectives of MSNBC for the next version of the interactive service include

- Personalization and customization of the delivered content via *client-side filtering*. In client-side filtering, a content provider transmits a large data stream, which the client filters, presenting the user with information relevant to the user's preferences. Such personalization might include a customized stock tracker as well as customized news headlines, weather, and traffic information.

- Modularization, which will provide different content types, spaces, and branding opportunities. For example, the current service is limited to one particular advertiser. Modularity would enable MSNBC to offer a flexible ad package to multiple advertisers.

- Limited show-specific content. Show-specific content would be tied to a particular show such as *Dateline NBC*, with content that is loosely synchronized with the video programming rather than completely independent of it.

- More use of quizzes, live voting, and other interactive content.

In the future, the MSNBC interactive team hopes to transmit both show-specific and channel-generic content. The success of MSNBC will be determined by both the extent to which it can offer a useful service and the extent to which it can serve the strategic goal of helping Microsoft build the interactive content market and associated platforms such as WebTV and WebTV for Windows. Although numerous questions remain to be answered, the first version production service created for MSNBC offers a great model for your own interactive service.

Credits

Frank Barbieri, Kevin Crumley, Peter Durham, Brian Keller, Rich Lappenbusch, Ted McConville, Chuck Mount, Beth Roberts, Rick Salsman.

Home & Garden Television, Food Network, and Do-It-Yourself: Making "How-To" Truly Interactive

Steve Hicks, Chief Technology Officer
Home & Garden Television
w w w . h g t v . c o m

Home & Garden Television (HGTV), Food Network (Food), and Do-It-Yourself (DIY) are premier television networks of over 44 million lifestyle enthusiasts. Interactive television is a natural outlet for such lifestyle "infotainment" broadcasting. This chapter describes how these three pioneering cable networks plan their ITV strategies and how they plan to deploy WebTV for Windows interactive content to better meet the needs of viewers.

In 1993, Ken Lowe was a broadcasting executive for The E.W. Scripps Company, experienced in identifying and predicting consumer viewing trends for Scripps' nine ABC and NBC affiliate television stations. Lowe recognized early the opportunity for category television in the lifestyle market. (The lifestyle market includes many activities that consumers do in their leisure time: hobbies, crafts, gardening, cooking, and home remodeling and decorating.) Advertisers in the $535 billion consumer market needed a more effective medium than print to communicate with customers. Lowe, a homebuilder himself, also knew that people wanted a place to get unbiased expert advice in a format that was easy to understand.

Home & Garden Television

Home & Garden Television, distributed via cable and satellite, was the medium that brought the advertiser and the consumer together.

Figure 20.1   The Home & Garden Television network logo.

Why Knoxville?

Lowe found a postproduction television facility, Cinetel Productions, that offered everything he needed to launch a cable network. Cinetel is one of nation's largest producers of cable programming and produces more than 800 shows annually for networks such as A&E, ESPN, and TNN. Cinetel, along with a group of independent producers, would provide HGTV with its original programming.

Lowe presented a business plan to the Scripps board of directors and began building HGTV in late 1993. He quickly hired a core group of senior managers and established headquarters in Knoxville, Tennessee. HGTV launched on December 31, 1994. By September 1998, HGTV would reach more than 44 million households, or approximately 59% of all U.S. homes with cable and satellite service. The *Beta Research Cable Subscriber Study*, 1997, ranked HGTV second among networks that viewers demanded from their cable companies.

Responding to Viewer Needs

From the beginning, Lowe insisted that the network be responsive to viewers. HGTV encouraged its viewers to call, write, e-mail, and fax the network about its programs. In 1995, HGTV created a magazine featuring a program guide and original content that complemented the on-air programming information. It also established a 1-800 line and encouraged its viewers to call anytime. The seven-person Call Center suddenly began receiving about 11,000 calls and 2500 letters per month. Viewers described themselves as "addicted" to HGTV, its how-to programming, and the ability to get detailed information easily. "Viewers felt they were a part of HGTV and began to think of us as something special, as an expert down the street," said Lowe. "We were feeding their passion for home and garden in a way that no other content provider had been able to achieve."

By late 1995, HGTV was finding it increasingly difficult to keep pace with the mail and telephone calls. So in 1996, HGTV established its Web site to give viewers a high-tech method of communication. Content was based on questions received through the mail and telephone and was enhanced with graphics, hyperlinks, and a search engine. In 1997, HGTV added chat, a question-and-answer feature, and links to other quality home and garden Web resources. By the middle of 1998, the Web site was receiving more than 21 million hits per month.

Targeting Viewer Interests

HGTV research found that home enthusiasts' interests can be classified into the following five categories:

- Building and Remodeling

- Gardening and Landscaping

- Crafts and Hobbies

- Interior Design and Decorating

- Specials

All content created by HGTV is classified into these categories, as are the program guide and the Web site (*www.hgtv.com*). The five categories meet the needs of viewers by matching lifestyle interests with the best viewing times for their demographic group. It also serves viewers who seek ideas for a project or on-air programs in a certain interest category.

In September 1998, HGTV redesigned the Web site and launched "The HGTV Village" (Figure 20.2), which enhances online navigation, gives sponsors an alternative to banner ads, and creates a storefront metaphor to advertise and sell products.

Figure 20.2   The Home & Garden Web Village.

The village concept is just one example of the creative ways that HGTV brings how-to information to viewers. Both viewers' needs and information means are considered when developing information products. "Information behaves differently in different media," says Channing Dawson, senior vice president of New Media. "Because television is linear, conveying information on TV is a little like stamping instructions in wet sand: they leave an impression that fades as soon as new instructions are stamped. Put the very same information in print or online, or in front of a telephone operator conveying it over phone lines, and that information — though not as visually stimulating — becomes preservable, actionable and useful. The instructions are saved for others to use."

The ITV Age

The HGTV Programming Department is responsible for creating content that provides information, ideas, and inspiration and for presenting content in an entertaining way. For this reason, HGTV content has been referred to as *infotainment* — programs that both entertain the viewer and deliver useful information and how-to advice.

Ideally, you could watch a television show on how to build a water garden, call up details on the screen that enhance your understanding of the building process, then download step-by-step information, materials lists, and resources. If the Internet is available on the same screen, you could also find experts in your area who could help plan and build the water garden.

Interactive television is perfect for the HGTV viewer who wants detailed instructions or resource guides for materials and retail sources. HGTV selected the Crafts and Hobbies category for the first interactive content sent over the VBI. We will soon branch out into the four other categories.

Ed Spray, executive vice president, says, "Our greatest advantage over other cable networks is the fact that we own the majority of our programs; we do not have to negotiate separate Internet license agreements. My biggest concern for this new technology is the amount of staffing we will need to hire in order to keep our interactive content fresh and dynamic."

Repurposing Content

Much of the information encoded for ITV resides at our Web site (*www.hgtv.com*) in HTML, CGI, Java, and JScript formats. "The challenge and opportunity for us as designers of HGTV interactive content is to create more entertaining and informative ways for the consumer to get involved with our network," says Marcia Irwin, new media creative director. The approach was to repurpose the HTML content to fit the ITV templates. We also created short content titles that linked to the actual Web page. Because our Web pages were originally created in HTML without the benefit of an authoring tool, it would be time consuming to recode pages for interactive television. We selected FrontPage 98 as our authoring tool to repurpose the original code if editing was required for ITV. Because FrontPage integrates into the ITV tools set, it eliminates the necessity of learning another authoring package.

Technically Speaking

A basic understanding of the Vertical Blanking Interval (VBI) helped our project team to understand both the capabilities and limitations that we were dealing with in deciding what content to encode. Ultimately, HGTV chose to use between three and five lines of the VBI to broadcast interactive content. This gave us flexibility in the placement of content within the available VBI space and the ability to accommodate future requirements.

As television producers move to a digital platform for broadcast, the VBI will be replaced with a high-speed data line, which will be sent along with the television signal. The industry will be operating in a hybrid state until 2006, when all broadcasters will convert to digital. In the current analog world, Web content is inserted into the VBI by using a computer connected to a Norpak VBI Inserter. The Norpak system allows selection of up to 10 VBI lines, scheduling of insertions, and number of times to send each packet of data. Because interactive television is technically a one-way broadcast transmission, it is recommended that the encoded data be sent more than once. This allows viewers to receive the enhanced content after the program begins.

HGTV's Network Operations is responsible for uplinking a high-quality signal to our subscribers, with or without enhanced content, 24 hours a day, 7 days a week, 365 days a year. Mark Hale, senior vice president of operations, says, "Engineers have had to become Internet-savvy to stay abreast of this new technology, so from a transmission standpoint, converging content in data form with our broadcast programming has become relatively easy. What's interesting to witness from a management standpoint is the skyrocketing value of a once relatively unused portion of the television signal. As competition for the VBI bandwidth grows, strategic planning is critical to ensure that the desired volume of data to be delivered is permissible within the available lines. Everyone in the organization needs to think in terms of these limitations, not just the engineers anymore." Figure 20.3 shows the layout of the HGTV network.

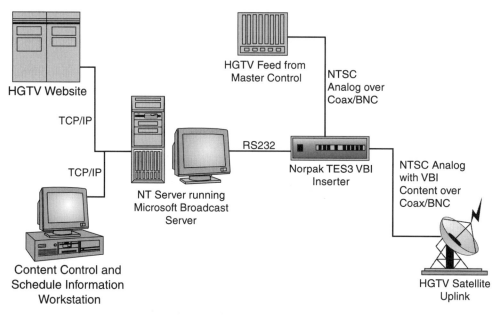

Figure 20.3 Network Operations diagram.

Going Live

HGTV created a closed-loop interactive television workstation where templates, content, and VBI insertion could be created and tested prior to live broadcast. The following lists the hardware and software used in the workstation setup:

Hardware

- NT Server

  Pentium II 350 MHz

  64 megabytes RAM

  Seagate 4.3 gigabyte hard disk

  Diamond Viper 330 AGP graphics card

  Intel EtherExpress PRO/100 PCI network card

- Windows 98 Test Workstation

  Pentium 200 MHz

  64 megabytes RAM

  Western Digital 2.1 gigabyte hard disk

ATI All-in-Wonder graphics card

Intel EtherExpress PRO/100 PCI network card. (Note: If the content is being encoded and broadcast, a network connection is not required for testing the broadcast signal.)

- Norpak VBI Inserter (TES3) — analog-serial connection (or TES5 digital-serial connection)

The enhancement network configuration is shown in Figure 20.4.

Server Software List and Installation Order

1. Windows NT Server version 4

2. NT Service Pack 3

3. Internet Explorer version 4

4. Windows NT Option Pack 4 (be sure to install FrontPage Server Extensions, Internet Information Server 4 with Internet Service Manager and WWW Server options, Microsoft Management Console, NT Option Pack Common Files)

5. Microsoft FrontPage 98

6. Microsoft Broadcast Router

7. Microsoft Interactive Programming Suite

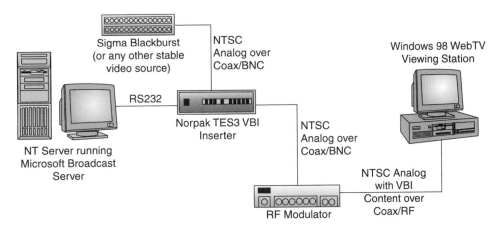

Figure 20.4 Enhancement network configuration.

Creating a Test Broadcast

1. Run the Microsoft Live Content Wizard.

2. Choose a design template.

3. Edit heading buttons. (These generally appear beside the video as "main menu" options and can do one of two things: bring up a list of subheadings or link directly to a URL.)

4. Define content (or subheading) items. (These generally appear at the bottom of the page and can contain one of three things: four items each with a link to a longer blurb of text; four items each with a direct link to a URL; or a listing of an upcoming schedule with time, title, and a brief description.)

5. Choose a custom graphic or advertisement to appear on the screen (normal Web graphics format), if desired. If you choose to include a graphic, it can be linked to a URL.

6. Define interactive icons. These are the icons that will appear in video feed when interactive content is being broadcast. The user can click this icon to receive WebTV content. You can create custom icons or use the defaults.

7. Define a background color (an NTSC-safe color is recommended, and dark colors tend to work better for display on television sets) or a background image.

8. Define default button colors, button highlight colors, and content area colors.

9. Choose font and font size.

10. Define a unique title and description for this program profile. These items will be used to identify the program for content editing and in FrontPage98.

Editing Content

To edit content, simply access the Microsoft Live Content Manager via a Web browser (generally localhost/console/login.asp). Log on to the Live Content Manager and you can revise broadcast schedules, edit content items on given programs, view the schedule of WebTV programs, and preview given shows. The Live Content Manager can be run from any workstation on the network and it is simple to use.

Previewing Broadcast via an IP Network Connection

1. On the Windows 98 workstation with WebTV for Windows installed, open Internet Explorer and go to the Live Content Manager.

2. Choose the View Schedule option, and pick the date and time from the schedule that you would like to preview.

3. Select the program, preview time, and preview size.

4. Select "Preview," and a window will appear with the same content that will be broadcast at the time you chose. The video feed you are seeing is the live content of whatever channel you are on, but the enhanced content is being served to you via the network — not the VBI.

Aaron Pickering, new technology specialist, says, "I think setting up a closed-end broadcast test system is a vital step toward going live with interactive television. Since this is an emerging technology, both broadcast engineers and Web designers will have a safe environment to experiment and explore new and old approaches before sending content to the viewing public."

Promoting ITV and Measuring the Results

For ITV to be widely adopted by the general public, it must be promoted on air in ways that will not distract from regular programming or advertisements. The early ITV audience will be small, but if the medium is promoted by the content providers and made available in a simple and easy way for viewers, it will grow rapidly. We have discussed several ways to promote ITV on our networks:

- We feel that it is important to let all viewers (not just those with ITV-enabled equipment) know that our signal contains enhanced content. Many of our viewers are so passionate about our programming that they will purchase ITV equipment just to get the enhanced content.

- Since we promote our Web site, phone number, and mailing address at the end of every program, it makes sense that we would promote ITV here.

- We have also considered showing the ITV icon at the top of each ITV program over our regular signal.

With any new technology, however, it is important to manage expectations. Developing a measurement methodology up front will help to address management's questions and help to evaluate the resources deployed for ITV. We plan to send enhanced content that will entice viewers to interact with our Web site. The URL will be available only to ITV viewers and will give us an easier way to measure ITV traffic.

Food Network

Food Network, with more than 32 million cable and satellite subscribers, is the most popular food site on the Internet (*www.foodtv.com*) and is considered to be among the top 25 entertainment sites on the Web.

Figure 20.5   The Food Network logo.

In the spring of 1996, Microsoft approached the network and discussed the creation of an interactive prototype. According to Erica Gruen, then the chief executive officer, "At that time we were a relatively small cable network with growing ratings, but we had one of the most visited sites on the Internet, and had under contract some of the most famous chefs in the world — a very strong combination for ITV."

Through the summer and fall of 1996, Microsoft developed sample screens for *The Essence of Emeril* series, one of the most popular food programs on cable. Over the following 6 months, Microsoft developed a prototype — a half-hour Emeril program enhanced with material provided by Food Network producers and by Microsoft's own research. Microsoft produced the graphics, page construction, and navigation. The prototype delivered background information on world-renowned chef Emeril as well as food preparation and cooking tips and recipe ingredients. It also provided examples of how enhanced content could be used to merchandise products used in a recipe. A sample enhancement screen is shown in Figure 20.6.

Microsoft also used the prototype to help developers create an enhanced content tool set. Food Network has decided to target four basic areas for ongoing ITV development:

- Delivery of recipes.
- Delivery of background information on the chef.
- Delivery of upcoming program information. (What is the chef preparing tomorrow?)
- Solicitation of viewer comments.

Figure 20.6 Screen shot of a Food Network enhancement.

The comments would be used to plan for additional enhanced content based on viewer feedback. The producers also decided to repurpose the Web content for VBI encoding.

Looking Ahead: DIY, the Do-It-Yourself Network

DIY will be one of the first networks launched over the new digital channels being deployed by cable operators. The digital compression technology delivers six or more channels over the same bandwidth that one analog channel occupied. With over a 600% increase in cable channel capacity, more channels will be targeted to

Figure 20.7 The DIY logo.

specific audiences and interests. The network is scheduled to launch in September 1999 and will have a strong Internet component supporting the video content. For the next several years, the Internet audience will be significantly larger than the digital television audience, so DIY will use the Internet as a vehicle to drive its brand and increase audience awareness. Susan Packard, chief operations officer for HGTV, leads the development effort.

DIY will devote its programming to in-depth, step-by-step instructions on home improvement, decorating, gardening, cooking, and other topics of the home lifestyle category. This will be the ultimate home and garden resource, condensing popular projects into easy-to-follow how-to segments and job-specific content. "The do-it-yourselfers in the audience for HGTV and Food wanted more information than fits in a 30-minute show," Packard says. The Web content will consist of detailed instructions, guides, illustrations, video-on-demand, and lists of materials and resources that will integrate with the on-air video. The network will also provide on-demand video over the Internet and offer a call-in help desk.

Glossary

Term	Definition
AC-3 algorithm	An algorithm developed by Dolby Laboratories for delivering audio in a compressed format.
ActiveX	A group of technologies that enable software components to interact with each other regardless of the language in which the components were created.
Announcement	A set of text that allows a server application to tell broadcast receivers, on a common address, about other addresses that will be used for actual data transmission. An announcement describes the type of content to follow and the address and port that will be used for actual data transmission.
Announcement filter	An announcement filter distinguishes between those announcements that are of interest to a particular broadcast client's user and the announcements that are not of interest.
Announcement listener	An operating system service that receives announcements of upcoming data and monitors them for upcoming transmissions. Stores announcements so that they are maintained across restarts of Windows. Listens for announcements on a set of addresses specified in the registry.
Announcement manager	A built-in component that indicates whether announcements are being received.
Application programming interface (API)	An application uses an application programming interface to direct a set of procedures by the operating system of a computer.

Term	Definition
Asymmetrical digital subscriber line (ADSL)	A method of transmitting high-speed digital communication across standard copper phone lines.
ATVEF	Advanced Television Enhancement Forum. A cross-industry alliance of companies representing broadcast and cable networks, cable and satellite service providers, consumer electronics, personal computers, and the software industry. ATVEF advocates an industry-wide specification for interactive television programming.
Back channel	The segment of a two-way communications system that flows from the consumer back to the content provider, or to a system component, to provide responses, often via a modem or other connection to the Internet.
Base page	The hypertext markup language (HTML) page that resides at the top level or base of the enhancement pages loaded into the Web browser or into WebTV for Windows.
bpc:	A pluggable protocol that supports Internet security zones. The bpc: protocol provides files stored locally to Internet Explorer (IE) rather than having those files come from the IE cache.
Broadcast Architecture	The underlying set of technologies, components, and standards that make it possible to display television, receive broadcast data feeds, provide interactive content, and display enhanced content. A fundamental component of Windows 98 and the foundation for WebTV for Windows.
Broadcast Router	A main component of the Broadcast Server. The Broadcast Router service forwards multicast or tunneled data to broadcast head-end hardware or to peer Broadcast Routers.

Term	Definition
Broadcast Server	The Broadcast Server allows the delivery of interactive content and broadcast data feeds. Uses Internet Protocol (IP) to encode and deliver data over networks that support IP Multicast. The three main components of the Broadcast Server are the Broadcast Router, Internet Channel Server, and Enhancement Tools.
CAB file	One file containing multiple compressed files. Keeps enhancement content (such as an HTML page) and associated dependencies together.
Channel	A path or link through which information passes between two devices. On television, a channel carries a specific sequence of programming broadcast by an individual television broadcaster. In Internet Explorer, a channel is a collection of links to World Wide Web pages.
Channel announcement	One of four types of enhancement announcements (along with current, future, and timeslice announcements). A channel announcement contains information about an enhancement for a current channel and enhances a particular channel.
Channel enhancement	An enhancement of a particular channel. An enhanced channel continuously displays enhancements whenever the user tunes to that channel.
Closed captioning (CC)	Textual information contained in line 21 of the Vertical Blanking Interval. TV Crossover Links and other interactive television features are embedded in closed captioning.
Codec	Combination of coder-decoder. A codec converts audio or video signals between analog and digital forms. Also a combination of compressor-decompressor. Compresses and decompresses audio or video data.

Term	Definition
Component object model (COM)	An object-oriented programming model for building software applications made up of modular components. The component object model allows different software modules, written without information about each other, to work together as a single application.
Current announcement	One of four types of enhancement announcements (along with channel, future, and timeslice announcements). A current announcement refers to a show that is currently on. Specifies that the triggers that are broadcast on the specified IP address apply to whatever show (episode) the viewer is currently tuned to.
Current enhancement announcement	Same as current announcement.
Data binding	Data binding links a data source to a Web page and allows presentation, manipulation, and updates of the page on the end-user side.
Digital television	The delivery of a television signal using the common binary system of combinations of 1s and 0s. As opposed to traditional analog television, digital television provides higher quality picture and sound and supports features such as interactive programming and Electronic Program Guides.
Direct broadcast satellite (DBS)	A satellite communication technology that allows use of a small (18 inches to 3 feet in diameter) receiver dish packaged as a consumer electronics product, enabling consumers to receive satellite television signals directly through the receiver.
Document Object Model (DOM)	A dynamic HTML feature that allows authors direct, programmable access to individual components of a Web document.

Term	Definition
Dynamic HTML (DHTML)	A variation of hypertext markup language (HTML) that allows a user's machine to reformat and redisplay Web pages (instead of the user waiting for a remote server to make changes and send them back to the user). Every element of a Web page is therefore changeable in real time on the end-user side.
Dynamic Link Library (DLL)	A file of code containing functions that other executable code requests. DLLs are not executable programs; rather, they are loaded only when called for and needed by the program. DLLs are compiled, linked, and stored separately from the computing processes that use them.
ECMAScript	Script based on the standards established by the European Computer Manufacturers Association. ECMAScript adds features to Web pages and is one of two main components of Microsoft JScript 1.1 (along with Document Object Model).
Electronic Program Guide (EPG)	A WebTV for Windows component that lists television shows. Users can browse and search the Electronic Program Guide. With the right hardware, they can view television programs through the Electronic Program Guide.
Enhanced television	The combination of a video program and multimedia enhancement elements such as hypertext links, graphics, text frames, sounds, and animations. Also referred to as interactive television.
Enhancement	A multimedia element, such as a hypertext link to a World Wide Web page, a graphic, a text frame, a sound, or an animated sequence, added to a broadcast show or other video program.

Term	Definition
Enhancement announcement	Informs a broadcast client that a show is interactive. Provides details about the show's enhancements, such as each enhancement's identifier, the show that the content enhances, and the page that contains the enhancement's starting point.
Enhancement announcement filter	An announcement listener filter that processes enhancement announcements. Enhancement announcements contain data about an interactive show and its enhancements, such as the name of an enhancement to come, and the show reference of the interactive show.
Enhancement Author	An interactive television authoring tool that creates a stream script (a file that synchronizes enhancement files with the main video broadcast of an interactive show) by sending triggers and files at specified times.
Enhancement cache	A storage location for enhancement files on the user's local hard disk. When files are located in the enhancement cache, it allows the enhancement engine to utilize the Internet Explorer security features while protecting the files from premature deletion in IE garbage collection.
Enhancement control	An ActiveX control that responds to enhancement stream events. Like a video control, the enhancement control is hosted in an enhancement page displayed by WebTV for Windows or by a Web browser.
Enhancement filter	A part of the Broadcast Architecture. When an enhancement filter receives an announcement, it calls an internal object of the Broadcast Architecture to load the enhancement data into the guide database.
Enhancement Listener control	Also known as the enhancement trigger control. An ActiveX control embedded in Web pages that expect to receive interactive content and triggers.

Term	Definition
	The enhancement listener control is one of two controls (along with the enhancement video control) that an enhancement utilizes.
Enhancement Player	A lightweight tool that plays finished stream scripts and transmits enhancements.
Enhancement stream	A continuous delivery of enhancement data.
Enhancement stream player	A basic tool for broadcasting preauthored interactive content. Utilizes a stream file to determine what announcements, files, and triggers to transmit.
Enhancement tools	Applications that make it possible to play and author interactive television content. Enhancement tools enable authoring and transmission of both synchronized and nonsynchronized content.
Enhancement trigger control	Also known as the enhancement listener. The enhancement trigger control processes enhancement streams and receives interactive content and triggers.
Enhancement video control	One of two types of video controls (along with the Video control). The enhancement video control is used in Web pages that are hosted in WebTV for Windows; the video control is used in Web pages that are not hosted in WebTV for Windows.
File Transfer Service (FTS)	A Microsoft NetShow component used for delivering files. File Transfer Service provides file transmission capabilities and sends files using a transfer mechanism based on IP Multicast that includes forward error correction (FEC).
Forward error correction (FEC)	An algorithm that increases the reliability of data transfer. Forward error correction inserts extra, or redundant, bits into a stream of data transmitted to another device. The redundant bits correct errors in the data.

Term	Definition
FTS data trigger	Initiates data reception. Indicates the subdirectory in which an enhancement is stored and the IP address and port on which files will be transferred.
FTS trigger timeout	A timeout value that specifies the time after which enhancement files will be removed from a user's hard disk.
Guide database loader	A module used to load program guide data into the electronic program guide database.
Head end	The physical location from which television and data are transmitted.
High-definition television (HDTV)	Television content that is of significantly greater resolution and clarity than standard television content.
Interactive Programming Suite (IPS)	A Microsoft product that provides a database-driven, template-based authoring system for creating basic interactive broadcasts. The three core functions of the Interactive Programming Suite are the Live Content Manager, the Live Content Stream Server, and the Live Content Wizard.
Interactive television	The combination of a video program and multimedia enhancement elements such as hypertext links, graphics, text frames, sounds, and animations. Also referred to as Enhanced television.
Intercast	An Intel-developed system that delivers interactive content in the Vertical Blanking Interval of a television signal.
Internet Channel Server (ICS)	One of three main components of the Broadcast Server, along with the Broadcast Router and enhancement tools. Internet Channel Server allows the transmission of industry standard channels and Web content over broadcast and other multicast-enabled networks.

Term	Definition
Internet Information Server (IIS)	An Internet server that enhances the functionality of Windows NT Server 4 and includes a complete set of tools for building server-based Web applications. An important feature of Internet Information Server is its Active Server Pages capability, which allows Web authors to combine HTML, server-side scripts, and ActiveX controls.
Internet Protocol (IP)	A standard for the delivery of data across networked computers, relying upon the delivery of packets of information.
Internet Protocol (IP) Multicast	A method of transmission used in conjunction with Internet Protocol (IP). A multicast sends information to many recipients at once, as opposed to typical unicasts, which are directed to a single recipient.
IP Tunneling	A connection-based method of transmitting data using Internet Protocol.
JScript	A scripting language used in Web pages.
Live Broadcast Editor	An application, included in Enhancement Tools, that broadcasts enhancement files with the main video broadcast of a live interactive show.
Live Content Manager	One of three core functions (along with the Live Content Stream Server and the Live Content Wizard) of the Interactive Programming Suite (IPS). The Live Content Manager allows a user to create, edit, and schedule interactive content. For example, the user can enter headings, subheadings, and links to Web sites.
Live Content Stream Server	One of three core functions (along with the Live Content Wizard and the Live Content Manager) of the Interactive Programming Suite. The Live Content Stream Server checks the Live Content Manager for live page content, collects the content, packages the files into a CAB file, and transmits the CAB files as encapsulated IP multicast data.

Term	Definition
Live Content Wizard	One of three core functions (along with the Live Content Stream Server and the Live Content Manager) of the Interactive Programming Suite. The Live Content Wizard allows producers to design custom live pages for interactive broadcasts. Users can add backgrounds, station logos, advertisements, and other graphics. Users can also set up buttons that viewers will click to see the types of interactive content viewers want.
MBONE (multicast backbone)	A collection of Internet sites transmitting real-time audio and video to each other. Special software allows the transmission and delivery of packets of data at high speeds.
Multipart MIME	A multipart format, similar to the design of CAB files, that supports "all-or-nothing" delivery of files. The ATVEF format for interactive television supports the use of multipart MIME, whereas the WebTV for Windows format supports the use of CAB files.
NetShow	A Microsoft product that allows a user to receive networked streaming multimedia content from the Web or an intranet server. NetShow delivers live and on-demand audio, video, and mixed multimedia to the desktop.
Network Driver Interface Specification (NDIS)	A low-level abstraction layer between data reception hardware and higher level parts of the operating system. The Network Driver Interface Specification allows programmers to write hardware device drivers independently of the target operating system.
Norpak inserters	A popular piece of hardware for inserting digital data in the Vertical Blanking Interval (VBI) of a television signal. Common inserters are the TES3, TES4, and TES5.

Term	Definition
North American Basic Teletext Specification (NABTS)	NABTS is an open standard that specifies the transmission of data in the Vertical Blanking Interval (VBI) of a television signal.
Open database connectivity (ODBC)	An interface providing a common language for Windows applications to gain access to a database.
PreloadURL	A tag that specifies the base page for a WebTV for Windows enhanced show.
Prepurposing	A term coined by Tribune and used by its employees to create awareness among producers and creators of content that Tribune can use their content in many different ways. For example, the camera operator who shoots a 10-second clip for a television newscast can also plan and shoot a lengthier clip about the same subject for a Web site featuring streaming video.
Repurposing	Repurposing is distinct from Tribune's use of prepurposing (the practice of creating awareness among content providers and producers, before content is provided or produced, that content can be used in many different ways). Repurposing means using content intended for one medium (such as newspaper) for another medium (such as true Web or interactive television). Interactive television professionals should always strive for prepurposing.
Script trigger	Triggers are notifications that are sent to broadcast clients at specific times during an interactive show. Script triggers are the primary triggers used in WebTV for Windows.
Session Announcement Protocol (SAP)	Along with Session Description Protocol (SDP), Session Announcement Protocol is used to announce data and interactive content streams.
Session Description Protocol (SDP)	Along with Session Announcement Protocol (SAP), Session Description Protocol is used to announce data and interactive content streams.

Term	Definition
Session Description (SDP) announcement	SDP announcements indicate the Protocol address and port for both triggers and data streams.
Show reference	A show reference is a formatted string that contains information about a broadcast episode such as the show time, channel, and network. You can use a show reference to specify a particular episode or episodes.
Spool folder	A storage location for enhancement files after they are received on the client during a broadcast. WebTV for Windows creates the spool folder during its installation.
Streamed video	Video sent using Microsoft NetShow over IP-based networks.
T.A.G. Editor	A Digital Renaissance product that allows the authoring of digital television shows. The T.A.G. Editor creates interactive content that can accompany both streaming and broadcast audio and video.
Ticker	A program feature that displays a continuous stream of information, usually running in a narrow strip along the bottom of a screen. Stock market tickers, which feature a continuous display of stock prices, are common tickers.
Trigger	Used to synchronize interactive content with video programming.
Tuning space	A feature of the Broadcast Architecture that separates channels available from different sources (such as cable, satellite, and broadcast).
Tunnel	A connection between two applications that sends data packets within other data packets. Tunneling allows packets encoded with one protocol to be transferred using another protocol.

Term	Definition
TV Crossover Link	A link to a Web site that is delivered as a hidden part of the closed caption part of a television signal.
TV tuner card	Computer hardware that is necessary to receive and display television broadcasts on a computer.
Uniform resource locator (URL)	An address for the location of resources on the World Wide Web. A uniform resource locator includes the protocol to be used (such as HTTP or FTP), the name of the server that the resource is located on (such as www.microsoft.com), and the path to a resource (such as dtv, for the Microsoft digital television site).
Vertical Blanking Interval (VBI)	A portion of the analog television signal. A television signal is composed of many horizontal lines that reset themselves. During the reset period, the electron beam that displays the image briefly blanks out, allowing the transmission of data instead of a picture.
Video Access server	A stand-alone process that runs on the broadcast client. The Video Access server handles device contention among multiple instances of the Video control.
Video control	An ActiveX component that displays video within a Web page or other container application. The Video control supports properties for setting input devices and channels.
WebTV for Windows	A component of the Windows 98 operating system that enables users to select television channels and that displays interactive television programs. WebTV for Windows uses an ActiveX control to display conventional television shows, and it hosts a hypertext markup language (HTML) browser to display interactive content for those shows at the same time.

Term	Definition
Windows Sockets Interface (Winsock)	An application programming interface that provides a network abstraction layer (such as a TCP/IP interface) to applications working above networking software. Winsock allows applications to receive and send network data without needing any information about the network involved.

Contributors

Before joining MSNBC, *Frank Barbieri* worked as World editor for MSN News, and prior to that pursued a master's degree in multimedia journalism at the University of Missouri. Frank has worked as a freelance and staff journalist all over the world, including a stint at *Asiaweek*'s Bangkok bureau and at the *Budapest Business Journal*. Frank can be reached at *fbarbier@microsoft.com*.

Kevin Beggs began working in television in 1991 as a production assistant on *Baywatch*. He quickly became a producer and has worked on the series for 8 years in all areas of production, including development, marketing, business affairs, and licensing. In 1995 Kevin was promoted to vice president of development for Berk/Schwartz/Bonann Productions. With Doug Schwartz, Kevin has developed and sold to the Fox Family Channel a package of classic film remakes, including Jules Verne's *Mysterious Island* and H. G. Wells' *The Invisible Man*. Kevin recently accepted a new job as senior vice president, drama development at Lions Gate Media/Mandalay Entertainment. Kevin can be reached at *klbeggs@hotmail.com*.

Manish Bhatia has worked at Nielsen Media Research since 1989, when he started his career as an analyst in the cable division (NHI). Manish then joined the newly formed Planning and Development group and helped develop new metering technologies (the Active/Passive meter, AMOLII) and other new business initiatives including AEM (Monitor Plus) and Agency Planning Systems (New Millennium). Since 1995, Manish has developed Nielsen Media Research's Interactive Business, focusing on surveys, site tracking, and panel-based research services. Manish can be reached at *bhatiam@nielsenmedia.com*.

Jonathan Boltax is the manager and producer of the NBC Enhanced Broadcast Group. He has headed the group since its inaugural broadcast of the 1996 Summer Olympic Games from Atlanta. Before joining NBC, Jonathan worked for the Apple New Media Labs in Boulder, Colorado, and at Commonground, a Colorado-based Internet marketing and development firm. He represents NBC in the Advanced Television Standards Committee (ATSC) Specialist Group T3/S17, Digital TV Application Software Environment (DASE), as well the Technical Working Group of the Advanced Television Enhancement Forum (ATEVF). Jonathan can be reached at *jonathan.boltax@nbc.com*.

As an innovative media company, ***Digital Renaissance Inc.*** provides the software content, tools, and expertise for the convergence of media and technologies. From broadband systems integration and media-on-demand architectures to electronic commerce-enabled solutions, to the creation of content across multiple mediums, Digital Renaissance is a leader in the creation and distribution of transactive media experiences.

Steve Hicks is chief technology officer for Home & Garden Television and is responsible for overseeing the network's technology infrastructure and computer-basedinitiatives. He is also responsible for research and development and for supporting hardware and software requirements for New Media. He advises the Food Network and DIY on technical issues and strategies. Steve joined HGTV in 1997 after consulting for numerous media companies including Times Mirror, The E.W. Scripps Company, North American Philips, and Greenberg Networks. He also served as chief technology officer and senior partner for Whittle Communications LP, an early pioneer in VBI-enabled targeted media. Steve can be reached at *shicks@cnnt03.scripps.com.*

Rob Martell is head of product development for Digital Renaissance and has been with the company since 1996. Prior to joining the company, Rob was the director of Canadian Broadband Marketing for Nortel. He had been with Nortel for over 13 years in various marketing, product development, and product management roles. Rob graduated from Queen's University, Ontario, Canada with a degree in electrical engineering in 1983. He can be reached at *rob_martell@digital-ren.com.*

Tim Millard began his career with Global Net Productions in Seattle as a developer of entertainment and documentary film and video projects. In the spring of 1993, Tim managed production of *Paul Keller: Portrait of a Serial Arsonist,* an award-winning special that was developed by CBS into a Movie of the Week titled *Not Our Son.* Tim cowrote the award-winning *The Fire Below Us,* a documentary purchased by National Geographic Explorer, and he produced an accompanying CD-ROM. As a freelance producer, Tim has worked for syndicated television shows as *American Journal* and *Inside Edition.* His corporate clients include AT&T, Boeing, Weyerhaeuser, Microsoft, Sierra Online, and Nintendo. Since October 1996, Tim has worked with Microsoft on the development of interactive television content. He has also developed interactive episodes for *The Essence of Emeril* on The Food Network, *Sci Squad* for Discovery Kids, and *The People's Court* for Warner Brothers Online. Tim can be reached at *timmillard@hotmail.com.*

Larry Namer started his career at Time, Inc., rose to the position of director of operations in the company's cable division, and then served as director of corporate development at Manhattan Cable Television. After leaving Time, Inc. in 1981, he moved to California and built the first 61-channel, two-way cable system in the United States, Valley Cable Television. While he was general manager of Valley, the company was recognized by *Forbes Magazine* as the national model for local programming.

In 1984, he and Alan Mruvka came up with the concept for MovieTime Channel, Inc. (later renamed E! Entertainment Inc.). Larry and Alan wrote the business plan, raised the financing, and launched the channel on July 31, 1987. After turning over management of E! to HBO, he formed Comspan Russia, which today is the largest producer of live entertainment events in the former Soviet Union. Comspan Communications has become one of two independent companies in the United States that can plan and execute the launch of new cable television channels. Most recently it helped launch The Recovery Network and will launch The Documentary Channel and HobbyCraft Network in 1999. From 1996 to 1997, Comspan was the primary consultant to MITV and helped Microsoft establish relationships (for enhanced TV development) with companies such as Spelling Entertainment, USA Network, Rysher Entertainment, Home & Garden Television, TV Food Network, and many others. In 1997 and 1998, Comspan helped the Microsoft Windows Group establish relationships with Tribune Company, Scripps Howard, and Neilsen Media Research to participate in testing the delivery of data (via VBI insertion into a TV signal) to Windows 98 beta users in multiple markets. Larry can be reached at *lnamer@comspan.com*.

Michael G. Samet is chairman of Brand Dialog, Young and Rubicam, Inc.'s global interactive practice. In June 1994, he was named executive vice president, director of media and new technologies, Young & Rubicam, New York. Previously, he had been director, strategic planning, for Whittle Communications' Special Reports Network (SRN), where he had also served as vice president, Sales. From 1989 to 1991, Michael was vice president and national sales manager for HealthLink Television, which eventually was purchased by Whittle.

In 1986, Michael cofounded Triad Futures, a New York futures and options trading, money management, and consulting firm, where he served as president until 1989. He also helped establish the Cable Health Network (today, Lifetime Television), where he served as vice president of sales from 1982 to 1985. Earlier, Michael worked at Benton & Bowles as senior vice president and manager of Media Services. He codesigned and implemented the industry's first media department minicomputer system. Michael is married and the father of two children. He holds a bachelor's degree from Brooklyn College and a master of science degree in operations research from Polytechnic Institute of New York. He can be reached at *mike_samet@brand-dialogue.com*.

Bill Sanders has headed creative affairs at Big Ticket Television, a division of Spelling Entertainment Group, a Viacom company, since the inception of Big Ticket in October 1994. He developed its first four on-air series and is leading Big Ticket's expansion into new media. Bill was supervising producer of HBO's *Dream On*, a comedy series that won multiple Emmy and CableAce Awards during its first six seasons. Bill is actively involved in interactive media. He created *Dream On* forums for several major online services and initiated the development of a *Dream On* interactive CD-ROM game. Bill also served as the only producer–member of a Universal Television Interactive Task Force and led efforts to establish Universal's online presence.

From August 1984 to January 1990, Bill was vice president, original programming, West Coast, for HBO. He developed and supervised production of pilots, specials, and series for HBO and Cinemax. Bill first worked with Larry Lyttle from April 1983 through August 1984 as director, comedy and drama series development, for Warner Brothers Television. Sanders began his career at ABC in New York City in 1977. In March 1980, he moved to Los Angeles and became director, Variety and Late Night Programs. He produced the successful programs *That's Incredible!*, *Ripley's Believe It or Not*, and *Fridays* (written by *Seinfeld*'s Larry David and featuring Michael Richards).

Bill received his bachelor of arts with distinction from Stanford University, where he majored in communication (broadcasting and film). He studied for 2 years in the master of fine arts program in television production at UCLA. Born in New York City, Bill resides in Santa Monica, California with his wife, Kerrie Klark, and their 5-year-old son Aaron, 3-year-old daughter Ardsley, and 1-year-old son Duncan. Sanders can be reached at *billsanders@jet.net*.

Jeff R. Scherb was named senior vice president and chief technology officer of Tribune Company in August 1996. Responsible for leading company-wide technology initiatives, Jeff also has overall responsibility for the company's existing information technology and systems. Prior to joining Tribune, Jeff was chief technology officer and senior vice president for research and development at Dun & Bradstreet Software. He was responsible for overall technology planning and created the SmartStream Web Series, the first enterprise applications based on intranet technology and the Java programming language.

His previous positions include vice president of systems development for Turner Broadcasting from 1994 to 1995; senior vice president of product development for Delphi Information Systems from 1992 to 1994; vice president of applications and technical support for Commodore International, Ltd. from 1989 to 1992; and various positions with Cullinet Software, Inc. and Computer Associates International from 1984 to 1989. Before becoming involved in technology development, Jeff was circulation promotion manager for Home News Publishing Company in New Jersey and technical director for an ABC affiliate television station in Naples, Florida.

A native of New Jersey, Jeff received a bachelor's degree in computer science and a bachelor's degree in business administration from Rutgers University. He is a member of the Board of Overseers of the Illinois Institute of Technology, Rice Campus, and serves on the Technology Council of the Field Museum in Chicago. He can be reached at *jscherb@tribune.com*.

Annette Schultz is a technical writer at Digital Renaissance. A graduate of the Honors Language and Literature program of Wilfrid Laurier University, Annette strives to bring creativity and storytelling skills to her technical writing efforts. She can be reached at *aschulz@digital-ren.com*.

Doc Searls is a computer industry analyst, writer, speaker and president of The Searls Group (*www.searls.com*), an organization that began as part of Hodskins Simone & Searls (HS&S), which Doc cofounded in 1978 and helped build into one of the top technology advertising and public relations agencies in Silicon Valley. Doc has advised dozens of leading companies in the computer industry, plus others in broadcasting, publishing, and related industries. His writings have appeared in *OMNI*, *PC Magazine*, *Upside*, *WEBsmith*, *Linux Journal*, *The Globe & Mail*, and many other publications, including his own Web journal, *Reality 2.0* (*www.searls.com/r2.html*). Doc and his wife, Joyce, live in Emerald Hills, California, and have four children, ranging in age from 28 to 2. Doc can be reached at *doc@searls.com*.

Matt Thompson is an Internet producer at WGN-TV in Chicago. Matt holds a bachelor's degree in journalism from Northwestern University. He previously worked at Tribune Media Services on a number of online and Internet products. Matt can be reached at *mthompson@tribune.com*.

Gary Wong was a senior developer in Tribune's Advanced Technology Group. Before joining Tribune in 1995, he was the science scheduler on NASA's Extreme Ultraviolet Explorer Project. Gary has a bachelor's degree in engineering physics from the University of California, Berkeley, and is currently working on his master of business administration degree at the University of Chicago. He is now manager of network communication at Classified Ventures LLC, and can be reached at *gwong@classifiedventures.com*.

Index